RED SQUARE AT NOON

RED SQUARE AT NOON

Natalia Gorbanevskaya

With an Introduction by

Harrison E. Salisbury

Translated by Alexander Lieven

HOLT, RINEHART AND WINSTON
New York   Chicago   San Francisco

Published simultaneously in Canada by Holt, Rinehart and Winston of Canada, Limited.
First published in France under the title *Midi, Place Rouge* by Editions Robert Laffont S.A.

Library of Congress Catalog Card Number: 79–138888
ISBN: 0–03–085990–5

First Edition

Natalia Gorbanevskaya's manuscript was conveyed to Editions Laffont by le Comité
International pour la Défense des Droits de l'Homme

Printed in the United States of America

CONTENTS

PART FOUR

*There is a map of Red Square and the surrounding area
on page* 44.

INTRODUCTION

In the past year or two I have been hearing a sad and sinister kind of speculation on the part of an occasional member of the Soviet intelligentsia. They have begun to discuss in frank fearful terms something which has long lurked close below the surface of their consciousness – the real possibility of the fascisation of the Soviet Union.

This fear is something quite different from the kind of intellectual argument which one might have heard in the 1930s, for instance, concerning the 'social fascism' of Stalin; or the police state which Stalin created; or the national socialism which was imposed in his time.

Nor is the current talk related, particularly, to the open manifestations of anti-semitism which have become so common with the increasingly vigorous struggle of Soviet Jews against the anti-Jewish policies of their government, although this bears some relationship to the new fears.

No. What some of the Soviet liberals are concerned with is a phenomenon much deeper, much more pervasive, much more dangerous. It is the conscious catering to repressive, racist and class strains in Russian society – a revival in lightly concealed forms of the kind of anti-intellectual, chauvinistic spirit which was epitomised in the last fifty years of the Romanov régime by the so-called *chernaya sotniya*, the Black Hundreds, the crude mobs, deliberately used by Plehve and others to carry out the *pogroms* which so disfigured Russian life during the last days of the Czars.

This is a strain of anti-intellectual, Slav supremacy which historically has deep roots in the Russian countryside. It was anathema to the forces which produced the Revolution, the

European, Marxist-oriented, cosmopolitan intellectual atmosphere which created Lenin, Trotsky, Bukharin, Radek and the other leaders of the Bolshevik movement. Even Stalin, for all his Georgian more-Russian-than-the-Russians spirit, would have turned his back on the kind of spirit which is represented by this revival of old hates and passions that are deeply linked with the roots of Muscovy.

But today if one looks about the Russian scene with a knowing eye there are tell-tale symptoms. Amid the most reactionary writers and ideologues there has even appeared a new Russsophilic movement, glorifying the Russian-ness of Russia, its ancient traditions, its architectural and cultural heritage. It is almost *pravoslavenny* (Orthodox) in its mood and one can well believe that its apostles devoutly adhere to the principles of *domostroi* (the ancient Russian doctrine of household management which preached regular beatings of wives by husbands for the mutual good of each).

In the guise of a movement for the preservation of ancient relics and antiquities the new Russophiles seem to hope to turn the clock back not merely to Stalin but to Nicholas I, the Iron Czar. They ruthlessly wage war upon every manifestation of liberalism, attack, slander and suppress writers who enjoyed a brief whirl during the Khrushchevian thaw and ceaselessly propagandise not merely for the return of 'law and order' à la Stalin but for a totally repressive society, backed by the terror and physical force of proletarian storm troops, imposing neo-fascism with fists and clubs. All this, of course, working in the closest association with the rapidly reviving police organs.

It is too early to assess the potential weight of the new fascist strains in Soviet society. It is apparent, to be sure, that the ordinary working man (like his counterpart in many western societies) is no paragon of liberalism. The American hardhat has his Russian hardhat comrade. And their political attitudes are remarkably similar. The Russian factory worker tends to think in terms of better material conditions. He has no sympathy for white-collar workers and particularly not for intellectuals whom he perceives as leading a lazy, easy life, making trouble for everyone and not patriotic to boot. He is easily aroused against 'yids' or any other kind of minorities. He strongly supports his government's chauvinism against the Chinese and readily agrees that the Czechs deserve anything they get – after all he went without in order to help them and he and his chums fought for Czech freedom. And the same goes for the Hungarians, the Poles, the Yugoslavs or any of the other 'little' peoples of eastern Europe. He has no more sympathy for eccentric Russians who demonstrate against their government than his American counterpart has for long-haired youth.

These attitudes on the part of the Russian lumpenproletariat are not necessarily new although they are in radical contrast with the kind of proletarianism which forced the backdrop of the Revolution and the early years of the Soviet régime. But Soviet Russia is a very middle-aged state today, looking back on more than fifty years of existence. Its citizens more and more tend to think in terms of a new car, a refrigerator, a better apartment, fine clothes, a pleasant vacation than anything upsetting like revolution. Nor do they like to be disturbed in their routine of gradually improving home life.

It is against this background that the remarkable document of Natalia Gorbanevskaya is to be read.

There may be those who will wonder why she and her friends went to such extraordinary efforts to compile this minute-by-minute, person-by-person account of what will seem to be, after all, a most trivial event – six or seven men and women sitting down on the parapet of Lofno Mesto, the old execution platform in Red Square, on 25 August 1968 just after noon and unfurling a few home-made signs and one home-made Czech flag, protesting the Soviet invasion of Czechoslovakia. What did it, after all, amount to? It lasted but a few minutes. Only a few score people witnessed it before plainclothes Soviet security agents roughed up the demonstrators and rushed them out of the square in commandeered cars. The participants were arrested, tried, sent away into exile or incarcerated in prison 'psychiatric hospitals'. What kind of a mark did it leave on the consciousness of Soviet society? Or of the world, for that matter?

Those are pragmatic questions but I think they miss the whole point of the matter. The keeper of the conscience of a great state is not always (or even usually) its government. The conscience is much more likely to be kept by a few not-well-known individuals who feel more keenly than their comrades and see life and the world with greater depth and vision.

In the fifty years before 7 November 1917 not a few obscure groups of Russian individuals risked their lives and well being to protest the criminal and cruel acts of their government. They were little people and the Russian government was vast and powerful. But, today, it is clear that the tiny bands, the young men and women of the Narodnik movement, the Narodnaya Volya, the Socialist Revolutionaries and even the more doctrinaire Mensheviks and Bolsheviks had an impact upon the course of events which far exceeded that of the Czar's Third Section, his Black Hundreds and all the reactionary obscurantist tradition which rallied to the support of the status quo.

This is worth remembering in evaluating not only what Madame Gorbanevskaya has done in making up this record but what the handful of her friends did – Pavel Litvinov, grandson of one of Russia's greatest men, Maxim Litvinov, Vladimir Dremlyuga, Vadim Delone, Larissa Bogoraz, Konstantin Babitsky and Victor Feinberg.

They are men and women of courage and as Aleksandr Ulyanov, brother of Lenin and himself executed for an unsuccessful attempt on the life of Alexander II, noted there will always be somewhere in Russia ten men who are willing to stand up and risk their lives if necessary for the sake of truth and justice.

No repression, however severe, has ever been able to smother all the sparks of the human soul. The Czars could not do it. Nor will the present Soviet government. Nor a future one even if it moves fatefully further towards fascism.

For perhaps the greatest revelation of the Gorbanevskaya document is the distance which Russia has already moved into fascist methods, fascist mentality, fascist practice. The virtue of the document is its meticulous detail; its crystal exposition of the rude violation of the letter of Soviet law; the wilful application of force and deceit; the use of the court as an instrument of injustice; the falsification and suppression of testimony; the deliberate provocation by state organs; and over it all the total banality of the system.

This banality is what is so strikingly illuminated by the sincerity and bravery of the protesters.

Listen to Pavel Litvinov's final speech in court: 'Some people may think that all our policy, including our government's mistakes, is determined by our social and state system. This is not how I see it. Even the Prosecutor would probably not say this, or he would have to admit that all the crimes of Stalin's day were determined by our social and state system.

'And what is happening here? Infringements of legality continue. The most fundamental of these is the infringement of trial in open court . . . I shall say nothing of other infringements. These will do.

'I believe it to be of the utmost importance that the citizens of our country should be truly free. This is important apart from anything else because ours is the largest socialist state and, for better or worse, all that happens here is mirrored in other socialist countries. The more freedom we have, the more there will be there and therefore in the world at large.'

Or listen to Vladimir Dremlyuga's final plea to the country: 'I do not know whether it is à propos to select an epigraph for a final plea, but if it is I would take for my epigraph the words of Anatole France from *The Opinions of Jerome Coignard*: "Do you think you can seduce me by the vision of a government of honest men that so hedges in all liberties that no one can enjoy them?"

'. . . All my conscious life I have wanted to be a citizen – that is, a person who proudly and calmly speaks his mind. For ten minutes I was a citizen (during the demonstration). My voice will, I know, sound a false note in the universal silence which goes by the name of "unanimous support for the policy of the Party and Government". I am glad that there proved to be others to express their protest together with me. Had there not been I would have entered Red Square alone. If there had been other ways, I would have used them.'

A government which ignores this kind of conviction, this kind of spirit, does so at its peril. Indeed, it is already far advanced into a régime which is based on the utter suppression of the human spirit, a régime, in short, of fascism.

But no one reading the Gorbanevskaya record can doubt that the human spirit will in Russia prove indestructible.

One footnote: After compiling the record of the Czecho-slovak protest Madame Gorbanevskaya (who was not then placed on trial or sentenced to prison, presumably because of her three-months-old child) has been subjected to the newest and most sinister kind of Soviet repression. She has been committed by a Moscow court to confinement in a 'special category' psychiatric hospital. The 'special category' hospital is, in fact, an institution operated by the secret police themselves. In addition to political prisoners like Madame Gorbanevskaya, the hospitals have a certain number of genuine psychiatric patients who are mixed in with the political prisoners – a new kind of bedlam which would have aroused the envy of Himmler's police psychiatrists.

New York   HARRISON E. SALISBURY
July 1971

PROLOGUE

To The People Of The Czechoslovak Socialist Republic

Yesterday, 20 August 1968, at about 11 p.m., troops of the USSR, the Polish People's Republic, the German Democratic Republic, the Hungarian People's Republic, and the People's Republic of Bulgaria crossed the state boundaries of the Czechoslovak Socialist Republic. This happened without the knowledge of the President of the Republic, the Presidium of the National Assembly, the Presidium of the Government, and the First Secretary of the Central Committee of the Czechoslovak Communist Party, and of all these institutions. During these hours, a meeting of the Central Committee, Czechoslovak Communist Party has been taking place, to prepare the 14th Congress of the Party. The Presidium of the Central Committee, Czechoslovak Communist Party calls on all citizens to remain calm, and not to offer resistance to the advancing forces, since it is now impossible to defend the frontiers of our state.

For this reason, our army, state security forces and people's militia did not receive orders to defend our country. The Presidium of the Central Committee of the Czechoslovak Communist Party considers that the accomplished act not only contradicts the basic principles of relations between socialist countries, but is a denial of the basic standards of international law.

All leading activists of the Party and the National Front are remaining at the posts to which they were elected as representatives of the people and members of their respective organisations, in accordance with the law and other decrees in force in the Czechoslovak Socialist Republic. The authorities are summoning a meeting of the National Assembly and the Government of the country without delay, while the Presidium of the Central Committee, Czechoslovak Communist Party is summoning a plenum of the Central Committee of the Party to discuss the situation which has arisen.

Presidium of the Central Committee,
Czechoslovak Communist Party.

Pravda, 21 *August* 1968 *Tass Statement*

Tass is authorised to announce that Party and State leaders of the Czechoslovak Socialist Republic have appealed to the Soviet Union and other allied states to render immediate aid to the fraternal Czechoslovak people, including aid by the armed forces. This plea is occasioned by a threat to the existing socialist system in Czechoslovakia, and to the statehood established by the constitution, by counter-revolutionary forces, who have entered into collusion with external forces hostile to socialism.

On several occasions events in and around Czechoslovakia have been the subject of an exchange of opinions between the leaders of fraternal socialist countries, including the leaders of Czechoslovakia. These countries are united in stating that a common international duty of all socialist countries is to support, strengthen and defend the socialist achievements of the people. Their common position was solemnly stated in the Bratislava declaration.

The further aggravation of the situation in Czechoslovakia affects the vital interests of the Soviet Union and other socialist countries and the security of the states belonging to the socialist commonwealth. A threat to the socialist system in Czechoslovakia also constitutes a threat to the foundations of peace in Europe.

The Soviet government and the governments of allied countries – the People's Republic of Bulgaria, the Hungarian People's

Republic, the German Democratic Republic, the Polish People's Republic – acting on the principles of indissoluble friendship and co-operation, and in accordance with existing treaty obligations, have decided to accede to the above-mentioned request to render the necessary aid to the fraternal Czechoslovak people.

This decision completely accords with the right of states to individual and collective self-defence, as set out in the treaties of alliance concluded between fraternal socialist countries. It also meets the fundamental interests of our countries in maintaining European peace against the forces of militarism, aggression and revanchism which have more than once brought the peoples of Europe to war.

Soviet military units, together with military units of the allied countries referred to, entered the territory of Czechoslovakia on 21 August. They will be withdrawn from the Czechoslovak Socialist Republic immediately the threat to the achievements of socialism in Czechoslovakia, the threat to the security of the countries of the socialist commonwealth, is removed and the lawful authorities consider that there is no further need for the continued presence of these military units.

The actions undertaken are not directed against any state, and in no way infringe the state interests of any country. They serve the aim of peace and are dictated by a concern to strengthen peace.

The fraternal countries firmly and resolutely set their invincible solidarity against any threat from outside. Nobody will ever be allowed to tear a single link from the commonwealth of socialist countries.

To the Communist and Workers' Parties of the Whole World

Comrades! Today, the Czechoslovak Socialist Republic was occupied by troops of the five countries of the Warsaw Pact, against the will of the government, the National Assembly, the leadership of the Czechoslovak Communist Party, and the whole people.

Since the Central Committee building, where the presidium of the Central Committee of the Czechoslovak Communist Party is meeting, is in the hands of occupation troops, the Prague City Committee of the Czechoslovak Communist Party appeals to all communist and workers' parties:

Comrades, protest against this unparalleled breach of socialist internationalism!

Demand from the Central Committees of the Communist Parties of the USSR, Poland, Hungary, Bulgaria and the GDR that, despite the temporary presence of occupation troops, the activities of the Central Committee under the leadership of A. Dubcek, and the activities of Cernik should not be paralysed!

Demand the immediate withdrawal of the occupation troops!

We call on you to discuss the need for the immediate summoning of a conference of Communist and Workers' Parties, which should take up a definite position towards this act of lawlessness against the Czechoslovak people and its Communist Party.

At the same time, the presidium has decided to inform the Romanian and Yugoslav embassies about the situation that has arisen and request them to send messages to the central committees of their parties. It is desirable that these countries should, at the earliest possible moment, consider the situation that has arisen in the Czechoslovak Socialist Republic.

The City Party Committee assures the inhabitants of Prague that it is fully operational, and asks for complete support for its measures.

Vecherny Praha 21 August   1968 Prague Committee of the
                                    Czechoslovak Communist Party

Pravda, 22 August 1968
In The Interests Of Socialism And Peace — Our Common Concern

The events in Czechoslovakia over the last few days have properly been causing increasing concern among the workers of the

Moscow 'Hammer and sickle' factory. Only yesterday, at the end of their shift, the metal workers gathered in the political education room of the metal-rolling shop. The speakers' words were pregnant with deep concern for the fate of socialism in the Czechoslovak Socialist Republic.

'Counter-revolutionary elements in Czechoslovakia and their instigators from the imperialist camp,' said lathe '450' operator, Alexei Belousov, 'have attempted to tear the Czechoslovak Socialist Republic from the socialist commonwealth, to take from the Czechoslovak working people their freedom and independence, won with the blood of Soviet soldiers and Czechoslovak patriots. Our people could not contemplate with indifference the fact that the forces of reaction have threatened the socialist system in Czechoslovakia and the statehood established by the will of the people.

'Therefore we, the workers, faithful to international solidarity and fully recognising the danger hanging over a fraternal people, warmly support the actions of the Soviet government and the governments of the allied countries, which decided to render the Czechoslovak Socialist Republic the necessary aid at the request of the party and government leaders of the Czechoslovak Socialist Republic.'

The workers unanimously adopted the resolution, which contains the following passage:
'We fully and whole-heartedly approve the action of the Soviet government and the governments of allied countries, which – acting on the principles of indissoluble friendship and co-operation, and in accordance with existing treaty obligations – went to the aid of the fraternal Czechoslovak people.'

Meetings and gatherings also took place at the Vladimir Ilyich and Likhachev Red Proletariat factories, at the second ball bearing factory and other plants; among literary and theatrical workers of the capital, and in many other collectives. Everywhere, Muscovites spoke of their warm approval for the actions of the Soviet government and the governments of fraternal countries aimed at the defence of socialist achievements and peace.

Leningrad, 21 August. (Pravda Correspondent, M. Korolev)

The working people of Leningrad unanimously support the decision of the governments of the ussr and allied socialist countries to render immediate aid to the fraternal peoples of Czechoslovakia in their struggle against the forces of internal counter-revolution and the intrigues of international imperialism. Mass meetings of workers were held today at the largest enterprises in all parts of the city. Unanimous support was expressed for the actions of the socialist states, dictated as they were by a concern to strengthen the positions of socialism in the world.

'This is a very correct and timely measure, undertaken by the socialist countries for the defence of the achievements of socialism in the Czechoslovak Socialist Republic' said N. V. Perlov, foreman of the milling machine operators in the heavy steam turbine shop of the 22nd Congress of the cpsu Metal works. 'I whole-heartedly and warmly approve this measure.'

'The decision of the governments of the socialist countries expresses the will of the peoples concerned and is in the basic interests of the Czechoslovak people', said B. P. Karaulov, head of the machine assembly section. 'We regard the defence of socialism in Czechoslovakia as our international duty.'

Those taking part in the meeting unanimously approve the energetic actions of the Soviet government and the governments of fraternal allied states in rendering immediate aid to the Czechoslovak people, at the request of the party and state leaders of Czechoslovakia.

To All Trade Union Organisations of the World

On the night of 20-21 August, the Czechoslovak Socialist Republic was occupied by troops of the Soviet Union, the Polish People's Republic, the German Democratic Republic, the People's Republic of Bulgaria, and the Hungarian People's Republic.

This occurred without the knowledge of the President of the Czechoslovak Socialist Republic, the government, the National

Assembly and the Central Committee of the Communist Party. Such an unmotivated and treacherous occupation of our country directly contradicts international law and the Charter of the United Nations. Our country was occupied because we aspire to a humane and profoundly just socialism, designed fully to correspond to our conditions and opportunities.

We call upon you in the name of five and a half million members of Czechoslovak trade unions, in the name of all workers, in the interests of humanity, to protest against this act of force.

> The Secretariat of the Central Council
> of Trade Unions and the Presidents of
> the central committees of Trade Unions.

Komsomolskaya Pravda, 22 August 1968
In Defence of the Achievements of Socialism

The Soviet people unanimously approve the actions of the government of the USSR and the governments of allied countries which decided to meet the request of party and state leaders of the Czechoslovak Socialist Republic concerning vital aid to the fraternal Czechoslovak people, in connection with the threat to the socialist system that had developed in that country.

Tass, 21 August   Baku

During the lunch break, several hundred workers of the Yu. Kasimov Baku oil equipment factory met to exchange ideas.

'We fully support and approve the actions of the Soviet government and the governments of other socialist countries, which decided to render fraternal aid to the Czechoslovak people', said lathe-operator Asif Guseinov.

Tashkent

'We know that the working people of Czechoslovakia are devoted to the ideas of socialism,' said foreman A. P. Krotov at a meeting of many thousands at the 'Tashtextilmash' factory. 'But we also know that the imperialists are weaving plots against this country and, using the support of a handful of renegades whom they themselves have reared, are attempting to stab the Czechoslovak people in the back. It is the duty of fraternal peoples to rise up in defence of socialist achievements in the Czechoslovak Socialist Republic.'

Appeal to the World Council for Peace

Dear Friends!

It is we who appeal to you this time, with grief in our hearts; we, who till this moment have stood in the front ranks of those who invariably condemned violence and aggression wherever they occurred; we, who have always expressed our active solidarity with the victims of violence.

Now it is we who are the victims of violence. Now it is we who call for solidarity. We are accused of something we did not do, and did not wish to do. If there is anyone who can be the judges in our cause, it is yourselves, who always co-operated with us; our views are known to you, and more than our views – our concrete actions.

Had we been seized upon by an imperialist army, it would have been painful; but to fall victim to aggression by one's best friends is unbelievable, and will cause dismay among all progressive and peace-loving powers.

We sought a free, socialist and democratic Czechoslovakia as an inseparable part of the socialist camp. We sought a deeply humane socialism in which the people would really rule. We are members of the Warsaw Pact, which should have defended us against aggression by imperialism, but did not defend us from occupation by our friends.

Since the World Peace Council has always taken a clear stand against every aggression, every breach of human rights, we expect it to do the same now. This we ask of you:

Support our clear and uncompromising demand that the forces of occupation be immediately withdrawn from our country, if anything is still to be saved.This is not only in our interests, but in the interests of the whole socialist camp, and of peace throughout the world.

We put our hope in you! Please inform all Peace committees – it is indeed a matter of peace throughout the world!

Prague, 22 August 1968   Czechoslovak Committee for
                                                  the Defence of Peace.

Pravda, 23 August 1968

The will of the Soviet people is united and unshakeable. All Soviet people firmly and resolutely support the actions taken for the defence of socialism and peace.

Balkhash

Thousands of workers of the Balkhash Order of Lenin '50th anniversary of the October Revolution' mining and metallurgical combine met and expressed their full support for the timely measures of the Soviet government and the governments of the socialist commonwealth in rendering help to the fraternal Czechoslovak people in their struggle with counter-revolution, and in defence of the achievements of socialism.

'The interests of the fraternal Czechoslovak people are dear to the Soviet people,' stated craftsman V. S. Vershinin. 'The defence of the socialist achievements of the peoples of the Czechoslovak Socialist Republic, and of other fraternal countries, is the common concern of all states and peoples of the socialist commonwealth, who are bound together by the indissoluble ties of internationalism.'

'We, the Soviet people,' said foundry worker D. Shakhataev, 'will never permit the achievements of the Czechoslovak people gained in the common struggle, its success in the building of socialism to be destroyed by counter-revolution supported by international imperialism.'

V. Ganyushkin
Pravda special correspondent.

Appeal by the delegates to the Extraordinary 14th Congress of the Czechoslovak Communist Party to the Communist Parties of the whole world.
(*22 August 1968, in the afternoon*)

We appeal to the Communist and Workers' Parties of the whole world, and in particular to the Parties and peoples of the Soviet Union, the Bulgarian People's Republic, the Polish People's Republic, the German Democratic Republic, the Hungarian People's Republic, whose troops have occupied our country.

In January, our party began the process of reviving socialism. It began to develop in broad measure the democratic and humane principles of socialism, in accordance with conditions at this new stage of our progress. It believed that the principles of sovereignty and non-interference would be respected, and that all difficult questions would be resolved by negotiation. The leadership of our Party worked on this assumption in all negotiations – bilateral and multilateral – that have taken place since January. This policy, which is set out in the 'Action Programme' of the Central Committee of the Czechoslovak Communist Party, attracted unprecedented authority and support for our Party. A subject for discussion at the 14th Extraordinary Congress, preparations for which were being completed, was to have been how to secure and accelerate this progress. On the eve of the Congress, without any grounds, without the agreement of the legal government and party organs, against the wishes of our people, troops of the USSR, Polish People's Republic, the People's Republic of Bulgaria, the German Democratic Republic and the Hungarian People's Republic forcibly seized our territory, caused disorder in the country, made – and continue to make – it impossible to continue the progress which we had begun. We stand before the bitter truth: troops of states which we have grown accustomed to regard as our friends are behaving like occupiers. The constitutional authorities of our state and the representatives of the Party are no longer able to carry out their functions. They are deprived of the opportunity to discuss in the normal constitutional ways the situation that has arisen. They have no access to the means of communication. Prominent leaders are interned. There can be no doubt that these actions must lead to fatal consequences for the entire communist movement. We declare that our people – and with it our Communist party – will never be reconciled to these actions; they reject them, and will do everything possible to secure the restoration of normal life in our country.

To this end, a large part of the delegates to the Extraordinary 14th Congress have met in response to the demands and wishes of Communists, and of society as a whole; they had been legally elected at regional and provincial conferences. They address the following appeal and request for help to you.

So that it may be possible freely to continue our socialist progress, it is essential that the following demands be fulfilled:
1. Immediately free all representatives of the party, the government, the National Assembly, the Czech National Council and the National Front who have been interned, and make it possible for them, as well as for the President of the Republic, to carry out their functions unhindered.
2. Restore all civil rights and freedoms immediately.
3. Begin without delay the speedy withdrawal of all occupying armies.

The Extraordinary 14th Congress of the Party declares that it recognises no representatives of the Party and government, except those elected by the appropriate democratic means.

In connection with the tragic consequences (for the cause of socialism), of the occupation of our country, we ask you, Comrades:

To support our just cause by political means, and express your views to the representatives of the parties responsible for the actions affecting our country. To consider the possibility and desirability of summoning a conference of Communist and Workers' Parties, in which a delegation of ours would also take part. To contact only those representatives of our Party whom this Congress will elect.

Defend the human face of socialism. This is our international duty.

The Delegates of the 14th Extraordinary
Congress of the Czechoslovak Communist Party.
Rude Pravo, 23 August 1968 (Special Congress edition)

To all Students of the World

I am a Czech student, I am 22 years old. As I write this appeal, large numbers of Soviet tanks stand almost under my windows. The muzzles of their guns are trained on a government building carrying the inscription 'For socialism and peace!' I remember this slogan on the building ever since I became conscious of my surroundings. Only seven months, however, have gone by since this inscription began to take on its original meaning. For seven months, my country has been led by people who, probably for the first time in history, set out to prove that socialism and democracy can exist together. It is not known at present where these people have been taken. I do not know if we shall see or hear them again. There is a great deal I do not know. I do not know, for example, for how long Soviet soldiers will be unable to silence the free radio stations that are informing our people truthfully. Nor do I know whether I shall again meet my friends abroad, whether I shall ever, as I had intended, finish my university education; but just now everything loses the meaning that it had. At 3 o'clock on the morning of 21 August 1968, I woke up in a world completely different from that in which I had gone to sleep a few hours earlier.

Perhaps you think that the Czechs behaved like cowards, because they did not fight. But one cannot face tanks with bare hands. I would like to assure you that the Czechs and Slovaks behaved as a politically mature people who can be broken physically, but morally – never. That is why I am writing this. You can help us only in one respect – do not forget Czechoslovakia. We ask you to support our passive resistance and gradually strengthen the pressure of public opinion throughout the world. Think of Czechoslovakia even when it is no longer a newspaper sensation.

The only Czechoslovakia we acknowledge is a Czechoslovakia that is free and neutral.

Student, 1st undated special edition, circa 23 August 1968.

PART ONE

RED SQUARE

On 21 August, troops from five countries of the Warsaw Pact carried out a treacherous and unprovoked attack on Czechoslovakia.

The aggressive actions of the USSR and its allies met with a severe rebuff from world public opinion. . . .

The most determined protest against aggression in Czechoslovakia (in our own country – Natalia Gorbanevskaya) was a sit-down protest, which took place on 25 August, at 12 noon, in Red Square.

Human rights year in the Soviet Union.
Chronicle of Current Events,[1] No 3, 31 August 1968.

EYE-WITNESS ACCOUNT OF THE DEMONSTRATION

Sunday 25 August 1968

Noon. Provincials and foreign tourists, policemen, soldiers on leave and excursions crowd into Red Square. It is hot, half the Square is closed and empty but for the queue for the Mausoleum.

As the clock is about to strike the guard changes at the Mausoleum; droves of onlookers and small boys run to the Spassky Gates, their eyes darting in every direction.

The clock strikes. A black Volga hurtles out of the Gates and roars down the street, past the GUM department stores.

Just then several people, seven or eight of them, sit down and unfurl banners by the mediaeval platform, the old Execution

Ground where a fair number of people are standing about, or sitting, or looking at St Basil's. One can make out an inscription from some thirty yards away – 'Stop Soviet interference in Czechoslovakia'.

In a few seconds, people – about ten of them – come rushing headlong towards the others from various points in the immediate vicinity. First they snatch away, tear, crumple the banners and snap off a little Czech flag, just like one of those distributed to people to welcome President Svoboda two days earlier. The new arrivals, having disposed of the banners, start hitting those sitting down about the face and head.

A crowd immediately gathers and displays the usual street corner curiosity about a row. 'What's up?' they ask one another.

In the thick of the crowd, several people aged between thirty and forty, dressed in everyday clothes, are sitting, surrounded by the first to have run up. Two are women, one young one with glasses, the other older, with greying hair. A baby, apparently a few months old, sleeps in its pram.

The onlookers cannot make out what is happening, since there is certainly nothing objectionable going on, except that the lips of one of the people sitting down are covered in blood. There is some speculation: 'Czechs, probably!' 'Well, they should be sitting at home', 'Why come here?' 'If they're not Czechs, off with them to the police, and that'll be the end of it!' But the prevailing mood soon sharpens. Presently, carefully articulated remarks spurt from the surrounding crowd: 'Anti-Soviets!', 'Off with them to the police!' 'Stamping on, that's what they need!' 'Dirty yids!' 'The tart's got herself a child – now she comes to Red Square' (the latter clearly aimed at the woman with the pram).

Those sitting down either stare in silence at the surrounding faces or try to explain to the onlookers that they are here to protest against Soviet aggression in Czechoslovakia. Their softly spoken words, hardly audible even to those who are closest, are drowned by shouts: 'Scum', 'What aggression? Everybody knows why we went in'. A woman tries to side with those sitting down, and is shouted at: 'She should be arrested too.'

Four or five minutes go by. A policeman with a whistle clears a way through the crowd for a light-blue Volga which had stopped some seven to ten yards from the Execution Ground, on the GUM side.

A number of people in plain clothes, with no insignia to distinguish them from the rest – some of them had followed the car through the crowd, others were standing beside those sitting down – obey orders from a few others and take four men and one woman (the one with the greying hair) to the car. Among those being led away, the first snaps: 'Don't twist my arm.' Another is half carried, half dragged along. A third, his lips bleeding, has time to shout 'Long live Czechoslovakia!' before they ram him into the car. All of them get hit over the head before being pushed through the left-hand rear door of the Volga; the last to be shoved in, a woman, has her neck jerked to make her crawl though the open door.

The car moves off. The woman in glasses stays sitting beside the Execution Ground. Another woman stands beside her, holding the pram by its handle. An argument starts up between them and the bystanders. Voices ring out: 'Hooligans!', 'You get given bread, don't you?' – She answers: 'My Czech flag had been broken.'

Some try to persuade the woman to leave; they ask the crowd to make room – 'Citizens, let's give the baby a chance to breathe'. Meanwhile, the abuse and shouting do not let up: 'Off to the police with them too'. A reasonably pleasant looking young blonde lays down the law: 'People like you should be stamped out. Together with your children, so they don't grow up as morons!'

Everyone stays put. Some eight to ten minutes go by after the men have been removed and before another light-blue Volga draws up, ten yards or so away, between the Execution Ground and the Mausoleum. A way is cleared and the women are carried away, not as roughly as the men.

They are bundled into the car, together with the pram.

The crowd, still unsatisfied, hangs about but a traffic policeman in the Square repeatedly asks the people to disperse. Heated arguments develop in some places: 'You are defending them are you?' A young man in glasses, with a tiresome, persistent voice, proposes: 'Let's talk it over, let's sort it out', but he cannot find a sparring partner. An excited man in a sports shirt says to his stout wife, in her Sunday best: 'If you don't understand anything, just shut up!' She had been trying to add her voice – which lacked the necessary professional touch – to the chorus of disapproval.

As the crowd begins to disperse (quarter past twelve has struck) whistles suddenly sound, traffic policemen begin to dash about. Two black Chaikas shoot out of the Spassky Gate, through the eight yard gap between the two sections of the crowd and down the street past GUM.

The car windows are curtained. On the middle seat of the second car a man in a hat half turns aside and beside him, on the rear seat, a face peers out through the right-hand window. This face is like a photograph of Dubcek. It was to be announced two days later, on Tuesday, that he had joined the Czechoslovak delegation for talks in Moscow.

Then another crowd gathers round a green Volga between the Execution Ground and St Basil's. Someone is trying to expose the film in a foreigner's camera, while he protests in Russian with a strong accent. The car moves off. The protests die down. The crowd slowly disperses.

Somebody says: 'Czechs are objecting because their flag has been broken'. A shrug answers the question: 'So what?' It is 12.22 by the Spassky Tower clock.

At 16.00, on 25 August, the BBC quoted in an English news bulletin a Reuter despatch from Moscow reporting that 'at least' four people had been detained in Red Square, 'apparently' in connection with a demonstration by a group of intelligentsia against Soviet intervention in Czechoslovakia.

Two days later, one of the radio stations broadcasting to the USSR reported that among those detained were Pavel Litvinov and Larissa Daniel, wife of the imprisoned writer. The detainees would be charged with 'violation of public order'.

Comments on the eye-witness account of the demonstration

Not everything is accurate in this account, but I did not know the author, had no right to edit what he wrote, and shall therefore merely point to the inaccuracies it contains.

The slogans were up for such a short time that the author evidently reconstructed the text of the slogan he saw from its meaning. He probably noticed the most striking slogan, in bold black and white – 'Hands off the cssr (Czechoslovak Socialist Republic)' – and remembered it as 'Stop Soviet interference in Czechoslovakia'.

There were not just two cars, and I was not taken away with another woman. Nine people had been removed in at least three cars before me, including three women. Then, only after a long wait, they took me away and they did not pile the pram into the same car as me, but tried to find another. The eye-witness also mistook the woman 'taken away' with me. She was in fact a kgb operative who had struck me on the mouth, but this was only noticed by people standing closest to the car.

The author of the account has, I think, described the crowd too luridly. It seemed more neutral to me, and most of the remarks he quotes were uttered by people who had come in that first group that tore down our banners and had then mingled with the crowd.

WHAT I REMEMBER OF THE DEMONSTRATION

It rained the day before. Sunday was fine and sunny from the start. I wheeled the pram past the Alexandrovsky Garden railing and the crowd was so thick that I had to leave the pavement for the roadway. The little one slept peacefully, with a bag at his feet and spare pants and nappies in it. Two banners and a Czechoslovak flag lay under the mattress. I was telling myself that if nobody was there to take the banners from me I would fasten them on either side of the pram and hold the flag in my hand.

I had made the flag as early as the twenty-first. When we went for a walk I stuck it on the pram and at home hung it from the window. Early on the twenty-fifth I got the banners ready, wrote on them, hemmed them and mounted them on sticks. One of the inscriptions was in Czech: 'Long live free and independent Czechoslovakia'. The other carried my favourite slogan: 'For your freedom and ours'. I am in love with Poland; and I found it particularly hard to bear during those days that, along with our own troops, soldiers of the Polish army had entered Czechoslovakia; the soldiers of a country that had struggled for centuries against imperial aggressors, and against Russia first and foremost.

'For your freedom and ours' was the slogan of the Polish insurgents in the fight to liberate their homeland and of Polish émigrés as they died in every corner of the world to gain freedom for other nations. It was also the slogan of those Russian democrats who came to understand in the course of the last century that a nation which oppresses others cannot itself be free.

The road between the Alexandrovsky Garden and the Historical Museum was barred by police because of the queue in front of the Lenin Mausoleum. This made me think that the whole of Red Square was crammed with people, right down to the church of St Basil. I went round the museum the other way and the Square opened up before me, spacious and almost desolate with the solitary Place of Skulls – the old Execution Ground – a white spot in the midst of it. As I went by the GUM stores I passed some people I knew, smiled at them and walked on without stopping.

I came to the Execution Ground from the direction of GUM just as Pavel, Larissa and a few others were approaching it from the Square. The clock began to strike and the demonstration started, neither on the first stroke nor on the fateful last, but at one of the twelve at random, or maybe even between two strokes. It took a few seconds to unroll all four banners – I gave mine to our friends and kept the flag for myself. Then, in a single movement, we sat down on the raised parapet round the Execution Ground.

Lara was on my right holding a white calico with 'Hands off

the CSSR' in clear black lettering. Pavlik sat to the right of her. I had deliberately given him 'For your freedom and ours' when I fetched out the banners, because we had once spent a long time talking about the inner meaning of this slogan and I knew that he too set store by it. Vadim Delone and Volodia Dremlyuga sat beyond Pavlik but I could hardly see them because the curve of the pavement followed the outline of the Execution Ground and one had to bend over to see the end of it. That is why I failed to see them later beating up Vadim. Kostia Babitsky, whom I had not met before, was beside the pram and beyond him Vitia Feinberg, recently arrived from Leningrad. I took all this in at one quick glance but, looking back, less time still elapsed between the raising of our banners and the moment when they started to rip. People had hardly begun to gather round us when those who were intent on undoing our demonstration came racing towards us, beating the nearest onlookers to it. They leapt on us and tore down our banners without sparing even a glance for what was written on them. I shall never forget the sound of ripping cloth.

I saw two people hitting Pavlik, a man with his briefcase and a woman with a heavy handbag. A powerful fist grasped my little flag. 'What?' I said. 'Are you trying to take the Czechoslovak official flag from me?' The fist wavered and relaxed its grip. I turned my head for a moment and saw them hitting Vitia Feinberg. The banners had gone and only I had succeeded in defending my flag. Then a tall, smooth faced man, one of those who had been hitting our friends, came to the aid of his hesitant comrade and angrily snatched at the flag. It broke and I was left holding a snapped piece of stick.

As they ran towards us these people shouted, less to give vent to their unbridled feelings than to provoke the crowd into copying them. I only made out two sentences, which I have quoted in my letter: 'They're all Jews!' and 'Beat up the anti-Soviets!' They used some less printable expressions as well: during questioning at the trial, Babitsky was reproved by the judge for quoting one of the insults directed at us.

Yet the crowd that had gathered made no move to 'beat up

the anti-Soviets'. It just stood around us like any other in-quisitive crowd.

For a short while, all those who had been hitting us and tearing up the banners, vanished. The bystanders were mostly silent. Here and there a hostile or puzzled comment could be heard. Two or three speakers who had stayed behind when the others left ranted on. They stuck to two main themes: 'We liberated them' and 'We keep them fed' – 'them' being the Czechs and Slovaks. New arrivals would ask, driven by curiosity: 'What's going on here?' 'This is a sit-down demonstration to protest against the occupation of Czechoslovakia', we would explain. 'What occupation?' some would ask in genuine surprise. The same two or three speakers went on shouting: 'We liberated them, we lost 200,000 men liberating them, and all they do is stage a counter-revolution.' Or again: 'We are saving them from Western Germany.' Or better still: 'We must hand over Czechoslovakia to the Americans, must we?' And so on, with the whole battery of imperial arguments, right up to the statement that 'they themselves asked us to bring in troops'.

It was difficult to hear which of my friends was saying what against the noise raised by the speechmakers. Somebody, I remember, explained that 'The letter from a group of the Central Committee of the Czechoslovak Communist Party asking for the entry of troops is a fake, it's no accident that it is unsigned.' My reply to 'You ought to be ashamed!' was 'Yes, I am ashamed – ashamed that our tanks are in Prague.'

The first car drew up some minutes later. People who had been present told me afterwards how those who had snatched away our slogans rushed around aimlessly in search of transport. Eventually they intercepted the odd cars coming from Kuibyshev Street towards the Moscow River bridge and chased them back to the Execution Ground.

They picked up my friends and carried them away to the cars. The crowd was round me and I could not see how they were being carted away and who was going with whom. Babitsky was taken away last. He was sitting next to the pram and earned a taunt from the crowd: 'He's hiding behind a baby!' I was left on my own.

The noise woke the baby, but it did not cry. I changed it and an unknown woman who was standing beside me helped me. The crowd was thick and close. People who had not been there at the start were pushing forward and asking what was going on. I explained that it was a demonstration against the invasion of Czechoslovakia, that my friends had been carted away and that my Czechoslovak flag had been broken. 'What are they, Czechs?' people asked one another. 'Well, why don't they go home to Czechoslovakia and demonstrate there?' I have been told that a rumour went round Moscow that very evening about a Czech woman with a baby demonstrating in Red Square.

I said in reply to the sermon of one of the licensed orators still present that the Constitution guaranteed freedom of demonstration. 'What about that?' volunteered someone in the crowd. 'She's right enough in that. No, I don't know what happened here earlier, but she is right in that.' The crowd kept quiet and waited for developments. I also waited.

'Go away, girl,' somebody kept on saying. I stayed put. I told myself that if it had suddenly been decided not to take me away I would stay until one o'clock and then go.

A voice was demanding that people should stand clear. In front of an approaching Volga came a man and the woman who had hit Pavlik with her handbag; she had later stood in the crowd cursing – and probably memorizing – any bystander who displayed sympathy. 'Well, what are you standing about for? Can't you see she's ill . . .' the man kept on saying. I was lifted up, the woman next to me hardly had time to press the baby into my arms and they pushed me into the car. My eyes met those of a redheaded Frenchman standing close by. He stared at me in horror and I thought: 'That's my last memory of freedom', while the man who had come for me pointed to the same thickset brawny woman and told her: 'Get in. You'll be a witness.' 'Take one more witness', I called to him pointing at the nearest bystanders. 'That will do', he answered and the 'witness' who, incidentally, was never seen again as a witness, sat down next to me. I threw myself at the window, lowered it and shouted: 'Long live free Czechoslovakia.' Half way through the sentence the witness took a swipe at my mouth. The man got in beside the driver and said: 'To the 50th police station.' I lowered the window again and tried to call out: 'They're taking me to the 50th police station,' but she hit me over the mouth again, which was both humiliating and painful.

'How dare you hit me', I cried each time and each time she answered, baring her teeth:

'Who hit you? Nobody hit you.'

The car made for Pushkin Street by way of Kuibyshev Street and past the Lubyanka.[2] I found out afterwards that the first cars went straight to the Lubyanka but had been turned away and sent on to the 50th station. The man said to the driver as we went along: 'What luck you came our way.' And when we got there the driver asked this 'casual representative of an infuriated crowd' to sign his duty log, or else he would be late.

'What is your name?' I asked the woman in the car.

'Ivanova', she answered with the same insolent smile she had put on when she said: 'Nobody hit you.'

'Well, of course, it's very easy to call oneself Ivanova.'

'Of course it is', she answered, with that smile again.

THE ACCOUNT OF TANIA BAEVA, THE EIGHTH
PARTICIPANT IN THE DEMONSTRATION

At the investigation, I told them: 'I was there by chance.' Why? Why was I not afraid to go to the Square, and why did I later deny it?

24th, in the evening

I knew that I would go – I made up my mind straight away. Why? Understanding, and the anger born of understanding, came later. I knew intuitively that violence had been done, that my country was once again the gendarme of Europe. I also knew that my friends were going. I went with my friends.

They chose to go with Czechoslovakia. They were giving their freedom to Czechoslovakia. And I gave it to my friends.

I understood that a camp lay ahead. I made ready for this. Late that night I cleaned my flat and wrote letters to my friends and to my parents, who were away. My mind was free of doubt.

25th in Red Square, at about 12 o'clock

We were all together, joking, smiling. Suddenly Vadik appeared. He had heard by chance. He had not been told. After all, he had just come out of prison. 'Vadik, go away!' 'No!' He smiled.

12 noon

We sat down. We had already crossed over to the other side. Freedom was now the dearest thing on earth for us. At the start, only ordinary people stood round us, without understanding. Natasha held a little Czech flag in her outstretched hand. She talked about freedom, about Czechoslovakia. The crowd was deaf. Vitia Feinberg smiled his vague, short-sighted smile. Then, suddenly, a whistle, and six or seven men – they wore plain clothes – came running from the Mausoleum. They all seemed tall to me, aged about twenty-six to thirty. They came pounding along shouting: 'They've sold themselves for dollars.' They snatched away the slogans and, after a moment's confusion, the little flag. With a shout of 'Beat up the Jews' one of them set about kicking Feinberg in the face. Kostia tried to cover him with his body. Blood! I jumped up, horrified. (Later, Tania bent down to wipe Victor's blood-covered face with her handkerchief – N.G.) Another was hitting Pavlik with a handbag. The crowd looked on with approval. Only one woman demurred: 'Why beat them?' The people in plain clothes faced the crowd and loudly voiced their indignation.

Some fifteen minutes later, cars drew up. People in plain clothes started to drag us to the cars, without producing any documents to prove their authority. I had only one wish – to land in the same car as my friends. I tried to rush towards them. Someone twisted my arms. Five were shoved into one car, to the accompaniment of hasty blows. They dragged me off and dumped me in another car with a frightened youth they had grabbed by mistake. Swearing, they drove to the Lubyanka, where they telephoned, cursed, and went back to police station No 50 – the 'Half-rouble'.

The Half-rouble

We were all together again, excited, laughing, joking, not thinking of what lay ahead – I perhaps, less than anyone else. We were together, that was what mattered. I looked at Vadik; he smiled, dark patches of sweat were spreading on his shirt. It was probably hardest of all for him, now. I looked through the window, people were walking past, free . . . I would get up and walk out, get up and walk out, get up and . . . I looked out of the window – the dusty pavement, the sun, voices. A policeman drew the curtain. I looked at my colleagues – Vitia smiled through his bleeding lips, the rest were talking away. I happened to glance into the custody cell: three men were squatting there, they watched us listlessly, coldly – we were from the other world.

I knew that prison awaited me. Suddenly a sentence caught my ear: 'Well, as to you, Tatka, they won't let you go!' Already, we had been sorted into those without hope and those who would return to freedom and the world. A thought sprang to my mind: 'What if I try?' I went to Lara: 'Lar, shall I try to get out of it?' 'Of course, dear, the main thing is done.' For me the main thing was over. For them, it was just starting.

Three hours passed. We asked in vain for a doctor for Vitia. Finally, they began to call us. Pavlik was taken away; he said goodbye and went. Vadik smiled at us from the door. Then, my turn. The second floor, the usual investigator's room. By now, I thought of nothing, and picked over memories of *that* life, while *another* began.

Interrogation

'I was there by chance.' (Who could believe this? Three demonstrations in my past already – and still 'by chance'). I told how we had been struck, how the slogans were taken away. I supported the views expressed. The interrogation dragged on half-heartedly. Suddenly: 'Why do you say you were there by chance? Are you afraid to answer for your actions? You are dishonest.'

Honesty – here? Do these people need honesty? I realized only later that it was a matter of being honest with myself.

Then the interrogation was over. They led me away. I saw Lara and she smiled encouragement.

They drove me home for the search. I travelled through Moscow at evening time, a Moscow I had never particularly liked. Now everything was dear to me: the noise, and the bustle, and the laughter – all these signs of freedom.

Nobody was at home. Now they began to address me familiarly, as 'Thou'. Police captain Bogotoba, who had interrogated me, and two people in civilian clothes, carried out the search. They had brought witnesses with them, two boys of nineteen – Andrei Istakov and Mikhail Antusyuk. The witnesses sat in silence, scared stiff. No woman was present. While they searched, I gathered my things in a string bag. They rummaged among my clothes, looked at family photographs, asked whether I kept a diary. I asked them if it was cold inside a cell: why not – was it not hot outside? They saw that I was collecting my things in earnest, stopped looking about and looked away. I ate in a hurry. I was not hungry, but when would I have another chance to eat? They were silent. I turned off the gas and the fridge. They were silent.

The search went on for three hours. They rummaged in my father's personal things and took two of his typewriters, and his greetings cards from foreign scientists. They took my exercise books, my note books, my tapes.

'You may stay at home', they said with a grin. And went away.

The interrogations went on, with nothing new for the record.

The last time, after the Pushkin Square demonstration, they had 'spared' me, so they said, but now I would 'not escape retribution'. Galakhov, the investigating officer, was not specially amiable, but seemed most anxious to bring the conversation round to my private life. He even produced a piece of paper to enumerate my 'lovers' because there were, apparently, so many of them that he could not remember them all. All my friends were included in the list: Galakhov obviously had no conception of the meaning of friendship. There were no more such questions after I said I would demand a change of investigators. He, and later Akimova, had a great deal to say about N. Gorbanevskaya: 'Her place is in a psychiatric hospital', 'What sort of a mother is that?', 'She would be in prison but for our humane approach'. Crude blackmail was the mainstay of the interrogation: 'But Delone says . . .', or 'We shall summon your father . . .' About Czechoslovakia, they said little. It would have been pointless to argue about clichés borrowed from editorials.

At the last session, they said: 'We have decided to spare you this time, but . . .' The usual threats followed.

As I gathered my things, taken away during the search (some of them had been sent to the KGB) I asked Akimova what she thought of the accused. Yes, she said, they were obviously good people, she liked them, but she did not understand what made them look for punishment. Why did they prefer prison to freedom, penal servitude to their favourite occupation, a camp to their family? What sort of a mother is it who puts her child in danger? The state exists, the law exists, the laws must be respected. 'Why then do you not respect the laws?' I asked, and Akimova answered somewhat stuffily: 'We too can make mistakes.'

A week after the demonstration I was expelled from the Institute. The notice stated that while an external student at the Moscow Institute of Historical Archives I had not been working. I sought the help of a lawyer in the Ministry of Higher Education, who confirmed that I was right to be indignant about this decision by showing me the actual letter of the law on the subject. But Themis, the Greek goddess of justice, was helpless

in the face of Senior Inspector Comrade Shumsky. He spread
his hands and said: 'But we didn't expel you for that . . .'

And so, they 'spared' me . . . Now my friends are *there*,
while I am here. My brave, steadfast friends – and I am here. I
bow before them – Lara, Pavlik, Natasha, Kostia, Vitia and
Volodia. And Vadik, only a boy, as we thought, but who paid a
dreadful price for growing up.

I recanted. Only my share in the demonstration, neither my
friends, nor my convictions – but I recanted. Now I am here.
Who am I?

NOTE   This book was ready, including an account by Tania; I had
asked her to recall where we had been sitting, how each of us had been
taken away, what she remembered about the Half-rouble station and the
investigation. Tania gave me a fairly short account, without knowing
why I wanted it, and I took it down. She was among the first to read
this book. When she saw what I had written, the brief factual report
that omitted the most important fact – we had kept quiet about it –
that she had taken part in the demonstration, she decided that the
truth must out. The investigation had not proved Tania's participation
and I therefore did not think it right to mention it. I am glad that
Tania did so herself.   N. G.

PART TWO

THE CASE:
VIOLATION OF PUBLIC ORDER

IN THE 'HALF-ROUBLE'

Police station No 50, commonly called the 'Half-rouble' (i.e. 50 kopeks) stands – or rather stood – on Pushkin Street, next door to the *Romen* Theatre. For some reason it has now been re-numbered 19, but the same gloomy policeman still stands at the entrance and tries to make the women sit to one side of the door and the men on the other. And let them not dare to meet.

This is the station nearest to Pushkin Square, the traditional place for demonstrations in Moscow. Our presence there was clearly also a matter of tradition.

I have tender memories of the three hours we spent together in the 'Half-rouble' before the interrogation began. We had held the demonstration and were happy. Larissa had become positively sombre during the last, difficult months with Marchenko's arrest,[3] that of her cousin Irina,[4] and finally 21 August, the day both of the invasion and of Tolia Marchenko's trial. She now visibly brightened. We were light at heart.

There were eleven people in the duty room. In addition to seven demonstrators, there were Tania Baeva, Maya Rusakov-skaya, Inna Korkhova and Misha Leman. Misha had obviously been taken for an acquaintance of ours and lumped in with us. There was no sign of the other witnesses, particularly of those 'witnesses' who had torn the banners and beaten up the boys. We saw nothing of them, although their interrogation reports were dated 25 August. Nor did we know what had happened to the banners. None of the names of the 'citizens' who detained us or handed the banners to the police later emerged in the evidence; details on this score were remarkably scarce. Yet those few 'citizens' who appeared in court confidently stated that they could read the slogans from a distance – even 'Freedom for Dubcek', written in pencil.

As to the slogans – 'What was the fourth one?', I asked one of the boys.

'Shame on the occupiers' on one side, 'Freedom for Dubcek', on the other, he said, but could not quite remember which side was showing – probably 'Shame on the occupiers'.

This was Volodia Dremlyuga. I should have asked him and avoided that annoying mistake in my letter.[5] The slogan was 'Down with the occupiers', and I omitted 'Freedom for Dubcek'; since it was on the back of the banner, it might as well not have been there. I wrote that letter immediately after the end of the Moscow talks and this may also have influenced me, because I already knew that Dubcek had taken part in them and that he had a share in the compromises arrived at. The name of Dubcek had already lost something of its magic.

We had demanded from the very start that Victor Feinberg be given a medical examination. The duty policeman wrote down all our names, surnames and patronymics in this connection and, as a result, the procedure of establishing our identities could be skipped. Presently a frightened doctor appeared, Victor was taken away, and we did not see him again. There was no medical examination report in the evidence, as I later discovered. Perhaps it was never made or was removed from the evidence along with the rest of the material about Feinberg. It would have provided solid evidence of the methods adopted to deal with demonstrations.

We also stated that the others detained with us had not taken part in the demonstration: they should be interrogated first and not held unnecessarily. They were indeed interrogated, but were not released, and were held, as we were, until late in the evening.

After three hours, Volodia Dremlyuga got up and calmly made for the door, to the great fury of our guard. Quietly,

Volodia explained that we could not be held for more than three hours without a detention order. We backed his statement. Policemen began to rush about. A head presently poked round the door:

'Is there a Litvinov here?'

Pavlik was taken away for interrogation. Larissa followed, and then it was my turn.

As we sat in the 'Half-rouble' the prophetic parody of the old song kept coming back to us: 'Once again, yet once more, many many times again, once more Pashka and Natashka and Larissa Bogoraz.'

I was interrogated by Vasilenko, an investigator of the Moscow

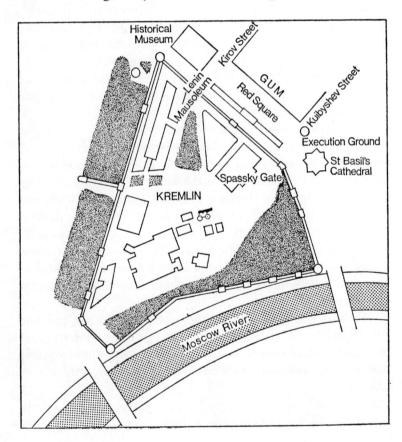

Protection of Public Order Department. I made statements about the way in which the demonstrators had been treated, how the banners had been ripped, about the violence I had witnessed and the woman who had struck me in the car. I refused to answer any questions about the demonstration itself, its preparation and organization, but stressed that it was a sit-down demonstration and that it was easy to distinguish the participants from people detained by mistake. I motivated my refusal to answer by pointing out that only those who broke up the demonstration and struck peaceful demonstrators had violated public order in Red Square: I would therefore confine myself to discussing their actions. To be consistent, I even refused to say when the demonstration had begun.

Eventually, Vasilenko picked up the report which he had completed, accompanied me from the third floor to an office in a corridor on the second floor and went in to consult someone. The wild, incomprehensible shouts of an investigator came from another office. 'Aren't you ashamed of yourself', was all I could make out. The other voice was so quiet that I could only spot the answers by the pauses between infuriated shrieks. I jumped to the conclusion that Larissa was being questioned there, and that hurt. I wished that they had been shouting at me. I do not know to this day who was getting such rough questioning.

I listened hard, but there was not a sound from downstairs, where I had left my baby.

Vasilenko emerged from his chief's office and we went back upstairs. He pulled out a new record sheet, filled in the personal details, then asked me about the demonstration all over again. I told him that I had given all the information I considered necessary. The interrogator was getting nothing from me, so he tore up the blank record sheet and took me down to the second floor again.

He did not, of course, accept my refusal to give evidence all that quickly on either occasion and employed every means of talking me round, including the classic: 'But your comrades are holding nothing back!'

'That is their business,' I told him with a smile. 'If they really

told all, it would make no difference to my evidence.' I
knew my comrades well, in any case. That evening I saw
Dremlyuga's record sheet – just the questionnaire – on Major
Karakhanyan's table during a confrontation with which I will
deal later. Even from what I saw it was clear that Dremlyuga
was being even more consistent than I. In the spaces for signature
– under the questionnaire and the warning about refusing to
give evidence or giving false evidence – the investigator had
been forced to write: 'Refused to sign'.

Yet it was as witnesses that they interrogated us. And as
'witnesses' that they identified us.

I was 'identified' at about nine in the evening, and remained
until then in an office on the second floor, completely out of
touch with my baby. First one policeman, then another stood
guard over me, both thoroughly annoyed at this chore, because
they clearly had enough on their hands without it. I asked the
fat middle-aged one about my baby, and whether he had seen it.
'Your girl friend is looking after it', he told me. I heard later
that Inna and Misha Leman had coped most of the time but that,
for a while, there was nobody with the baby except a young – and
fortunately kindly – policeman. The baby, incidentally, behaved
in exemplary fashion, though it might well have cried. I had fed
it last in the middle of the day; out of the food left, one small
bottle of yoghurt was spilled when the pram was searched and
the cream cheese turned sour in the heat so that, while I was
away, my friends had to make do with what was left.

I chatted about Czechoslovakia with the fat policeman: 'Now
you are saying that there is a counter-revolution going on and
that troops must be sent in, because that's what the papers
write. In a month they will write that troops should not have
been sent – and you will just repeat it after them.'

Finally, the policeman handed over guarding me to lads from a
vigilante squad.[6] Whenever I had seen such lads at work – at
Bukovsky's trial, at the trial of Galanskov[7] and Ginzburg[8] – I
was driven to thinking that they must have joined the squad
out of some feeling of inferiority. Now, seeing them again and
reluctantly listening to their talk, I became more than ever

convinced that I was right. Two of them, I gathered, were assistants in book shops. This in no way improved their minds. They only really woke up when one of them announced that a friend of his had brought a pornographic book from West Germany. They began a most knowledgeable discussion about how such books were produced over there, and who had seen what book. Because I was present, they did not use the word 'pornographic' and resorted instead to some conventional but completely transparent euphemism.

I also obtained clear confirmation that, as we had thought, squad members were now being used as witnesses during searches. While I was there the investigator twice detailed two lads as witnesses, and lads from the same lot served as witnesses when I was being identified.

I saw and heard my guards, but my mind was wandering. I had no idea as yet that I might be released, and looked out of the window, trying to fix the threadbare view in my memory for ever: the yellow, peeling walls enclosed a bare courtyard. Two trees rose high behind the wall. At a certain moment a clear feeling came to me that I would be released. I was very calm and only longed to be back with my baby again soon.

At about 8 o'clock, I was called for identification. They sat me down beside two beautiful girls some 10 years younger than I and asked a certain Oleg Konstantinovich Davidovich, a thin-faced, thin-lipped young man in civilian clothes, to pick me out from the 'three people presented for identification'. He did identify me, of course. He then stated under what circumstances he had seen me and what I had been doing, briefly at the identification, in great detail when we were confronted immediately afterwards. It was to the evidence of this very Davidovich, a senior KGB lieutenant from the strict régime camps in the Komi ASSR, that the court later gave more weight than to any other. At that time, in the 'Half-rouble', I was aware of only those parts of his evidence which directly concerned me: that I had arrived at the Execution Ground together with all the demonstrators, that I was holding a banner, that nobody had hit the demonstrators, that they had been sent to the station by members of the police, etc. – in a word, nothing but lies. He stated that I had made 'anti-Soviet speeches' and compared the introduction of Warsaw Pact forces with the Hitlerite invasion.

If one adds to this statements by him which were not known to me then – that he had entered Red Square from GUM (GUM is closed on Sundays), that Larissa was not holding a banner – it becomes pretty certain that either he was not in the Square at all, or else appeared only to help take away the demonstrators.

Before identification and confrontation I was led into a corridor and saw Larissa for the last time. They were taking her away for the search. 'Lara', I called. She smiled and waved her hand. She had never stopped smiling.

I saw Pavlik for a moment when the confrontation was over. He too was in a brighter mood, not joyfully animated like Lara, but radiating a kind of special tenderness. And so I parted from my two dearest friends.

Then I was told: 'You are free. Go with this comrade.' Without bothering too much how free I was, free in general or only from the confrontation, I went downstairs, accompanied by this 'comrade', to my baby who by this time had just done for the last of his dry pants. The entire pram was draped with wet nappies. They packed us and the pram into a police car and drove us home for the search.

THE SEARCHES

Eight searches were carried out that night in the six Muscovite demonstrators' homes and those of two people detained with us, Tania Baeva and Maya Rusakovskaya.

As usual, any *samizdat* texts, note books, scraps of paper with addresses, telephone numbers, personal notes were taken. From Dremlyuga they took, of all things, the Criminal Code. From me they took a typewritten collection of Mandelshtam's poems, from Dremlyuga and Maya Rusakovskaya – an American edition of Mandelshtam. For the first time over a long period of searches they again took my poems. Delone's poems had been removed

before and they were removed again this time. From Delone
they also took a cross.

It was Larissa's third search that month; there was practically
nothing left and, so as to get something, anything, they dug
everywhere short of ripping up the cushions. They turned Maya
Rusakovskaya's whole flat upside down. Five men – and no
woman – went to search Tatka's. I do not know how the
searches went at Pavlik's, Vadim's and Volodia's because nobody
was at home there that summer Sunday. Sanka Daniel arrived
home from the Baltic during the search, just in time to say
goodbye to his mother.

All the searches were carried out – or at least completed –
at night. Mine began at 10 o'clock in the evening, already
officially night time. A very correct young police captain was in
charge of the search. The witnesses were two young girls who
sat without stirring throughout the proceedings, not even daring
to eat the apples they were offered. Two men who did not
identify themselves searched the room, together with the captain.
One of them was completely mute and got through the evening
without saying a word, the other was the reverse, and garrulous.
For instance, he found the receipt for a letter of mine addressed
to a camp.

'Who's this Ginzburg?'

'My friend.'

'Is he in prison too?'

'In a camp.'

'Oh? What's the difference?'

I patiently explained the difference, not for the benefit of this
buffoon but for that of the girls, who did not seem to be squad
members.

'And what's he in for?'

'Article 70.'[9]

I again expounded the article and what Ginzburg had done and
why it was a 'White Book'.

'Ginzburg didn't give it that title. For some reason, it
acquired the name during the investigation. He simply called it
a collection of documents in the case of Sinyavsky and Daniel.'

A while later, he blandly asked again:

'But why did he call it a "White Book"?'

'Didn't I tell you? He did not call it that, the KGB did. So why not ask the KGB?'

At that, for the first and only time, he burst out:

'We're not KGB.'

'I didn't say that you were KGB. I said you should ask the KGB.'

The mute remained mute. He, it appeared, was KGB.

The chatterer found a box of watercolours.

'Was that what you splashed it on with?'

'What is this,' I asked, 'an interrogation, or a search?'

'Ah well!' He was offended but spoke almost gently. 'If you had said no, we'd have left it.'

The captain looked through my books and nodded at a collection of Gleb Gorbovsky's poems:

'That's a good poet.'

By then it was nearly two in the morning. The girls sat bolt upright and fought against sleep. Little Oska had been asleep on the divan for a long time. Yasik, my elder son, had not woken up when we arrived and slept on despite the light and the talk. My mother's face was like a stone mask but, even so, she was more calm than I had expected. The search came to an end. I made my protest against the carrying out of a search at night and the removal of the original signatures from the letter to the State Prosecutor about the trial of Ginzburg and Galanskov.

I should add that little enough of the mass of exhibits accumulated during the searches was produced as evidence: the paints and brush taken from me, and the board removed from Babitsky, which still carried the imprint of a banner that was never taken to Red Square – that was about all. Not everything removed during the searches was returned, however: the items taken from Bogoraz, Litvinov and Rusakovskaya were sent 'for checking' to the KGB as well as some belonging to Tania Baeva. The rest was returned. In defiance of all existing legislation a search of the home of Volodia Dremlyuga's mother was carried out in Melitopol on 7 October, long after the investigation was over.

On the morning after the search, a piece of material I had overlooked, inscribed 'For your freedom and ours', turned up in my dressing-gown pocket. Not liking the lettering, I had written it out again and forgot to throw away the draft. It is by no means easy to make a thorough search of our small, untidy room cluttered with books. And, strange as it may seem, there was a touch of humanity about the way in which it was done. As they were leaving, they told me: 'You may thank your children that the search was over so quickly.' I was told to present myself next day before Investigator Streltsov at 38, Petrovka.

PRELIMINARY EXAMINATION

By the morning of 26 August I already knew who had been searched and who arrested, or rather – formally speaking – detained. It would finally become clear on the twenty-eighth whether our friends were to be released.

I set out in the morning to register Yasik at school. Towards one o'clock I left for Petrovka, having asked a friend to sit with the baby. The promised pass was not at the pass office and the young man at the window said: 'Get Streltsov on the phone for yourself.' I explained that I had no need of Streltsov – it was he who had need of me. Then I wrote a statement on similar lines to the head of the department: I had presented myself, obtained no pass, had no intention of ringing around, and was off. This so that it could not be said later that I had failed to come. Thereupon, taking advantage of some spare time (I was tied by the baby's feeding times), I went about my business.

I do not usually notice that I am being followed and therefore tend to believe that it is not happening to me. But my shadows would have been hard to miss. Moreover, these were not callow novices, but hardened veterans, no doubt happy to shed the weary burden of ceaselessly following Litvinov and Bogoraz. The effect was most comic while these ageing yokels were around: you would stop and turn round and they would be overcome by confusion and start admiring the sky and the trees, or looking earnestly at their feet. I nipped into an editorial office I knew and, from the window, spotted this earnest person on the opposite side of the narrow street. By the time I came out again he and another like him were perched on benches on either side of the door and, willy-nilly, I marched past this guard of honour.

As soon as I reached home, the telephone rang:

'Natalia Evgenyevna? Fedorov, Deputy Prosecutor of Moscow, speaking. Why didn't you come? I came specially to talk to you.'

'I left a statement,' I explained and told him what it contained, but promised to come when I had fed the child.

Whether Fedorov changed his mind about talking to me or had never intended to do so I do not know, but that evening there were only two identifications and one confrontation, nothing else. As I walked to the investigator's office, Streltsov – who was standing with a boy behind the door leading into the building – pushed the lad away sharply, so that I should not see him. The lad, Vladimir Udartsev, a 19-year-old worker from Rostov, later identified me. They also confronted me with him. He was stuffed full of newspaper verbiage and kept mixing up aggression and escalation. He went on and on saying that I had been protesting against 'escalation in Czechoslovakia'. When I asked him whether he had seen how the demonstrators were detained and beaten, he curled up like some small scared animal and screamed angrily: 'You should all, all of you, be killed'. The investigator addressed him as 'thou', off-handedly. I imagine that the boy had been picked up in Red Square, held for a night in the lock-up, intimidated and turned into a good witness who hated us. After all, it was on our account that he had been picked up, wholly innocent though he was. But this, of course, is mere psychological guesswork.

Another thing he said was: 'They were beating themselves.' This story cropped up again during the investigation: 'He struck himself with his own fist', 'They hit each other', but no use of it was made in court.

By the time he had finished giving his evidence, my eyes were wide open – so far through astonishment, rather than horror. He said that when they set about detaining me I had knocked a man's glasses off and *begun to strangle my own child* to injure him, so as to be able to claim later that we had been beaten up. This struck me as such unmitigated rubbish that I said to him: 'You probably don't know how one should hold a child.' This, I decided, was what he thought he had seen and was honestly describing.

I later found that other witnesses in the case also testified that I had been 'strangling the child'. A number of people could not independently have thought they had seen anything like this. This was undoubtedly evidence fabricated at the instigation of those in charge of the examination and investigation who, in due course, obviously realized that this tale was too unlikely and decided to abandon it. Udartsev, incidentally, went back on these statements in court.

The same day, I was identified by Tatiana Mikhailovna Velikanova, Babitsky's wife. She had come looking for her husband, but they immediately interrogated her as a witness and even involved her in the identification procedure. It was in this memorable way that we became acquainted.

Instead of Streltsov, my interrogator turned out to be a man whose name I have forgotten and who was the first to tell me that we had been 'rescued'. When I said that we were beaten up while being detained he replied that, if we had not been taken into custody, the crowd would have torn us to pieces. This theme of the investigation was later repeated by the Prosecutor in court. It bore no relation to reality, but was deemed to justify the behaviour of those who had used force.

Streltsov was in charge of the investigation. He signed the order to institute proceedings 'on the fact of the organization of, and active participation in, collective actions which violated public order at 12 noon on 25 August 1968 in Red Square'. The egregious Fedorov and Investigator Gnevkovskaya of the Prosecutor's office were already throwing their weight about and giving orders in the Petrovka offices. On my way out I heard Fedorov say about Udartsev: 'Give him a pass, but we shall still need him.' At that time I did not know who these people were and decided they must be from the KGB, judging by their bossy ways.

THE LETTER

I decided to write a letter because I realized that, apart from vague rumours, nothing was known about our demonstration. Western radio mentioned through the jamming an attempted demonstration and, even so, only 'according to rumours'. I had remained free and must therefore see the matter through to the end; the import and purpose of the demonstration, its slogans and its participants must not remain merely the subject of rumours. I wrote my letter and despatched it on 28 August when I became certain after three days that there was no intention of releasing the demonstrators.

I have already explained the reason for my mistake about the text of the banner. I also do not regard as completely satisfactory that sentence in the letter which explains the presence of KGB agents in the Square entirely by the fact that they were on duty in expectation of the Czechoslovak cars. It later became clear that the first to rush up to us were people who had been shadowing Pavel, Larissa and possibly others amongst us. They all belonged to the same military unit 1164, of an unspecified arm of the service. But what arm of the service employs officers to shadow people like Litvinov, Bogoraz, Yakir and Grigorenko?

TO THE CHIEF EDITORS OF:

Rude Pravo
Unità
Morning Star
L'Humanité
The Times
Le Monde

The Washington Post
Neue Zürcher Zeitung
The New York Times

Dear Editor, I ask you to publish my letter about the demonstration in Red Square, Moscow, on 25 August 1968, since I am the only participant in that demonstration still at liberty.

Those taking part in the demonstration were Konstantin Babitsky, linguist; Larissa Bogoraz, philologist; Vadim Delone, poet; Vladimir Dremlyuga, worker; Pavel Litvinov, physicist; Victor Feinberg, art historian; and Natalia Gorbanevskaya, poet. At 12 noon we sat down on the parapet near the Execution Ground and unfurled the slogans: 'Long live free and independent Czechoslovakia' (in Czech), 'Shame on the occupiers', 'Hands off the CSSR', 'For your freedom and ours'. Almost at once a whistle blew and KGB agents in civilian clothes rushed up to us from all sides of the Square: they had been on duty in Red Square, waiting for the Czechoslovak delegation to leave the Kremlin. They shouted as they ran towards us: 'They're all Jews! Beat up the anti-Soviets!' We sat quietly and offered no resistance. They tore the slogans from our hands, struck Victor Feinberg in the face until he bled, and knocked some of his teeth out. Pavel Litvinov was struck in the face with a heavy suitcase and they tore and broke a little Czechoslovak flag I was holding. They shouted: 'Disperse you scum!' but we went on sitting. After a few minutes cars arrived and all, except for me, were pushed into them. I had my three-month-old son with me and was therefore not seized immediately; I sat at the Execution Ground for roughly another ten minutes. In the car, I was struck. Some members of the crowd who had expressed sympathy with us were also arrested – these were released late in the evening. That night, the homes of all those detained were searched, on being accused of 'collective actions gravely violating public order'. One of us, Vadim Delone, had earlier been conditionally sentenced under this article for his part in a demonstration on 22 January 1967 in Pushkin Square. I was released after the search, probably because I have two small children. I am still being summoned to give evidence. I am refusing to give evidence about the organization and course of the demonstration, since it was a peaceful demonstration which did not violate public order. But I have given evidence about the gross and illegal actions of those who detained us; I am prepared to testify about this before world opinion.

My colleagues and I are glad that we were able to take part in this demonstration, that we were able to break through the torrent of unbridled lies and cowardly silence if only for an instant and show that not all citizens of our country agree with the violence which is being committed in the name of the Soviet people. We hope that the people of Czechoslovakia have learned, or will learn of this. And the belief that, in thinking of Soviet people, Czechs and Slovaks will think not only of the occupiers but also of us, gives us strength and courage.

28 August 1968   Natalia Gorbanevskaya
                            Moscow A-252 Novopeschanaya, ul.,
                                             13/3, kv. 34.

THE INVESTIGATION

And so the case was handed over to the Moscow Prosecutor's office on 28 August. The team of investigators was headed by the notorious Ludmila Sergeyevna Akimova, at one time in charge of the investigation concerned with the Pushkin Square demonstration before it was handed over to the KGB. Gnevkovskaya, a member of the team in our case, had also been involved in the earlier case. I think that then, as now, she was mostly concerned with Delone. Apart from these the team included Investigators Galakhov, Lopushenkov and Solovev.

I was already acquainted with Akimova, who had interrogated me on 23 August in the case of Irina Belogorodskaya. Larissa had seen her on the previous day. Akimova remembered me particularly because I had come with my child, who had bawled so loudly that someone had rushed in to ask: 'Ludmila Sergeyevna, what's going on here?'

'It's a witness in the Irina Belogorodskaya case', she answered, biting off every word, as much as to say: you can imagine what sort of pernicious witnesses there are in this case.

It was not a matter of perniciousness, however – I just did not have anybody to leave the baby with.

After 26 August, I was not summoned again for interrogation until 3 September, but was then treated as a 'suspect' under article 190/3 of the Criminal Code of the RSFSR.[10] This was also the only article mentioned in the original charge against our friends.

It should be stressed that all those detained with us in the square – Tania Baeva, Maya Rusakovskaya, Misha Leman and Inna Korkhova – were interrogated as witnesses. The decision to suspend criminal proceedings against them was, however, only announced when the investigation had been completed, the grounds being that it had not been established that they had known in advance about the demonstration, or 'taken an active part in it'. If proceedings are suspended, they must have been started and all four should therefore have been interrogated as suspects and not as witnesses. This is no mere technicality: under the law, a witness must testify, while a suspect, like an indicted person, is entitled to tender explanations and is not held responsible for refusing to give evidence or giving false evidence. Thus, the legal position of these four people was breached and their rights were grossly violated. What is more, these four in particular were interrogated repeatedly. Inna and Maya were twice confronted with Pavlik. The investigation was striving to discover someone who could be described as the organizer of 'collective actions' and the only tenuous line to which it pinned its hopes was finding out who had heard about the demonstration from whom. Inna Korkhova's evidence was the same as later in court. She really had not known about the demonstration in advance. Her sad remark in the 'Half-rouble': 'Oh friends, if I'd known beforehand, how I would have tried to talk you out of it,' is etched into my memory. Just in case it might lead to something, the investigating team summoned for interrogation people known to it from the Pushkin Square case, such as several friends of Delone who were, of course, wholly ignorant about his part in the demonstration, since Vadim himself had only heard about it on the morning of the twenty-fifth. One of these was Ilya Gabai,[11] who had been on an archaeological expedition in Moldavia on 25 August. Galia Gabai, Ilya's wife, accompanied me when I was summoned for interrogation on 3 September; she sat under the wall of Lefortovo prison holding my baby while I was being questioned. Interrogator Galakhov kept on and on asking: 'Who is it who came with you?' I told him they should not worry about which of my girl friends was holding my child: 'If you have to, ask her yourself.' He let me go and called Galia for questioning, just in case. I waited for her with the baby in the witnesses' room. A very young man was sitting there, Sasha Epifanov, a friend of Vadim's as it later turned out. 'What's that, also a witness?' he asked, pointing to little Oska. 'No – a suspect,' I told him.

Having learnt Galia's name, Galakhov was somewhat nonplussed. He was even more surprised when it turned out that Galia could provide actual evidence, because she had been in Red Square that day with her son Alioshka. However, Galia was a long way from the demonstration and only saw the demonstrators being put into the cars.

Piotr Yakir[12] was also summoned for questioning. The record of that interrogation is exceedingly brief: he had not been in Red Square; he knew about what had happened at the demonstration from Tatiana Baeva, a friend of his daughter Irina, and from Gorbanevskaya's letter which he had heard over the Western radio.

Deputy Prosecutor Fedorov came into the room during the interrogation and insolently said:

'What, not giving evidence?' then to Yakir: 'Don't make up tales about the police, we know that you are the organizer of the demonstration anyway.'

As it happened, Yakir had not said a word about the police. Fedorov came in half way through the interrogation and merely blurted out what he already knew, namely that on the morning of 25 August Piotr Yakir had been stopped in the street and detained for over an hour in a police station 'for a document check'. Many rumours connected with this incident were circulating in Moscow. Those who believed that the proposed demonstration was known about before it took place used this as their main argument. There was naturally great interest in whether there had been foreknowledge of the demonstration or not, but we shall never, I think, know for certain unless the KGB archives are thrown open some day. In my opinion there had been no foreknowledge of the demonstration. I find it surprising that people should say: 'But why were you seized so quickly?' Given the circumstances in which we live, we were not seized quickly enough. There are always members of the KGB and the Ministry of Internal Affairs guard (this ministry was then still called Ministry for the Protection of Public Order) in Red Square. KGB operatives, who were constantly shadowing them, followed some of the demonstrators to the Square. They could, had they so wished, have prevented the demonstration altogether. Had they known about it, but been ordered to let the demonstration begin in order to provide grounds for arrest, they could have done everything much more efficiently. They could have torn up the banners and hit us straight away and also brought up cars immediately instead of rushing around the Square and its vicinity looking for them. Moreover, experience shows that members of the KGB prefer to work at second hand in such cases, usually through members of the vigilante squads. Only surprise and unpreparedness forced them to hurl themselves at us. This meant that some of them could not stay out of the limelight as agents should, but had to appear in court as witnesses. This 'mistake' was soon corrected during the trial: two of them left on duty trips between the first and second days in court and a third simply disappeared.

The fact that Yakir was detained also proves nothing. Several current theories use this incident to prove that the proposed demonstration was known about in advance. The first is that it was decided to 'save' him; not to lock up an old camp inmate; not to increase the outcry. The second is that they decided not to lock him up so as not to increase the gravity of the affair.

Neither theory has much substance. Yakir himself considers
that there was no foreknowledge of the demonstration and has a
very simple explanation for being taken into custody. He had
left the house together with his wife. They were shadowed by
one car with three occupants; such light shadowing is in itself
an indication that the surveillance service was entirely without
suspicion, since Yakir was usually tailed by two cars. The Yakirs
then met three friends, none of whom took part in the demonstration and they diverged in three different directions. One
KGB man went off after each couple, and the remaining man was
stuck at the wheel of his car with Piotr on his own. Tailing is
difficult when there is only one man to cover another and the
solitary KGB man asked the nearest policeman to hold Piotr 'for
a document check', so that he should not give him the slip.

Yakir was driven to the interrogation by Investigator Galakhov
in an official car belonging to the Prosecutor's office and tailed
right up to Lefortovo by two other cars. The investigator did
not react when Yakir drew his attention to this, but told
Akimova when they arrived that Piotr Ionych said that there
were – and indeed there had been – two cars. Akimova answered,
with a sweet smile: 'Ah well, that's a different government
department.'

The shadowing was intense and extremely blatant just then –
and for a long time to come. I would walk with the pram to the
children's polyclinic; to the crèche to discover when they could
take my baby; to the school to meet Yasik; to the shops – all
this within the area of two blocks. And all the time first one
and then another Volga would be doing U-turns along Novo-
peschanaya Street and the narrow Chapaevsky Lane. It's amusing
while it's new, like a game. It's fun, for instance, to shed one's
tail by going into the 'Detsky Mir' children's store to buy things.
Later, one tries not to notice – one gets bored with the
KGB types.

The shadowing reached its peak the day I tried to have my
baby christened, a week before the trial. I was not the first to
be tailed – a car drove up in the wake of Vera Lashkov, Oska's
godmother, and followed us to the church thereby earning five

stalwart and fat KGB men their sizeable wages. What is more, they did not just confine their attentions to us. One of them entered into a spirited argument about art with a skinny youth and a bearded artist outside the church. He then changed his field of operations and came into the registry for christenings and other rites. As a result, I was refused a christening for my child. But I am digressing from my account of the investigation.

A number of people were summoned for interrogation because they knew us, for instance, Valentina Savenkova (Piotr Yakir's wife) and Yuli Kim. Kim was stopped in the street, together with a colleague, Gertsen Kopylov, a doctor of science and physicist at Dubna who had not been in the Square and did not know any of us. They were taken to the nearest police station, No 52, where Galakhov arrived and questioned both of them, just to be on the safe side.

Tatiana Velikanova, Babitsky's wife, stated during her interrogation that two of her friends had been present in Red Square – Medvedovskaya and Panova, together with Krysin, one of Babitsky's colleagues at the Russian Language Institute, and that all three were prepared to give evidence. The investigation team interrogated Panova and Medvedovskaya (Krysin was on holiday) but, like all the other inconvenient witnesses, they were not called to give evidence in court. Panova was not even called when the court satisfied certain requests by counsel and accused to call additional witnesses. Yet her evidence gave a very full picture of the demonstration and of how the demonstrators had been treated. She had seen how Feinberg was beaten up and distinctly remembered who had hit him, later recognizing the man concerned near the court building. She saw me and the baby being pushed into the car and it appeared that I had pointed straight at her when asking that 'another witness' should be taken. I knew neither Panova nor Velikanova at that time and was simply pointing to the nearest kindly, human face.

While the investigation team was summoning us and our acquaintances, it was also carrying out its basic assignment – the collection of evidence against us. Those who had detained us were the chief witnesses in this case, together with others present in the Square. I do not know exactly how the latter were picked. One of the statements in court mentioned that a man with a cine-camera was registering witnesses in the Square. A cine-camera – what a thought! Maybe there is a film of our demonstration lying about somewhere in the archives of the Prosecutor's office, or the KGB. If there is, it is unique, since the films of foreign tourists taking pictures in the Square had been exposed.

The evidence provided by the few officials is peculiar.

On 25 August, Captain Strebkov of the motorized police was attending to his duties in Red Square, together with Sergeant Kuznetsov. He stated in his report that, at about 12 noon, he 'was ordered' – Strebkov does not indicate by whom – to drive to the Execution Ground where 'a group of people were indulging in hooliganism'. He went on: 'An unknown man was put into my car and I delivered him to police station No 50. At police station No 50 a banner "Hands off the CSSR" was taken from these people.'

Strebkov and Kuznetsov had taken away Babitsky, in other words, this was the penultimate car. Moreover, these representatives of the police, the only ones to have been close to the demonstrators, took no part in detaining people – someone told them to drive to the spot, someone put a man in their car. The statement that the banner was taken away at the police station was so obviously contrary to the facts that on the same day, 25 August, Strebkov had to write a second report.

This read as follows: 'I was given the order' – yes, but who was it that gave this order? – 'to drive to the Execution Ground and render assistance to policemen' – aha, only now do we hear about policemen supposed to have been detaining us. 'In the police station, I saw a banner, brought by an employee of the Committee who said that he had found it during a search – I do not know where.' When a policeman talks about 'an employee of the Committee', he is not referring to someone from the Committee for science and technology, or physical culture and sport. He means an employee of the Committee of state security (KGB). Therefore, it was an employee of the Committee who brought the banner and said that he had found it during a search. We were, however, not searched at the police station and by then we no longer had the banners, anyhow.

And so, the question of the banners remains a mystery. All four banners and the little flag were in evidence and produced in court, but where the investigation got them from remains unclear. Dolgov, the only witness from military unit 1164, testified that he had confiscated two banners.

The forensic examination's findings were no less odd. The experts seemed unable to make definite statements or simply came to the wrong conclusions. If the evidence which our friends eventually gave in court had been available to them, or even if they had been aware of what I knew for certain, they might have fitted their inferences to the facts. But as no evidence of any kind was elicited on this score during the investigation, the experts tossed their conclusions together in the dark.

It was concluded from an expert examination of the fabrics that material of the same general type was used in making the banners, except for 'Freedom for Dubcek' and 'Hands off the CSSR'. The materials used for these differed from each other and from the fabric used for the other two banners and the flag. It could, however, not be established whether the material of the latter two – manufactured by me from the same old cot sheet – was the same. Was the fabric of the banners identical with the piece of material taken from Babitsky? – It was impossible to tell. Were the banners manufactured on the board in question? – It was impossible to tell, but 'something had been made on it'.

Experts on dyes had no difficulty in establishing certain obvious facts: 'Down with the occupiers' and 'Freedom for Dubcek' were written in pencil, while 'Hands off the CSSR' was in china ink. It was further concluded that the flag was painted with china ink, but whether this was the same ink as that used for 'Hands off . . .' could not be established. I should have thought no expert was needed to tell watercolour from china ink – the blue wedge and red band on a white background were simply painted with a child's watercolour.

The hand-writing experts found it impossible to establish who had written the texts on the banners. In this connection the investigation took samples of hand-written capitals from some, but not all, the accused. Litvinov, to my knowledge, refused to provide a sample and others, in order to stick to the general principle of refusing to co-operate with the investigation, may have done the same. But Vadim Delone did write out his poem 'Farewell to Bukovsky' in block letters. Akimova spotted a 'criminal quality' in it and immediately put it on file, adding a certificate that it had actually been written by Delone.

Apart from these pieces of expertise, examinations of the poles for the banners and the flag, the paints, wash, organic dye, threads and brush were also carried out and were equally indeterminate in their conclusions. As I see it, the only purpose of this mass of expertise was to make a show of thoroughness in the investigation. Bearing in mind that the texts – and only the texts – of these banners served as evidence for indictment and conviction under article 190/1[13] of the Criminal Code of the RSFSR, it is clear that the only important expertise was omitted: an examination of the text, meaning and content of the banners. Did the slogans concerned slander the Soviet system? It is much more convenient to leave such accusations unsubstantiated – that way, at least, one does not get tangled up.

I must now come back again to my own story. My position was extremely obscure. I was the only member of the demonstration left at liberty. I realised that this was done on account of my children, but it was hard to tell how long it would last. Be that as it may, my friends arranged a sort of guard for me. They accompanied me wherever I went, particularly if it was for interrogation. This, for some reason, irritated the investigators and KGB men. On 26 August, one of my friends waited for me in a nearby square while I was at Petrovka. Someone carrying criminal investigation department identification approached him, checked his documents, and told him that the stamp in his passport was not in order. As a result, this young man was kept at the nearest police station until half an hour or so after I left, having failed to find him when I came out.

On 3 September, I was called for unexpectedly to be taken away for questioning, but succeeded in telephoning my friends and Galia Gabai accompanied me. I was interrogated by Galakhov, a crude and stupid investigator; I knew about him from people who had been with him. I refused to give evidence of any sort, saying that I considered the investigation illegal and I had already testified about the violation of public order committed by those who broke up the demonstration and assaulted the demonstrators.

By now I was rated as a suspect, no longer as a witness, and was therefore not bound to give evidence or even explain my refusal to do so. Galakhov, nevertheless, went on and on questioning me and noting that I refused to answer, while reminding me every now and again that he was in no hurry, that he had the whole working day before him while my child was in the street in a stranger's hands. He sometimes made more outspoken threats: 'Don't get ideas – we have prisons where people with infants in arms can be put.' To save myself from such a prison, I was presumably supposed to start giving evidence on the spot.

It was then, incidentally, that I discovered a curious psychological effect. The investigation usually employs custody as a way of putting pressure on the accused. It might seem easier to process and to extract evidence useful to the investigation from an individual who has been isolated and given a taste of prison. It struck me that my position was also meant to weigh on my mind. When one is free, and one's freedom seems to depend entirely on oneself, liberty, the air one breathes, the trees under which one walks, all become particularly precious. Yet the threat of losing my freedom did not sway me, any more than the Lefortovo prison cells had swayed the friends. We simply treated it all very sensibly and calmly.

Fedorov, who was following the investigation on behalf of the Moscow Prosecutor's office, came in towards the end of the interrogation. He too began to question me, but when faced with another refusal did not go through a routine like Galakhov. He simply said: 'Very well, write down: "I request you not to put any more questions to me as I refuse to answer'', and give reasons for your refusal.'

And now, at the fall of the curtain, not for the record, he put the most idiotic question, a question that had become in some sort the refrain of this investigation: 'Who is the father of your children?'

Everybody who knew me even in the slightest was quizzed about me, about my psychology, about any deviations they might have noticed (or else those questioned were told, straight out: 'Ah well, Gorbanevskaya – she is sick'). They were asked about my children, and then just about everybody was asked who was the father of my children. I told Fedorov that I would not discuss this subject even with my closest friends, let alone him. 'Come, come,' he said, 'after all, if we were to detain you in custody, we must know who would look after them?' 'They'll be looked after', I assured this humanitarian.

And, in conclusion, they informed me that I would have to go to the Serbsky Institute for a psychiatric examination. They would telephone to let me know the day before and would come to fetch me.

PSYCHIATRIC EXAMINATION

As far as I know, all the accused were subjected to this examination but, except for Victor Feinberg, only as out-patients. I think they were not even taken to the Serbsky – the experts came to Lefortovo prison instead. After his examination Victor became an in-patient.

As for me, I was only examined as an out-patient. They called for me on 5 September at eleven in the morning – unheralded, needless to say. While Investigator Lopushenkov stood at the door, I fed the baby, got him ready and telephoned my friends for someone to come with me to the Serbsky Institute and someone else to stay with Yasik while his grandmother was out. Then I went to meet Yasik at the school and missed him. Meanwhile a car with a detective tailed me and the pram, in case I ran away. Yasik eventually turned up. My friends arrived. 'Have you come for my birthday?' Yasik joyfully asked them and just as joyfully started a game of football with them.

My friends promised that Galia Gabai would go straight to the Serbsky. She did in fact get there, but could not get in – entry was by pass only. By chance she met Akimova, whom she knew well from the time when Ilya had been in Lefortovo during the Bukovsky case. Akimova took me to the main entrance where I handed the baby over to Galia. But by then the examination had almost reached its final stage, after a lengthy interview with the house doctor and just before the session with the commission of experts. All this time the baby was quiet, ate and slept, and Akimova was faintly surprised.

The house doctor, a pleasant young woman who had recently returned to work after spending a year at home with her little son, talked to me for a long time. I think she found the conversation interesting – not medically, but for its own sake – and I think that she even liked me, until I made it clear that I knew I might well be arrested and had gone to the demonstration nevertheless. That really horrified her. We talked for so long that every time Akimova walked through the room she asked impatiently whether we would soon be done.

My medical history from the district health-centre lay in front of the house doctor. I had not been to the centre since the previous autumn, when the doctors had shouted at me, insisting that I should not have the impudence to give birth. I cannot be sure whether the health-centre was directly involved in my enforced hospitalization at Kashchenko the following February. On 12 February, the women's section doctor had suddenly demanded that I should go to hospital; she diagnosed 'anaemia threatening miscarriage'. I was forcibly transferred on 15 February to a psychiatric hospital from the maternity home in which I had been. Now, while talking to the doctor at the Serbsky Institute, the last entry in the health-centre's account of the case caught my eye: 'Conversation with a KGB representative', dated 12-2-69, thus providing a neat proof that the entire business over the hospital was directly the work of the K G B.

I had a long wait before the commission of experts interviewed me. They were probably reading the house doctor's report and listening to her conclusions.

It was a commission of three: the house doctor – who had evidently had her say and asked no questions; a fair-haired middle aged woman, who had only one question: 'Why did you take your child to the Square? Was there no one to leave him with or did you simply want him to take part in the demonstration?' 'I had no one to leave him with,' I answered truthfully. 'Besides, he had to be fed at two'. 'Well, two o'clock was a long time away. You could have left him with friends.' I shrugged my shoulders. To leave a three-month-old baby with friends? And I certainly did not think that I would be able to reach my friends by two o'clock.

I have said that there were three people and have so far mentioned only two. The third, who was in charge of the examination, was the notorious Professor Lunts. I knew very well what Lunts stood for and how little the outcome of the examination would depend on anything I said. Nevertheless, I behaved properly and answered all the questions – about my past illness, about Czechoslovakia and whether I liked Wagner. I do not like Wagner. What possible import can such a question have during an expert examination? Who is to be declared sane – he who likes Wagner, or he who does not? No – that is just me asking myself questions now. Then, I simply told Lunts that, no – I did not like him. 'Whom do you like then?' 'Mozart, Schubert, Prokofiev,' I told him.

On 12 September, a week later, on the day the investigation closed, I heard the result of the examination and my own strange fate. The report on my case, signed by Professor Lunts, stated that 'the possibility of low profile schizophrenia is not excluded'. A marvellous diagnosis! I would dearly like to know whether there are many people, particularly intellectuals, about whom it could definitely be written: 'the possibility is excluded, etc.' This puzzling diagnosis was followed in the same unwavering hand by the recommendation: 'Should be declared insane and lodged in a special category psychiatric hospital for compulsory treatment.'

I do not know whether the Moscow Prosecutor's office is more humane than Professor Lunts', or whether an order went out from the upper reaches to avoid an outsize scandal (it is indeed a very scandalous thing to send the mother of two children to a prison hospital, but no greater than sending troops into Czechoslovakia). Be that as it may, the Prosecutor's office simply issued an order to close the case in view of my insanity and the fact that I had two children. I was placed under my mother's guardianship. 'The possibility is not excluded' that Professor Lunts' conclusion may yet re-echo in my life.

As soon as the trial of the demonstrators was over, I was called to the health-centre. Without even enquiring how I felt, Shostak, the senior doctor, asked me a single eminently medical question: did I regard my behaviour as correct? 'Yes', I told her.

'And your action in August?' – she could not bring herself to utter the word 'demonstration'.

'Yes,' I said.

'Well, you cannot remain at home.'

I shrugged my shoulders. At this, we parted. So far, I am still at home.[14]

END OF THE INVESTIGATION

On that same day, 12 September, the investigation was completed. Tatiana Velikanova was first told on the previous day that the accused would be indicted under two articles of the Criminal Code: 190/3 and 190/1. We spent a long time guessing how the use of article 190/1 would be substantiated. Some *samizdat* documents, maybe, discovered during the searches? Not a bit of it: the application of this article was based solely on the fact of the demonstration, as can be seen from a look at the indictment.

In other words, it was just as the investigator Galakhov had told the accused Dremlyuga: 'Give us the man and we'll find the article.'

The case against me was closed. I do not know when the cases against Baeva, Korkhova, Leman and Rusakovskaya were closed. The case of Feinberg, then undergoing psychiatric examination as an in-patient in the Serbsky Institute, was separated for special treatment. All the lawyers and accused protested against this.

Feinberg's lawyer, S. L. Ariya, submitted a petition which argued that Feinberg's actions were directly related to those of the others named in the indictment; that the verdict on the latter would determine whether his actions had been illegal; and that it would be impossible for Feinberg to defend his interests at this crucial stage in the proceedings. Feinberg's procedural rights and his chances of an objective trial would be impaired by the segregation of his case. The lawyer therefore petitioned for a rescinding of the order to try Feinberg separately and a halt to the investigation, pending the announcement of the findings of the court's psychiatric experts. The other lawyers petitioned in the same terms.

These petitions were rejected on the grounds that 'the actions of each of the accused are particularized in the documents in the case' and that 'a decision by the court establishing the guilt of the accused would not automatically decide the question of Feinberg's guilt'. The reader may judge for himself the extent to which the actions of each of the accused were 'particularized': the indictments of each of the five accused were identical repetitions of the same wording. There was no mention whatsoever of what had been said by whom, of who had held which banners, and so on. In the sentence which it delivered, the court went even further by adopting the phrase 'they all' and describing the actions of the demonstrators as a group, contrary to Soviet law on criminal procedure, even when collective actions are involved.

Now that the investigation had been concluded and they could acquaint themselves with the case against them, the accused submitted their petitions.

Vadim Delone requested a further investigation to identify those who had in fact violated public order in Red Square by beating up and insulting the demonstrators. The reply alleged that the investigation did not have at its disposal any evidence that any illegal acts had been committed by anyone against the accused while they were being detained and conveyed to the police station, and that there was therefore no need to identify such people.

Larissa Bogoraz petitioned that evidence concerning her in the case of Irina Belogorodskaya be joined to the evidence in the present case, so that the indictment under article 190/1 should bear on the whole range of the actions charged against Bogoraz. The investigation, it was claimed in reply, was not concerned at the present time with Bogoraz's criminal responsibility as regards these documents; much other evidence had been found during a search of Belogorodskaya's home. A similar petition by Litvinov received the same answer. A few months later Irina Belogorodskaya was sentenced for disseminating the very letter in defence of Marchenko referred to in the petitions of Bogoraz and Litvinov.

Litvinov further submitted the most basic and, to my mind, necessary petition: that the case be discontinued in the absence of indictable matter. This was rejected – the case could not be stopped since 'guilt is proved by the evidence in the case'.

While the investigation was ending and almost up to the beginning of the trial the lawyers came under heavy pressure. Not wishing to suffer the fate of Zolotukhin,[15] Advocate Popov refused to defend Babitsky. Advocate Ariya refused to defend Dremlyuga. P. G. Grigorenko[16] and A. E. Kosterin[17] dealt with this in a letter which, having been confiscated during a search of Grigorenko's home, now no longer exists.

The date of the demonstrators' trial was announced at the beginning of October.

WHO IS BEING TRIED AND FOR WHAT IN THE MOSCOW CITY COURT ON WEDNESDAY, 9 OCTOBER 1968?

The prosecution's answer to this question is: A simple criminal case will be heard – a violation of public order.

Is it so?

Will people in fact appear before the court who have violated *public* order, i.e. hooligans who have offended against the *public* – society as a whole – rather than against individuals?

To answer this question, let us ask what action is imputed to the accused as a violation of public order and who are the people accused.

On 25 August this year, a group of young people arranged a sit-down protest demonstration in Red Square against the occupation of Czechoslovakia by Soviet troops. In other words, they expressed their attitude to this event in a way provided for by the USSR Constitution. A gang of hooligans attacked the demonstrators and assaulted them. No one took their side, and none of the hooligans was arrested. The demonstrators themselves were arrested and are now on trial. The assault on them and their arrest are described in a letter by the poet Natalia Gorbanevskaya and a political assessment of their action is set out in a letter by the translator Anatoli Yakobson.[18] Both letters are attached.

Thus, the application by citizens of their constitutional rights is called a violation of public order. Jokers! But these dangerous jokers sit in the Moscow City Prosecutor's office.

In elaborating this case contrary to the law, these jokers have tried to blacken the accused in every way and to present them as people on a low moral level. They have not even hesitated to collect dirty rumours for this purpose. But the means they are trying to use are worthless.

Despite direct threats by the KGB, the linguist Larissa Bogoraz has spoken out boldly and fearlessly on several occasions against the arbitrary behaviour of the camp administration in the place where her husband, Yuli Daniel, is imprisoned. She signed, together with Pavel Litvinov, the celebrated 'Appeal to world public opinion', as well as the letter of the twelve 'To the Presidium of the Consultative meeting of Communist Parties in Budapest'. Copies of both documents are attached.

The physicist Pavel Litvinov is known to the world at large

as an initiator of the open and courageous struggle against all illegal repressive actions in our country, as an indomitable and fearless fighter against all arbitrary behaviour. As a result, he has been subjected to various forms of persecution (summons to the KGB, dismissal from work), but he has not bowed before the effects of arbitrary action.

The remaining accused – the linguist Konstantin Babitsky, the poet Vadim Delone and the worker Vladimir Dremlyuga – have also frequently spoken out against all arbitrariness on the part of the authorities.

A feeling of sympathy towards the process of democratization of public life in the Czechoslovak Socialist Republic, towards the Czechoslovak people and its driving force – the Communist Party of Czechoslovakia – developed in them and gradually strengthened since January this year. Their attitude was expressed in writing long before the events of 21 August 1968. They were all in sympathy with a letter from a group of Soviet Communists 'To the members of the Communist Party of Czechoslovakia and the whole Czechoslovak people' (attached). And one of them, Vladimir Dremlyuga, was among some young people who accompanied P. Grigorenko and I. Yakhimovich, the representatives of this group, to the Czechoslovak embassy.

As we can see, this trial is purely political.

Once again, as in the trials of Sinyavsky and Daniel; Khaustov;[19] Bukovsky,[20] Delone and Kushev;[21] Ginzburg and Galanskov; and others, people are accused not on account of their actions, but of their convictions. The *conscience* of our people is on trial.

We resolutely protest against this lawlessness and demand that the court should immediately terminate this case in the clear absence of indictable matter.

Comrade Judges! ! !

If the interests of the motherland and our people are dear to you, you will at once put an end to this unscrupulously fabricated case.

We ask all citizens of the USSR and the whole of progressive mankind to support our demand.

In the appendix, five documents mentioned in the text.

Ilya Gabai
Alexander Kaplan
Piotr Grigorenko
Nadezhda Emelkina
Alexei Kosterin
Ivan Rudakov
Piotr Yakir

NOTE *I am not inserting the enclosures. Two of these, closely connected with the subject of the present book — my own and Anatoli Yakobson's letter — are quoted elsewhere in this volume.* N.G.

PART THREE

THE UNJUST JUDGE

Moskovskaya Pravda, 10 October 1968 – page 4

IN THE MOSCOW CITY COURT

On 9 October, in Moscow, the trial of the criminal case of Babitsky, K. I., Bogoraz-Bruchman, L. I., Delone, V. N., Dremlyuga, V. A., and Litvinov, P. M. began. They are accused of violating public order in Red Square, Moscow, on 25 August of this year.

A LETTER TO THE AUTHORITIES

To: The Secretary General of the Central Committee CPSU, Comrade Brezhnev, L. I.

The Chairman of the Council of Ministers, USSR, Comrade Kosygin, A. N.

The Chairman of the Presidium of the Supreme Soviet, USSR, Comrade Podgorny, N. V.

Today, 9 October 1968, we, the undersigned, went to attend the trial of L. Bogoraz, K. Babitsky, V. Delone, V. Dremlyuga, and P. Litvinov, who had protested against the despatch of Soviet troops to the Czechoslovak Socialist Republic and the shedding of Soviet and Czech blood, but we were unable to enter the courtroom. The trial, it seems, has deliberately been switched to the Moscow Proletarsky District People's court where no courtroom can accommodate more than 30 people. What is more, members of the public selected by the KGB were admitted first to the court-room.

It is beyond doubt that this was done to turn what had been announced as an open trial into a closed trial for practical purposes, in the same way as the trials of Sinyavsky and Daniel, Galanskov and Ginzburg and others. We are convinced that the court could not have taken such a decision on its own and that this was done on orders from above.

In view of this, we are entitled to assume that unlawful retribution is being prepared in this case also. Clean business is not transacted under cover of darkness. If these people really have committed a crime, the court must demonstrate this openly. Without a public hearing there is no court, merely an unlawful reprisal. To prevent this we ask you to intervene at once and put an end to illegality: to stop the hearing in closed session; to transfer the court to adequately roomy accommodation: to re-move all KGB agents from the courtroom and its approaches.

If you fail to do this, the entire guilt for the resulting arbitrary action will fall on you personally, for neither we, nor any honest person in the world, will be able to credit that such a thing could have been done without your knowledge or, more correctly, without your direct instructions.

This letter carries 56 (fifty-six) signatures all told. The copy with the original signatures is being sent to the Secretary General, Central Committee, CPSU, Comrade Brezhnev, L. I.

The reply should be addressed to: Piotr Grigorevich Grigorenko, Moscow G–21, Komsomolsky Prospekt 14/1, kv. 96.

A TALE TOLD ANONYMOUSLY

I was summoned to the Party district committee a few days before the trial, together with a few active Party members from our works. Some thirty people assembled. We were told that a group of people who had slandered the Soviet system were to be tried and that we were to attend the hearing. We were told how to behave: make no notes, sit together, try not to answer questions from others present. If we could not avoid explaining how we got into the courtroom, we should say that it was our day off, that we had gone in by chance that morning and became interested. We were then asked to split into three groups, to decide which day we would be going. I got the second day.

Assembly was at eight. A covered van drove up and delivered us to Serebrennichesky Lane. We left the van at some distance from the court building. Some man went ahead and led us into the building, to a large room on the third floor. There we sat for an hour and a half, together with many young people who were smoking and playing dominoes. Afterwards, we found out that they had been on duty all day in the building. At about ten we were taken into the courtroom.

The courtroom contained fifty people altogether. One could immediately tell the relatives of the accused from those who had got there as I had. The relatives looked at us with dislike. I became uncomfortable about complete strangers like ourselves becoming witnesses to their grief.

It is impossible, looking back, to remember exactly what went on during the court session. There were many speeches and they produced different impressions but one's chief feeling was that it was impossible to understand what was going on. Among the accused, I liked a good-looking boy with a non-Russian name best. The accused called Pavel – I do not remember his surname – was, I was told, a famous artist's grandson, and the woman was also the wife of some celebrity. It seemed to me that all the accused were decent people.

When – very tired – we left by the main entrance of the court, we saw a huge crowd in front of the building. I don't know about the others, but I was very ashamed. We walked through the crowd in single file and someone said, pointing at us: 'Look at the types they've raked up.'

SESSION OF THE MOSCOW CITY COURT

9–11 *October* 1968
In the premises of the Moscow Proletarsky District People's court.

The court:

PRESIDENT: V. G. Lubentsova
PEOPLE'S ASSESSORS: P. I. Popov and I. Ya. Bulgakov
STATE PROSECUTOR: Assistant Moscow City Prosecutor, V. E. Drel
DEFENCE ADVOCATES: D. I. Kaminskaya, S. V. Kallistratova, Yu. B. Pozdeev, N. A. Monakhov.
CLERK OF THE COURT: V. I. Osina.

9 October 1968 – 9.00 *a.m.*

The first day of the trial. The Proletarsky District Court building, 15, Serebrennicheskaya Embankment, on the third floor. A small room, seating about forty, now with difficulty accommodating sixty to seventy people. As a member of the public put it: 'Judge Lubentsova is a grey-haired woman in a grey suit, markedly and easily polite, like a schoolmistress or the head-teacher in a good school.' Popov and Bulgakov, a metal worker and an engineer, the two assessors, were described by the same spectator: 'One is rather young, looks like a boxer, the other is grey-haired, long-nosed . . . censorious, with a grating voice.' Prosecutor Drel, in a dark purple uniform, 'thickset, flat-faced, pedantic, verbose, his loud voice carrying a permanently offended note'. Delone, Dremlyuga and Bogoraz were in the front of the dock, Babitsky and Litvinov at the back. Two escorting soldiers, without their rifles, stood on either side of the dock.

The hearing began with the handing over of the accused. They had been held since their arrest in the KGB's investigation isolator.

Judge: Bogoraz-Bruchman, Larissa Iosifnovna.
Clerk of the court: Present.
Judge: Litvinov, Pavel Mikhailovich.
Clerk: Present.
Judge: Delone, Vadim Nikolaevich.
Clerk: Present.
Judge: Babitsky, Konstantin Iosifovich.
Clerk: Present.
Judge: Dremlyuga, Vladimir Alexandrovich.
Clerk: Present.

The composition of the court was then announced. There were no objections to its members. The statement of petitions followed.

Bogoraz: I have several petitions. First, I ask that additional witnesses be called. The investigation picked as witnesses only those it required and did not include any whose testimony coincides with the explanations given by the accused. I ask that Baeva, Rusakovskaya, and Leman be called; they were present in the Square, and saw how it all happened.

Secondly, I decided in advance that I would undertake my own defence in court. Before the trial, I needed to consult a lawyer and did so. I have complete confidence in advocate Kaminskaya, but I said nothing about my motives at the preliminary investigation and she remains in ignorance of them. I refuse an advocate and ask the court to allow me to exercise the right to defend myself provided by article 3 of the USSR Constitution and article 19 of the RSFSR Code of Criminal Procedure.

Thirdly, on studying the case, I read Delone's petition for a supplementary investigation and I support him, since I consider it necessary to establish the identity of, and institute proceedings against, those who actually violated order in the Square and used physical violence against us.

On the basis of article 18 of the Code of Criminal Procedure, I ask that our friends be admitted to the court room.

Delone: I petition that the case be referred for supplementary investigation in order to discover those persons who actually violated order in Red Square on 25 August 1968 by their acts of hooliganism. I have in mind persons who assaulted Feinberg, myself and Litvinov and insulted the demonstrators with shouts of 'Hooligans! Bandits! Anti-Soviets' in an attempt to provoke the crowd into unconsidered action. I include those persons who testified at the preliminary investigation that they had snatched banners from peaceful demonstrators and interfered with the course of the demonstration, in other words with the implementation of their constitutional right provided for by article 125 of the USSR Constitution. These persons were in plain clothes and either did not carry, or did not display, any warrant of authority; if they had any authority, they exceeded it by using physical violence against us. I consider it essential to demand an explanation of their unlawful actions and determine their criminal liability.

If the court rejects my first petition and the hearings begin, I ask that Velikanova, Rusakovskaya, Baeva, Leman, Panova and

Medvedovskaya be called as witnesses. Their evidence is substantially different from that of the witnesses summoned by the court from the list compiled during the investigation.

I also ask that my friends be admitted to court.

Litvinov: I entirely associate myself with the petitions submitted by Bogoraz and Delone. I consider it essential that the case be referred for supplementary investigation, since the preliminary investigation has not discovered those persons who took a hand in detaining us and who assaulted the demonstrators, thereby violating order in Red Square. I consider it absolutely essential to call Panova and Baeva as witnesses: criminal proceedings were instituted against Baeva in the present case and only closed on 12 September; Panova offered to testify and gave evidence at the preliminary investigation.

I also petition that our friends be admitted to the courtroom. They have more right to be here than those we see before us.

Babitsky: supported all the petitions submitted.

Dremlyuga: I ask for the presence of my friends in the courtroom. Friends, and not the comrades who have gathered here. I do not even ask for this, I demand it, because I have no relatives at all in Moscow.

Advocate Kaminskaya: (Counsel for Bogoraz and Litvinov) As to the petition of Bogoraz, and since she wishes to conduct her own defence, I ask the court to grant her request in accordance with article 50 of the RSFSR Code of Criminal Procedure. I fully support the petition for a supplementary investigation and the summoning of additional witnesses. The list appended to the indictment does not include a single witness whom the investigation regards as being acquainted with the accused. Yet, article 20 of the RSFSR Code of Criminal Procedure places the onus of a full, comprehensive and objective examination of the circumstances of the case on the investigation and the court. I therefore request that Baeva, Velikanova, Panova, Medvedovskaya, Leman and Gabai be called as witnesses.

A supplementary investigation is essential in accordance with article 20 of the RSFSR Code of Criminal Procedure since the authorities in charge of the investigation have disregarded statements by the accused and other evidence in the case which throws light on the circumstances in which the accused were detained. No attention has been paid to the testimony of a number of people who were the first to witness the events, nor to testimony about the behaviour of those who were the first to detain the participants. In particular, the defence wishes to establish whether members of the police took part in detaining the accused, since the evidence of witness Strebkov that a member of the police helped to put Litvinov, Delone and others into a car conflicts with the evidence of other witnesses.

Further action is also required to consolidate the present case with that of Feinberg. The investigation wrongly decided to separate the case of Feinberg, at present under legal-psychiatric examination in hospital. The experts have not yet pronounced on Feinberg's fitness to plead. If Feinberg is fit to plead, his evidence would be of great significance in inquiring into the circumstances of the case.

Advocate Kallistratova: (Delone's counsel) The list of people liable to be summoned to the hearing was compiled by the investigator in clear breach of article 20 of the Code of Criminal Procedure. All those witnesses who support the evidence of the accused and refute the indictment have been omitted from the list. I insist that the following eye-witnesses interrogated during the preliminary investigation be called: Velikanova, Panova, Rusakovskaya, Leman, Medvedovskaya, Baeva, Gabai. In addition, I consider it essential that witness Krysin, summoned by the investigator but not interrogated because he was on holiday, should be called. Krysin is now in Moscow and could appear in court to give evidence about the events of which he was an eye-witness.

The separation of Feinberg's case is in breach of article 26 of the RSFSR Code of Criminal Procedure. Each accused in the present case, including Feinberg, states in evidence certain details about the event in connection with which all the accused are charged and which the prosecution describes as collective action. The separation of Feinberg's case, therefore, inevitably impedes the full and comprehensive examination of the circumstances of the case. I petition that his case be referred for supplementary investigation, with a view to consolidating the cases.

I also support Vadim Delone's petition to refer the case for supplementary investigation. As an advocate, it is out of character for me to demand that anyone should be indicted, particularly when the Prosecutor is involved in the case. But the accused deny guilt and indicate that those actually responsible for the violation of public order were the persons who detained them. It is therefore essential to establish the identity of these persons and verify the statements of the accused. This can only be done in the course of supplementary investigation.

Advocate Pozdeev: (Counsel for Babitsky) I support the petitions of my colleagues, since the object of the trial is to establish the truth.

Advocate Monakhov: (Counsel for Dremlyuga) I support the petitions presented. I consider it essential that the case be referred for supplementary investigation. I do not link a supplementary investigation with the indictment of any other persons; a supplementary investigation is essential to establish the actual circumstances of the event which took place in Red Square.

Prosecutor: I do not agree with the petitions of the accused regarding a supplementary investigation. The authorities in charge of the investigation took exhaustive measures to establish the truth. There are no grounds for the further investigation of the actions of those who terminated the criminal acts of the accused. If the court establishes that any of these persons acted incorrectly, it may promulgate a separate decision on the basis of article 321 of the Code of Criminal Procedure. I can see no substantive connection whatsoever between the criminal acts of the accused and the acts of citizens who intervened against them. The court has no grounds for supplementary investigation.

As to calling new witnesses, seventeen people have already been called to give evidence and have all testified to a sufficient extent. I ask the court to reprove the advocates who are not listening to me –

(the Judge reproved advocates Kallistratova and Kaminskaya). The available witnesses have provided exhaustive evidence, but taking into consideration the petitions, I would nevertheless entertain the possibility of calling Velikanova and Medvedovskaya as additional witnesses.

I object to the consolidation of the present case with that of Feinberg. It is not out of the question that he may be pronounced insane. His evidence would then be meaningless. It is clearly impracticable to wait for the result of the examination, since this would involve a considerable delay in hearing the case. The separation of Feinberg's case does not infringe the rights of the accused.

(The court retired for consultation. After half an hour its ruling was promulgated.)

Ruling of the court: To satisfy Bogoraz's petition to be granted the opportunity to conduct her own defence. To reject the petition that the case be referred for supplementary investigation. To reject the petition to consolidate the present case with the case of Feinberg. To summon and interrogate as additional witnesses Velikanova, Leman, Medvedovskaya. To reject the petition to summon other witnesses.

Judge: Accused, your petitions to admit your friends and relatives to the courtroom shall be dealt with as part of the proceedings. Since this does not relate to the substance of the case, it is not included in the ruling.

Litvinov: But the petitions have been integrated in the case?

Judge: They are entered in the record.

The judge read out the indictment.

INDICTMENT

Indicted:

BOGORAZ-BRUCHMAN, Larissa Iosifovna

DELONE, Vadim Nikolaevich

LITVINOV, Pavel Mikhailovich

BABITSKY, Konstantin Iosifovich

DREMLYUGA, Vladimir Alexandrovich

Under articles 190/1 and 190/3 of the RSFSR Criminal Code.

Criminal proceedings were instituted on 25 August 1968 by the Investigation Administration of the Directorate for the protection of public order, Moscow City Executive Committee, arising from collective actions in Red Square grossly violating public order. *Bogoraz-Bruchman L. I.*, *Delone V. N.*, *Litvinov P. M.*, *Babitsky K. I.*, *Dremlyuga V. A.*, and *Feinberg V. I.* were arrested in this connection and charged with a criminal offence. The evidence concerning *Feinberg* was referred for separate treatment. Criminal proceedings against *Gorbanevskaya N. E.*, an active participant in the collective actions in Red Square, were discontinued, a forensic psychiatric examination having declared her insane.

The investigation established that:

Bogoraz-Bruchman, Delone, Litvinov, Babitsky, Dremlyuga and *Feinberg*, disagreeing with the CPSU's and Soviet government's policy of rendering fraternal aid to the Czechoslovak people in defence of its socialist achievements, which was approved by all the workers of the Soviet Union, entered into a criminal conspiracy aimed at organising a collective protest against the temporary entry of troops of the five socialist countries into the territory of the Czechoslovak Socialist Republic. To gain wide publicity for their schemes, they prepared in advance on white material banners with the following texts: Hands off the CSSR, Down with the occupiers, For your freedom and ours, Freedom for Dubcek and Long live free and independent Czechoslovakia (the latter in Czech), i.e. texts containing deliberately false fabrications discrediting the Soviet state and social system.

Further, after previous agreement, *Bogoraz-Bruchman, Litvinov, Dremlyuga, Babitsky, Feinberg* and *Delone*, having concealed about them the above-mentioned banners, reached the Execution Ground in Red Square on 25 August of this year at 12 noon where, to give effect to their criminal conspiracy, they actively took part in collective actions, unfolded the banners and addressing the public present in the Square began to shout out slogans similar to the banners, thereby grossly violating public order and disrupting the normal movement of traffic. By these actions

Bogoraz-Bruchman, Delone, Litvinov, Babitsky, Dremlyuga and *Feinberg* aroused the indignation of citizens present in Red Square.

The participation by the above-mentioned persons in collective actions in Red Square is confirmed by the statements of witnesses interrogated in connection with this case. Witness Yastreba stated that, being present in Red Square near the Execution Ground on 25 August of this year at 12 noon, she became an eye-witness to the following: Coming from the direction of the Spassky Gates, Bogoraz, Litvinov, Delone and some others approached Gorbanevskaya at the Execution Ground. After a conversation with Bogoraz, Gorbanevskaya herself sat down by the Execution Ground and Bogoraz, Delone, Litvinov and Feinberg at once ostentatiously sat down beside her. Literally in a flash, they all jointly threw up their hands. In Litvinov's hands was the slogan: 'For your freedom and ours'. A three-coloured flag was in Gorbanevskaya's hands. The slogans were taken away from them almost immediately. Litvinov, Delone, Bogoraz, Gorbanevskaya and Feinberg did not even rise to their feet, but remained sitting. A large crowd of citizens, angered by their behaviour, gathered around them. More than a hundred people had assembled all told. Similar statements were made by witnesses *Dolgov, Bogatyrev, Savelev, Ivanov, Fedoseev, Veselov, Davidovich, Udartsev, Savilov, Vasilev, Besedin, Kuznetsov, Strebkov, Kuklin, Rozanov. Korkhova*, who was interrogated as a witness and is acquainted with the accused *Litvinov*, stated that on August 25 this year, having been informed by *Litvinov* in advance, she had come to Red Square together with him and observed the collective actions violating public order organized by the accused. The illegal actions committed by the accused are additionally confirmed by material evidence removed from them when they were detained and during searches, by documents and by the conclusions of forensic examinations which established that the plastic cover removed from *Babitsky* was used for the preparation of banners.

The accused *Bogoraz-Bruchman*, manifesting her dissent even before the aforesaid collective actions, on 22 August 1968 addressed a statement expressing protest against the above-mentioned decision by the Soviet government to the director of the institute and the trade union organization at her place of work.

Bogoraz-Bruchman, Delone, Litvinov, Babitsky and *Dremlyuga* do not deny the fact of coming to Red Square with banners of the above-mentioned nature on 25 August of this year and the fact of unfolding them, as stated in the indictment. Nevertheless, they do not regard these actions of theirs as a crime and therefore do not acknowledge themselves guilty. The accused have refused to make statements about the organization and preparation of the collective actions in Red Square. The crimes committed by the accused are confirmed by the proof collected in the case, an analysis of which is quoted in the descriptive part of the indictment.

The accused *Litvinov, Dremlyuga*, and *Delone* have not recently engaged in socially useful work. *Bogoraz-Bruchman* was dismissed from work in August 1968 for absenteeism. *Litvinov* and *Dremlyuga* are noted as being socially undesirable. *Babitsky* was conscientious in his work, but had expressed unhealthy, anti-social sentiments to his fellow workers.

On these grounds as above, are indicted:

Bogoraz-Bruchman, Larissa Iosifovna; born 1929; native of Kharkov; Jewish; non-Party; married; one dependent son, born 1951; higher education; previously employed as senior scientific assistant in the All-Union Scientific Research Institute for Technical Information, Classification and Coding; no previous convictions; present address: Moscow, Leninsky Prospekt 85, kv. 3; in that she, disagreeing with the CPSU's and the Soviet government's policy of rendering fraternal aid to the Czechoslovak people in defence of its socialist achievements which was approved by all the workers of the Soviet Union, did on 22 August 1968 send two statements about this to her place of work, addressed to the Director and the trade union organization of the All-Union Scientific Research Institute for Technical Information, Classification and Coding; and further, with the object of organizing in the town of Moscow a collective protest about the aforesaid questions, did enter into a criminal conspiracy with the other accused in the case—*Litvinov, Babitsky, Dremlyuga, Delone, Feinberg* and *Gorbanevskaya* – having previously prepared banners with texts containing deliberately false fabrications discrediting the Soviet state and social system, namely: Hands off the CSSR, For your freedom and ours, Down with the occupiers, Freedom for Dubcek, Long live free and independent Czechoslovakia (the latter in Czech), did appear on 25 August of this year, at 12 noon at the Execution Ground in Red Square, where, together with *Babitsky, Delone, Dremlyuga, Litvinov, Feinberg, Gorbanevskaya* and other persons, she actively took part in collective actions which grossly violated public order and disrupted the normal movement of traffic: unfolded the above-mentioned banners, shouted out slogans similar to the banners, thereby arousing the indignation of citizens gathered around her – that is, in perpetration of crimes envisaged by articles 190/1 and 190/3 of the RSFSR Criminal Code.

(The indictment of the other accused is identical with that of Larissa Bogoraz-Bruchman, except for the two statements she despatched on 22 August.)

Delone, Vadim Nikolaevich; born 1947; native of Moscow; Russian; non-Party; secondary education; single; no fixed employment; sentenced by the Moscow City Court to one year's deprivation of liberty suspended for a probationary period of five years; present address: Moscow, Pyatnitskaya ul. 12, kv. 5.

Litvinov, Pavel Mikhailovich; born 1940; native of Moscow; Russian; non-Party; one dependent child, aged eight; higher education; physicist by profession; no fixed employment; no previous convictions; present address: Moscow, ul. Alexeia Tolstovo 8, kv. 78.

Babitsky, Konstantin Iosifovich; born 1929; native of Moscow; Jew; non-Party; higher education; married; three dependent children, born 1953, 1955 and 1958; junior scientific assistant at the Russian Language Institute, Academy of Sciences, USSR; no previous convictions; present address: Moscow, ul. Krasikova 19, kv. 86.

Dremlyuga, Vladimir Alexandrovich; born 1940; native of

Saratov; Russian; non-Party; secondary education; married; no fixed employment; previously tried by the Leningrad Zhdanov District People's Court under articles 174 and 154 part 1 of the RSFSR Criminal Code, sentenced to two years' deprivation of freedom suspended for a probationary period of five years; present address: Moscow, Metrostroyevskaya ul. 7, kv. 44.

The present criminal case is to be forwarded to the Moscow City Court for hearing in substance.

The indictment was compiled on 20 September 1968.

Senior investigator of the Moscow City Prosecutor's Office, Judicial Councillor Akimova.

Agreed: Deputy Head, Moscow City Prosecutor's Office Investigation Department, Judicial Councillor Fedorov.

The Judge asked all the accused in turn whether they understood the charge and whether they admitted their guilt.

All the accused gave the same answer: 'I understand the charge, I do not admit my guilt.'

Judge: Comrade Prosecutor, what have you to say about the order of the court hearing?

Prosecutor: I propose that we start by questioning the accused in the following order: Bogoraz-Bruchman, Litvinov, Babitsky, Delone, Dremlyuga, followed by the questioning of the witnesses as listed in the indictment.

Judge: Accused Bogoraz, do you object to the order of hearing proposed by the Prosecutor?

Bogoraz: I have no objections as far as the order of questioning the accused is concerned. As to the order of questioning the witnesses, I ask that officials and members of the police – Strebkov, Kuznetsov, Rozanov, and Kuklin – be questioned first. *Delone, Litvinov, Babitsky, Dremlyuga* supported Bogoraz's suggestion. *Dremlyuga* asked that a further five witnesses from military unit 1164 – Dolgov, Bogatyrev, Ivanov, Veselov and Vasilev – be grouped separately. *The lawyers* supported the requests of the accused. After consultation, the court announced that witnesses would be called as listed in the indictment.

Recess

EXAMINATION OF THE ACCUSED

Bogoraz-Bruchman, Larissa Iosifovna

Judge: Accused Bogoraz, stand up. What can you say about the matter charged against you?

Bogoraz: On 25 August 1968, at about 12 o'clock, I came to Red Square, bringing a banner which stated a protest against the despatch of troops to Czechoslovakia. At 12 o'clock I sat down by the Execution Ground and unfolded the banner. Almost at once people ran up who were not personally known to me although I had frequently seen them in my vicinity in various places. Having run up to me, they took away the banner. On my left I saw Feinberg. His face had been knocked about. His blood spattered my blouse. I saw a bag flashing by as someone hit Litvinov. A crowd gathered. I heard a voice: 'You mustn't hit them – what's going on here?' I answered: 'I am holding a peaceful demonstration, but my banner has been removed.' I did not see the others. A citizen in plain clothes came up to me and suggested that I should go to a car. He produced no documents, but I followed him. I saw Litvinov being led away and hit on the back. Four people were in the car. I was seized by the hair and shoved head first into the car. I also saw Feinberg in the car, with his teeth knocked out. At police station No 50 where we were taken we all demanded a medical examination for Feinberg. He had been hit in the face and his teeth had been knocked out. In the evening, I was driven home from the police station for a search.

Judge: What was on the banner you raised?

Bogoraz: I refuse to quote the text of my banner.

Judge: Why?

Bogoraz: It is immaterial which particular banner I held. I do not disclaim responsibility for any of the banners. (She quoted the texts of all the banners.)

Judge: Who was with you in Red Square?

Bogoraz: I refuse to answer questions concerning the other accused. I am answering only on my own behalf.

Judge: Did you know that other people would come?

Bogoraz: No, I did not know. I had earlier decided that I, for my part, would go. I did not even know on the twenty-fifth whether others would come.

People's Assessor: You knew what you would get for this? You knew that it would happen precisely in Red Square?

Bogoraz: Nothing was known to me in advance.

People's Assessor: When did you come to know about it?

Bogoraz: When I went to Red Square.

Judge: Did you all sit down round the parapet simultaneously?

Bogoraz: I don't remember. I find it difficult to answer.

Judge: Did you sit down and raise the banners simultaneously?

Bogoraz: It is difficult for me to say.

Judge: Were you employed?

Bogoraz: Yes, I was working at the All-Union Scientific Research Institute for Technical Information as a senior scientific assistant. I only heard of my dismissal when I was in prison. On 22 August, on Thursday, I made a verbal statement to the head of my department that I was declaring a strike in protest against the despatch of troops to Czechoslovakia; on Friday, I handed in a written statement about this to the management and the trade union committee and was not informed that I was dismissed. The twenty-third was Friday; the Institute did not work on Saturday; I was therefore dismissed after my arrest.

Prosecutor: Why did you choose Red Square in particular?

Bogoraz: This protest was addressed to the government, and by tradition what is addressed to the government is usually put forward in Red Square. Secondly, there is no traffic in Red Square.

Prosecutor: But you know the location of the Central Committee building and the Council of Ministers' building. They are not in Red Square, are they?

Bogoraz: I repeat that there is no traffic in Red Square and that the tradition happens to be that the government is addressed in Red Square.

Prosecutor: How long have you known the accused?

Bogoraz: Litvinov, a year and a half to two years; Babitsky, six, seven, maybe eight years; Delone, about a year or a year and a half; Dremlyuga, some two months.

Prosecutor: Why, when supporting your petition, did he refer to you by name – Larissa?

Bogoraz: Because that is my name. Apart from that, better ask him.

Prosecutor: Describe your relations with the accused.

Bogoraz: Very close, friendly relations with Litvinov; Babitsky I also regard as my friend, if he does not object. My relations with Dremlyuga are good, and also with Delone, in so far as the difference in our ages permits.

Prosecutor: When did you last see the accused before the twenty-fifth?

Bogoraz: I refuse to answer this question and find it difficult to answer.

Prosecutor: Why?

Bogoraz: I refuse to answer anything concerning the others and I will only answer on my own behalf. In fact, have you not already separated Feinberg's case?

Prosecutor: How can you explain that you turned up together at the Execution Ground?

Bogoraz: Apparently by the fact that each of us wished to express his protest there in particular.

Prosecutor: Did you have a preliminary conversation about this?

Bogoraz: I refuse to answer.

Prosecutor: Does it not seem a strange coincidence to you that you all turned up at the Execution Ground together? Could not advance agreement be assumed?

Bogoraz: It does not seem strange to me; it was either a coincidence or a predictable event. I would accept either.

Prosecutor: Which banner were you holding?

Bogoraz: I have already said that I refuse to answer. I accept responsibility for *all* the slogans.

Prosecutor: How can you accept responsibility for all the other banners if you had no previous agreement and could not have known what was written on them?

Bogoraz: I know the texts of all the banners and each of them expresses what I might have said.

Prosecutor: How do you know about them?

Bogoraz: I saw them in Red Square and they are known to me from the evidence in the case.

Prosecutor: But you all sat in a row?

Bogoraz: Feinberg sat beside me, Babitsky a little to the back, next to him Gorbanevskaya – I don't remember exactly.

Prosecutor: But how then could you have seen the banners?

Bogoraz: I looked to the right and left, and saw them. The case contains evidence from some witnesses who saw these banners while standing with their backs to them.

Prosecutor: What were the dimensions of your banner?

Bogoraz: I refuse to answer.

Judge: What colour was the banner? Describe it. Was it executed on white material?

Bogoraz: I refuse to specify, but can say that it was done on white material with a brush.

Prosecutor: What colour was the writing?

Bogoraz: I refuse to answer.

Prosecutor: Why do you refuse to answer about the banner which you were holding?

Bogoraz: I do not wish to disclaim responsibility for all the other banners.

Prosecutor: As you walked to the Square, did you, personally, have anything in your hands?

Bogoraz: A banner.

Prosecutor: How were you holding it?

Bogoraz: Wrapped up in a newspaper.

Prosecutor: Who prepared the slogan?

Bogoraz: I did.

Prosecutor: When and where?

Bogoraz: The day before, at home.

Prosecutor: Was what you were doing known to anyone?

Bogoraz: I don't think so. No.

Prosecutor: Did you meet any of the accused on the twenty-fourth?

Bogoraz: I don't remember.

Prosecutor: And did you see any of them on the morning of the twenty-fifth?

Bogoraz: Probably not.

Prosecutor: And in Red Square, which of them did you see first?

Bogoraz: It's difficult to say. I arrived 20 minutes early and walked around Red Square.

Judge: Did you all get to the Execution Ground at the same time or did someone arrive first?

Bogoraz: It's difficult to say.

Prosecutor: Now, you have said that your protest was addressed to the government and that you therefore came to Red Square where, by tradition, it is usual to address the government. Have I understood you correctly?

Bogoraz: Yes. But also because there is no traffic in Red Square.

Prosecutor: And why did you not address a letter to the government?

Bogoraz: I have had occasion to address the government before in other connections and not a single one of my letters has received a reply.

Prosecutor: And why did you not choose another square or a quiet street? The place you selected lies in the path of traffic from the Spassky Tower towards GUM.

Bogoraz: Had I known this, I would have chosen another place. I have frequented Red Square and have never seen any traffic.

Prosecutor: Did you imagine that your actions would attract the attention of holiday-makers and other citizens? Did you not foresee that your public appearance would arouse the citizens' indignation and represent a violation of public order?

Bogoraz: I thought that it might attract attention, but did not reckon that the citizens would rush forward with their fists and set about removing the banners.

Prosecutor: What did you think? That the citizens would react favourably to your actions?

Bogoraz: I do not know what was, and what might have been, the actual reaction of the citizens if there had been no interference by those who hurled themselves upon us.

Prosecutor: If you read the papers, if you listen to the radio, our Soviet radio, you must know how Soviet workers feel about the policy of the party and the government.

Bogoraz: Yes, I had read the papers and listened to the radio.

Prosecutor: Well, were you not clear about it then?

Bogoraz: I too am a Soviet worker, but I felt quite differently about it. But I was not able to express my feelings in the newspapers. And I am not in the least sure that all that has been written in the papers expresses the views of all citizens. Unfortunately, nobody outside this courtroom will get to know of my attitude to these questions.

Prosecutor: Do you have a university degree?

Bogoraz: Yes, I am a post-graduate student of philology.

Prosecutor: When did you defend your thesis?

Bogoraz: I defended my thesis in February 1965.

Prosecutor: There is a reference from your place of work among the documents in the case noting that you were systematically late or failed to appear at work. What have you to say to this?

Bogoraz: I have happened to be late, but no oftener than others.

Prosecutor: We are not hearing the case of your other colleagues and this reference is about you.

Bogoraz: My reference means that I am no different from my other colleagues.

Advocate Kaminskaya: Do you acknowledge as correct the wording of the indictment concerning disagreement with the Party's and Government's policy of rendering fraternal aid to Czechoslovakia?

Bogoraz: No, I do not acknowledge this. The indictment alleges that I did not agree with the policy of rendering fraternal aid. This is not true. My protest related to a specific action of the government. I am in complete agreement with the rendering of fraternal aid – say, economic aid – but I do not agree with the introduction of troops.

Kaminskaya: Do you acknowledge as correct the wording of the indictment concerning your entering into a criminal conspiracy?

Bogoraz: No.

Kaminskaya: Do you confirm that, as stated in the indictment, you shouted out slogans?

Bogoraz: I do not confirm it.

Advocate Kallistratova: And did any of the others next to you shout out slogans? Delone, in particular?

Bogoraz: No, I heard no shouts whatsoever; in particular, I did not even hear Delone's voice.

Kallistratova: Tell me, while your banners were being taken from you did any of you physically resist? Delone, in particular?

Bogoraz: No, neither Delone, nor any of the others offered resistance.

Judge: Question the accused Bogoraz about her own actions. You will have time enough to ask about your client.

Kallistratova: I take note of your remark. Tell me, Bogoraz, do you consider that the texts of the slogans contain deliberately false fabrications discrediting our social and state system?

Bogoraz: No, I do not. There were no fabrications whatsoever in these slogans.

Kallistratova: When you made up your mind to protest openly did you think that you might violate public order?

Bogoraz: I gave this special thought, because I knew about the liability for violating public order and did everything not to violate it. Nor did I violate it.

Advocate Pozdeev: How long did this event at the Execution Ground last?

Bogoraz: No more than ten minutes, probably rather less.

Pozdeev: Did any vehicles drive through the Square during this time?

Bogoraz: No, there was not a single vehicle during this time, except for that fetched to take us away.

Pozdeev: Do you remember how Litvinov was dressed?

Bogoraz: A white shirt and grey trousers, I think.

Advocate Monakhov: Tell me, were you sitting in the roadway or on the parapet?

Bogoraz: On the parapet. Up against the wall of the Execution Ground.

Monakhov: Could you have impeded the movement of vehicles?

Bogoraz: No, we could not. Apart from which, there were no vehicles there anyhow.

Judge: As to the crowd which gathered around you, was it on the side or in the roadway?

Bogoraz: There is no roadway there in my opinion, but the people who had gathered were not on the parapet.

Litvinov, Pavel Mikhailovich

Litvinov: I shall deal briefly with the motives for my action. On
21 August, Soviet troops crossed the frontiers of Czechoslovakia.
I consider these actions of the Soviet government to have been a
gross violation of the standards of international law and an
infringement of the article of the Constitution concerning the
right of nations to self-determination. As a Soviet citizen, I
thought it necessary to protest one way or another. A demonstration is a lawful way of expressing protest. On 25 August, I
therefore went to the Execution Ground and raised a banner.
As soon as we had sat down a group of people immediately rushed
at us. They came running fast and from several directions.
When they reached us they tore away the banners. The first to
reach me were a man with a briefcase and a woman with a bag.
The man hit me several times with the briefcase, including about
the head. The woman may have struck me as well. There was a
crack and, on looking round, I saw Feinberg's bleeding face on
my left. His teeth had been knocked out. Five or six people
rushed at us for a start, then others followed. The woman with
the bag kept shouting around, obviously to collect a crowd.
These people shouted: 'Hooligans, parasites, anti-Soviets!' The
rest of the crowd was puzzled. Some citizens were asking questions. In fact, they could not make out what was going on, because they had not had time to see the texts of the banners.

People asked us why we were there. We replied calmly and
explained the reason for the demonstration. Only those citizens
who had attacked us shouted and made a noise. We were then
dragged to the cars and pushed into them by these very same
citizens. We offered no resistance to them, although they wore
no badges and carried nothing to prove their right to arrest us.
We saw nobody in uniform. Nobody showed us documents. I
was shoved into a car with about six people in it. We spent the
whole day in police station No 50 where, as soon as we arrived,
we immediately demanded a forensic-medical examination in
connection with the knocking out of Feinberg's teeth.

Judge: You had a banner in your hands. Where did it come from?

Litvinov: I do not disclaim responsibility for any one of the banners in the Square, and see no reason to answer this question.

Judge: Did you come to the Square alone?

Litvinov: I refuse to answer.

Judge: Was there previous agreement with the other accused about the time and place of meeting?

Litvinov: There was not.

Judge: The documents in the case indicate that you are not employed anywhere. What means are you living on? You have, after all, a child to assist.

Litvinov: I was dismissed at the beginning of this year, formally for absenteeism, but actually not for this reason since no adverse remarks whatsoever had been made to me at work. Nevertheless, I was dismissed. I make a living from translations and private lessons. I do not propose to disclose the names of people to whom I gave private lessons. Throughout, I was trying to find a job. I put in for entrance examinations to two Institutes of Higher Education. I applied to the employment commission of the City Executive Committee. There, I was offered employment, but I was not accepted for it because it did not fit my speciality. I then embarked on the procedure for entering the Mining institute, but the procedure was held up. In August, I was trying to get a job in a factory. Various people tried to help me, but without success. I tried to earn something by lessons and translations and gave money to support my child, but less than usual.

Judge: Did you telephone any of your acquaintances on the eve of the twenty-fifth?

Litvinov: Yes, I phoned my acquaintance Inna Korkhova on the twenty-fourth and, without explanation, arranged to meet her at the 'Prospekt Marx' metro station at half past eleven. When we met we went towards Red Square and I still gave her no explanation. I merely said: 'Stay on the side and watch whatever happens.' After that I only saw her at the police station.

People's Assessor: Why did you choose Red Square in particular?

Litvinov: The chief reasons were lack of traffic and the appropriateness of Red Square as a place for publicising an appeal to the government.

People's Assessor: Who chose the time and place?

Litvinov: I refuse to answer.

Judge: How long have you known the other accused and what are your relations with them?

Litvinov: Bogoraz for about two years – we are friends. Babitsky for six months or a year – I do not know him well, but we are on good terms. Dremlyuga for four to five months – we did not often meet, but were on good terms. Delone I have known for some fifteen years, but have seldom met him recently and our relations were not close.

Prosecutor: When did you last see each of the accused before 25 August?

Litvinov: I don't remember and refuse to speak about the others. When last we met is not relevant to the case.

Prosecutor: Where did you meet Bogoraz?

Litvinov: Not far from the Execution Ground.

Prosecutor: Was there any previous agreement between you?

Litvinov: There was not.

Prosecutor: So it was pure coincidence?

Litvinov: I think that it was not pure coincidence.

Prosecutor: How can you talk like that? Now as a physicist, you ought to reason logically. If it was not a coincidence, then there was previous agreement.

Litvinov: No, that does not conflict with logic. I can suggest several alternative versions of other possibilities. For example – I do not insist that it was so – the following version is possible: some third person informed both me and Bogoraz that a demonstration was proposed for 25 August. We could have met there without any previous agreement but, equally, not by chance.

Prosecutor: Had you been alone, would you still have gone, regardless?

Litvinov: Undoubtedly.

Prosecutor: How do you explain that you turned up in Red Square at precisely 12 o'clock on the twenty-fifth?

Litvinov: This, in my opinion, is not relevant to the substance of the case.

Prosecutor: You must be concerned to clarify all the circumstances connected with this case, yet you constantly refuse to answer.

Litvinov: I see nothing prejudicial either in my actions or those of the other accused.

Prosecutor: If you see nothing criminal in them, it is all the more incomprehensible that you should not wish to talk about them.

Litvinov: Since the prosecution regards them as a crime, I do not wish to assist it.

Prosecutor: But I am asking about your actions.

Litvinov: I refuse to say anything about myself which might serve as an aggravating circumstance for others.

Prosecutor: Which slogan were you holding?

Litvinov: The text of the slogan was: 'For your freedom and ours', but I do not disclaim responsibility for any of the slogans.

Prosecutor: What did the banner look like?

Litvinov: A piece of canvas with sticks of about 8–10 ins.

Prosecutor: How were you dressed?

Litvinov: In a white shirt and grey trousers.

Prosecutor: Could you have concealed the banner in your clothing?

Litvinov: I refuse to answer.

Prosecutor: Why do you refuse to answer? This has a direct bearing on the actual circumstances of the case.

Litvinov: In my opinion, the actual circumstances consisted in our sitting down on the parapet and raising banners.

Prosecutor: How long have you known Korkhova and when did you meet her for the last time?

Litvinov: We have known each other for about two years. We met sometimes often, sometimes infrequently. We had last met about a week before 25 August.

Prosecutor: The reason for your telephone call to Korkhova?

Litvinov: I wanted there to be a person in the Square who knew nothing. I was convinced there would be provocation and wished someone to be present who could report objectively on what had happened.

Prosecutor: What are your relations with Rusakovskaya?

Litvinov: De facto marriage for several months.

Prosecutor: Do you know that Rusakovskaya was in the Square? How and when did she learn of the proposed event? Did you inform her?

Litvinov: I did not inform her, but refuse to answer for the rest because Rusakovskaya was rejected as a witness.

Prosecutor: Did you realize that your presence near a motor road might lead to traffic disruption?

Litvinov: I did not realize this, because I knew there was no traffic there.

Prosecutor: And did you know that what you were undertaking represented a breach of the law?

Litvinov: I am acquainted with the Constitution and the law. I consider that article 190/3 does not cancel the freedom to demonstrate guaranteed by article 125 of the Constitution. I did not intend to infringe the law and consider that I have not infringed it.

Prosecutor: You know the articles of the Constitution concerning your rights so well, but do you know article 130 of the Constitution?

Litvinov: I do not know it by its number, but probably know its content.

Prosecutor: Article 130 obliges every citizen to obey the laws.

Litvinov: I wished to obey the law and consider that I obeyed it.

Prosecutor: Do you know article 112 of the Constitution?

Advocate Kaminskaya: I object to the Prosecutor's question. We are hearing a specific indictment and there is no reason whatsoever for holding an examination in knowledge of the Constitution here.

Judge: Your next question, Comrade Prosecutor.

Prosecutor: How do you explain that you infringed your basic constitutional duty to work?

Litvinov: I am not to blame for that. Those who dismissed me illegally or did not accept me for work are guilty.

Prosecutor: If you considered that your dismissal was wrong, did you lodge a complaint with the appropriate department?

Litvinov: I applied to the city trade union council and was told that the case was not actionable in court.

Prosecutor: On what means did you subsist?

Judge: Comrade Prosecutor, the court has already dealt with this question.

Prosecutor: Did you provide material assistance for your child?

Litvinov: While working, I gave 30–40 roubles a month, depending on earnings. Lately, when I was not working, slightly less.

Advocate Kaminskaya: What post did you hold in the institute?

Litvinov: Assistant.

Kaminskaya: That is a post open to competition?

Litvinov: Yes. Dismissal from a post open to competition is not actionable in court.

Kaminskaya: Do you consider that you deviated from your constitutional duties?

Litvinov: Certainly not. I tried to find work.

Kaminskaya: Why do you say you were formally dismissed for absenteeism?

Litvinov: Because it was common practice with us for teachers to stand in for each other during laboratory work. I missed two days after arranging it in advance. I was reprimanded by the Studies Staff for failing to inform it. After this I was, nevertheless, sent on a duty trip for an exchange of views, as being the best teacher. On my return I was dismissed for the two days on which I had been absent.

Kaminskaya: Did you shout out slogans similar to the texts of the banners?

Litvinov: I did not shout out anything and did not hear anybody shouting anything.

Kaminskaya: Do you consider the texts of the slogans to be false or slanderous?

Litvinov: I do not consider them false and do not consider them to be of a slanderous nature.

Kaminskaya: Did you see even one car leaving the Spassky Gates?

Litvinov: No, I did not.

Kaminskaya: Did you offer resistance to the people who were detaining you?

Litvinov: I did not.

Kaminskaya: How did you counter the blows which you were struck?

Litvinov: In no way. I remained sitting, just like my comrades.

Kaminskaya: Did you see anybody offering resistance?

Litvinov: No, no one offered resistance.

Kaminskaya: Could you identify the people who detained you?

Litvinov: Some of them I can identify.

Advocate Kallistratova: You said you were holding a slogan. Were you holding it alone or with someone else?

Litvinov: Two of us were holding it. The other was Delone or Feinberg.

Advocate Monakhov: Did you, from the moment you unfolded the banners, remain on the parapet? Or did you move into the roadway?

Litvinov: I did not leave the parapet and, in any case, I did not know that there is a roadway there.

People's Assessor: You said that there would be provocation.

Litvinov: Yes, I was convinced of it.

People's Assessor: Why did you not tell those responsible for preserving public order so that you might be protected against provocation?

(Laughter in the courtroom)

Judge: I ask you to stop laughing. There is nothing funny going on here.

Litvinov: As the provocation was to be connected with my actions, what was I to report, whom was I to warn?

Advocate Kaminskaya: Did you foresee as you went to the demonstration that you would be treated as you were treated? And did you know that, by acting as you did, you would incur the risk of legal action?

Judge: Comrade Advocate, the court reprimands you. You are suggesting answers to the accused.

Kaminskaya: How do you explain that you went to the Square knowing that serious unpleasantness awaited you?

Litvinov: I was deeply convinced of the rightness of my actions and, as a Soviet citizen, was bound to protest against the gross error perpetrated by the government.

Babitsky, Konstantin Iosifovich

Babitsky: On the assumption that the entry of troops into Czechoslovakia would, first and foremost, severely damage the prestige of the Soviet Union, I thought it necessary to inform the government and citizens of this conviction of mine. For this purpose I appeared in Red Square at 12 noon on 25 August, sat down on the pavement near the Execution Ground and raised a banner. Very soon, after a minute and a half or two minutes, there were five to six people in plain clothes around us who very rudely and sharply tore our banners away from us. None of us offered resistance. Meanwhile, the people in plain clothes shouted coarse abuse. One of them was shouting: 'Oh, you bitch, you anti-Soviet.'

Judge: Babitsky, please do not repeat these expressions in the courtroom. You are university educated, you work at the Russian Language Institute. They may be printable, but they should not be used in a courtroom. No more need be said than that they were coarse expressions.

Babitsky: All right. The man who snatched the banner from me and Feinberg, twice hit him in the face and in the teeth. As a result, his teeth were knocked out and he bled. Then people crowded round. We sat for about three minutes, surrounded by a fair crowd, some fifty people. There was an exchange of views just then between those who were sitting and those who were standing. The people who had removed the slogans could be heard shouting insults. To a woman annoyed by the texts of the banners I said: 'Friends, it is a huge mistake, we are losing our best friends, the Czechs and the Slovaks.' I think that I said no more. All was said quietly, there was no need to shout. For the most part, the crowd was puzzled: 'What's happened?' Then they started to lift us and lead us away, swearing and hitting us in the sides and back as they went. They got me to the car and two people pushed me in.

Judge: You do not deny that you were in Red Square and held a slogan? Which slogan did you hold?

Babitsky: I have already quoted it at the preliminary investigation: 'At žije svobodné a nezavislé Československo'.

Judge: Where did the banner come from?

Babitsky: I would prefer not to answer this question. I assume that the task of the prosecution is to prove the fact of a crime and that of the court to assess it, since a judicial error might otherwise be committed.

Judge: The testimony of an accused in conjunction with all other evidence will help a court to make its assessment. If you do not wish to answer, you need not answer. Did you bring it with you?

Babitsky: That is the same sort of question.

Judge: Who prepared this slogan?

Babitsky: I refuse to answer.

Judge: Did you prepare any slogan at home?

Babitsky: Yes, but it did not appear in Red Square.

Judge: What was the text of the slogan which you prepared at home?

Babitsky: The text is known, and so I have no alternative to answering: 'Down with intervention in the cssr'.

Judge: Did you use the plastic board found during the search to make it?

Babitsky: Yes.

Judge: Did you concert in advance with any of the accused?

Babitsky: No, I came to Red Square on my own initiative. There was no previous agreement.

People's Assessor: How do you explain that your disorderly assembly was so quickly and efficiently dispersed?

Babitsky: We were obviously expected.

People's Assessor: With whom did you confer about the visit to Red Square?

Babitsky: I refuse to answer.

Prosecutor: When did you make the slogan which was left at your home?

Babitsky: I refuse to answer.

Prosecutor: What did you prepare it for?

Babitsky: In order to bring it to the Square. I had a moment's hesitation and did not bring the slogan with me.

Prosecutor: Where is it?

Babitsky: Destroyed, I suppose. I do not wish to say any more.

Prosecutor: Did you bring a slogan when you came to Red Square?

Babitsky: I refuse to answer.

Prosecutor: Why?

Babitsky: Because this question has no bearing on the substance of the case. There was a demonstration and there was the rout of the demonstration; the rest is unimportant.

Prosecutor: When and where did you meet Bogoraz and Litvinov?

Babitsky: At the Execution Ground. I don't exactly remember the time.

Prosecutor: Did you know in advance that Bogoraz and Litvinov would be in Red Square?

Babitsky: I refuse to answer. I have already explained once why – I consider that it has no bearing on the substance of the case.

Judge: You are accused of entering into a conspiracy and these questions touch on the substance of the indictment against you – they are not the result of idle curiosity. You must therefore answer these questions.

Prosecutor: Did anyone apart from the accused know that you were preparing to go to Red Square?

Babitsky: I refuse to answer.

Prosecutor: Did you understand that you were preparing to violate public order by your actions?

Babitsky: Not only did I not intend to violate public order, but I took every step to avoid its violation.

Prosecutor: What was your education?

Babitsky: I graduated from the Communications Engineering Institute in 1953 and completed the course at the Moscow University philological faculty in 1960.

Advocate Pozdeev: What were you wearing?

Babitsky: As now, except for the jacket.

Judge: 'As now' cannot be written into the record. Clarify it.

Babitsky: White shirt, grey trousers.

Pozdeev: During your scientific activity were any of your learned works published and, if so, how many?

Babitsky: Twelve have been published, three are printing.

Pozdeev: Did you see the texts of the slogans? You know the texts?

Babitsky: I would not say that I saw them all – I came to know them from the evidence produced by the investigation.

Pozdeev: Translate the text of your slogan.

Babitsky: 'Long live free and independent Czechoslovakia.'

Pozdeev: Did you honestly believe that you were right? Or did you have other aims in view?

Babitsky: I will make bold to say that our aims were . . . (hesitating) lofty. Would one go to prison for the sake of something which one did not honestly believe?

Pozdeev: Do you consider that the slogans contained lying fabrications and slandered our social system?

Babitsky: By no means. I resolutely deny that the texts of the slogans cast a slur on the social and state system. Not a single slogan contains either slander or fabrication. Nobody in the USSR would argue against a demand for the freedom and independence of Czechoslovakia. No right thinking person would, I think, protest against the text of this slogan. The same can be said about the other slogans.

Pozdeev: Who put you into the car: the people in plain clothes or members of the police?

Babitsky: I was brought to the car by people in plain clothes. A policeman was inside – he opened the door.

Pozdeev: Did you attempt to offer resistance?

Babitsky: No, I offered no resistance whatsoever, neither to the police nor to the civilians who had been acting like hooligans – not even to the scoundrel who knocked out Feinberg's teeth.

Judge: Accused, I have warned you.

Babitsky: I apologize.

Pozdeev: Apart from the phrase about 'a grave mistake', you said nothing?

Babitsky: I do not remember any other phrases. I think I said nothing more.

Pozdeev: Did you hear shouts?

Babitsky: I heard no shouts at all and what the others were saying was difficult to catch.

Advocate Monakhov: Did you move from the parapet to the roadway before the moment when you were detained?

Babitsky: I did not rise. I did not even rise when I was detained – I was lifted.

Monakhov: Why did you go on sitting round the parapet?

Babitsky: I did not rise, nor did anyone else. We sat so as not to violate public order even by the slightest movement.

Advocate Kaminskaya: While you were sitting there did even a single car pass by?

Babitsky: I have *never* seen cars passing there and that is why I picked that place.

Kaminskaya: Did even one of your colleagues offer resistance?

Babitsky: No one offered resistance of any kind, not even Feinberg.

Judge: It is already perfectly clear to the court that none of the accused offered resistance.

Advocate Kallistratova: Would you recognize any of those who detained you and took away the banners?

Babitsky: I would probably recognize the individual who struck Feinberg and took away my banner. And another, who was swearing.

Delone, Vadim Nikolaevich

Delone: I wish to say first of all that I do not plead guilty. The indictment must be objective and based on facts. I regard the indictment against me as groundless, legally inept and unsubstantiated. I stated at the preliminary investigation that, because I did not agree with the government's actions, I took part in an expression of protest against the introduction of troops into Czechoslovakia and held one of the slogans. Everything else in the indictment differs from the real state of affairs.

First, my protest was not against fraternal aid, but against the introduction of troops into Czechoslovakia. It is stated in the indictment that, in order to publicize my criminal intentions, I entered into a criminal conspiracy. I did not enter into any sort of criminal conspiracy – in fact, there was no criminal conspiracy, because there was no criminal matter. It was only on the twenty-fifth that I heard of the possibility of a demonstration or meeting and there is nothing in the evidence in the case to controvert this. The investigation has at its disposal accurate information showing that I was not even in Moscow on the twenty-fourth.

I did indeed take part in the protest and unfolded one of the banners. I do not consider that the texts of the banners contain deliberately false fabrications casting a slur on the actions of the Soviet government. We put forward no facts in the texts of the banners, merely our attitude to them. They therefore cannot be false, let alone deliberately false, and could not mislead anyone.

The indictment against me is that I violated public order. But it is clearly without substance.

Yes, I did indeed appear in Red Square at 12 noon, but there was no violation of public order, either by my friends or me. I shouted no slogans and there is nothing about this in the evidence of the witnesses. I could not have disrupted the traffic since not a single car left the Spassky Gates heading for GUM. What is more, I was not even aware that this part of Red Square is a thoroughfare. On the contrary, people gather in great numbers in the Square, often even form crowds, tourist guides bring large parties to the Execution Ground and stay there a fair time. Had we been in the roadway, we might conceivably have disrupted traffic, but we sat on the side and stayed there right up to the time when I was dragged to the car.

The indictment refers to indignation on the part of a number of citizens. How did this manifest itself? In the blatantly disorderly and intentionally provocative actions of a few people. The texts of the slogans were, of course, unusual and bound to attract attention, but it was up to each citizen's conscience to react to the limit of his inclination and powers of self-restraint. These citizens should have acted in an orderly fashion, even if they did not like the slogans. True, I did unfold a slogan. But then, you are all aware of instances when crowds of people appear in Red Square with various slogans.

(*Movement in the courtroom*)

Judge: Accused Delone, the court must interrupt you. You should be elucidating the substance of the case. Instead, you are already analysing it. You will be given an opportunity for this later.

Delone: I want to explain the motives for my action. On 21 August I heard about the introduction of troops into Czechoslovakia and felt indignant about this government action. It conflicts with the right of nations to self-determination and all standards of international law. It seemed to me that, if I failed to voice my protest, I would tacitly be supporting this action. I therefore had to make a public protest. As early as 21 August I was already thinking about various forms of protest. I last saw all the accused on 21 August, but there was no talk at all of a demonstration at that time. On 25 August, I returned from the country and called on a friend. There, I heard some sort of meeting had taken place in Red Square on the twenty-fourth and that there might possibly be another on the twenty-fifth. I arrived in Red Square at roughly twenty to twelve without meeting anyone beforehand. At about twelve I met my acquaintances – Bogoraz, Dremlyuga and Litvinov – near the Execution Ground. Someone said that he also proposed to demonstrate. I was handed a banner – I do not wish to say by whom. Having established that the text completely tallied with my convictions, I raised it. I can now quote this text – 'For your freedom and ours'. As soon as we had raised the banners, several people rushed at us, three men for a start and then two more. They came running from the direction of GUM as fast as they could; they had clearly been standing by and were apparently specially detailed to stimulate resistance. They snatched away the slogans. The man who snatched away mine used unprintable language and twice hit me with his briefcase. Litvinov was also struck. Feinberg's whole face was covered in blood. I neither moved nor got up. Turning to the crowd, these people in plain clothes were shouting: 'Hooligans, anti-Soviets' thereby trying to arouse it. I saw no representatives of authority. None of us tried to run away. One of the first to arrive gave orders for a car. Cars drove up. We did not intend to run away and remained seated. We began to be manhandled with great roughness. My arm was twisted behind my back, clearly in order to inflict pain. I was thrown into a car. Definitely thrown, so that my face struck the seat. Then Litvinov was also thrown in. It seemed to me that he was struck or, at any rate, pushed very hard. I assume, although I cannot be certain about it, that these were members of the KGB. At the police station these people in plain clothes produced booklets – state security identification, in my opinion. One of them told the policeman in a very commanding way: 'Don't let anyone go'.

Prosecutor: Elucidate your purpose in going to Red Square.

Delone: I went to find out whether anything would happen or not. On the way I decided that if there were to be a demonstration about Czechoslovakia I would take part and would behave with great restraint.

Prosecutor: What is the surname of the acquaintance who informed you that a demonstration was being prepared?

Delone: I refuse to give the surname of my acquaintance.

Prosecutor: If you did not know what would happen, how did you propose to express your protest?

Delone: I hoped to hold one of the slogans and that is what did happen.

Prosecutor: So you knew that there would be banners?

Delone: I did not know, but assumed it. I had been told there might be a meeting or demonstration. A demonstration implies banners. I decided that if there were to be a demonstration, I must express my protest one way or another.

Prosecutor: Who gave you the slogan?

Delone: I refuse to answer.

Prosecutor: How do you explain that you and Litvinov were holding the same slogan: 'For your freedom and ours'?

Delone: Well, I held one end and Litvinov the other.

Judge: Who gave you the slogan?

Delone: Maybe I do not even remember.

Prosecutor: How was this slogan made? Was it specially prepared for display?

Delone: Yes, it was canvas mounted on slats.

Prosecutor: What size was the banner?

Delone: 12–15 inches.

Prosecutor: There are certain contradictions between your statements in court and your statements at the preliminary investigation. Why?

Delone: What contradictions?

Prosecutor: First tell me why and I will then tell you which.

(*General laughter in the courtroom*)

Prosecutor read out statements made on 28 August in which Delone stated that he had shouted out slogans.

Delone: I did shout once, or rather said in a loud voice: 'Freedom for Czechoslovakia!' But that was not in Red Square – I said it when the car in which I was being driven away was already some distance from the Execution Ground.

Prosecutor: To whom was the slogan addressed?

Delone: It was an emotional reaction to the use of force against me.

Prosecutor: And who was with you in the car?

Delone: Two people in plain clothes.

Prosecutor: And of your acquaintances?

Delone: Litvinov and Dremlyuga.

Prosecutor: Then to whom was it addressed – Litvinov or Dremlyuga?

Delone: There was no point in addressing it to Litvinov or Dremlyuga. I was addressing our escort.

Prosecutor: The record of your interrogation states that you shouted several times.

Delone: I said: 'I may have shouted several times', because I did not want to make wrong statements. And I now insist that it was once only.

Prosecutor: Were any citizens nearby while you were shouting slogans?

Delone: No, there were no citizens nearby.

Prosecutor: The record of your interrogation on 28 August

contains your statements that you were shouting these slogans while still at the Execution Ground.

Delone: This is where I had an amendment to the record.

Prosecutor: But not on this point.

Delone: Yes, precisely on this point.

(*The Judge* searched for the relevant amendment to the record.)

Prosecutor: When and on what grounds were you previously indicted on a criminal charge?

Delone: I was arrested on 27 January 1967 for taking part in a protest demonstration.

Prosecutor: You were not sentenced for a demonstration, but for collective actions grossly violating public order. You therefore knew about the illegal nature of such actions?

Delone: I did not – and do not – consider that the actions we undertook in Red Square violated public order. And I consider the previous sentence unjust. Bukovsky was wrongly sentenced.

Judge: The sentence has taken legal effect and you have not the right to discuss it.

Prosecutor: Was the meaning of this measure of conditional punishment explained to you?

Delone: Yes, the sentence was explained.

Prosecutor: In which higher educational establishment did you last study?

Delone: In Novosibirsk University, from January to June 1968.

Prosecutor: Why did you leave it?

Delone: For several reasons: I went there on the insistent advice of my family; linguistics did not suit me as a profession; apart from this, I found out when I was in Moscow in May 1968 that I had forfeited my right to be domiciled in Moscow. Then there was an article about me in *Vechernyi Novosibirsk* which was extremely tendentious, to put it mildly. After this, I felt awkward about staying there.

Judge: When were you expelled?

Delone: I left in June 1968. I should like to add something about the text of the indictment. It states that I have not been engaged in socially useful work. But it is just because I had literary work in Novosibirsk that I stayed on there. There was a long delay before I was granted registration in Moscow. I registered on 7 August and only received my passport on the twelfth. I was therefore unable to find permanent employment.

Advocate Kallistratova: With whom did you discuss the possibilities of employment?

Delone: At the Moscow University Geography faculty, about joining an expedition to Norilsk because this did not require a permanent Moscow registration. I had already received travel instructions.

Kallistratova: The profession which Novosibirsk University offered you did not attract you. What profession did in fact attract you?

Delone: I write verse. Creative work attracts me. I was constantly at work on my verse. I wrote articles in Novosibirsk and took part in literary competitions.

Kallistratova: Did your literary work receive any sort of recognition?

Delone: I won the second prize in a competition organized by the Novosibirsk 'Pod Integral' club and the Soviet district committee of the Komsomol for the Fiftieth Anniversary of the October Revolution.

Kallistratova: Have your poems been published anywhere?

Delone: No, they are lying about in various editorial offices and have not yet been published.

Advocate Pozdeev: Have you known Babitsky long?

Delone: No, I had not met him before 25 August.

Advocate Monakhov: Do you confirm the statements of the other accused that none of you moved from the parapet?

Delone: Yes, I confirm that nobody moved.

Monakhov: Can you remember whether anyone's glasses were broken there?

Delone: No, I don't remember.

Bogoraz: I wish to ask the accused Delone whether he knew for a fact that we in particular would be taking part in the demonstration?

Delone: No, I did not know.

Bogoraz: And was it when you arrived at the Square that you realized that we intended to demonstrate?

Delone: Yes, I realized it when I saw and heard you and the others.

Bogoraz: And did you, on 21 August, guess my intention to protest against the despatch of troops?

Delone: There was no actual conversation about this, but knowing you well enough. . . .

(Laughter in the courtroom)

Prosecutor: (addressing Bogoraz) You say that you already expressed your attitude on 21 August. How could you have known? The news was only in the press on the twenty-second.

Bogoraz: My memory is clear – the introduction of troops into Czechoslovakia was announced by both radio and press on the twenty-first. I well remember the day. On that day we all met at the trial of my friend Anatoli Marchenko.

Prosecutor: The news was published on the twenty-second.

Bogoraz: No, the twenty-first.

Prosecutor: No, the twenty-second.

Judge: Comrade Prosecutor, the court will enquire and establish this point.

Dremlyuga, Vladimir Alexandrovich

Dremlyuga: Unfortunately, I have to speak last. I can add nothing to what has already been said here. I shall merely have to dwell on the motives of my actions. I decided to take part in a demonstration a long time ago, at the beginning of August. I heard from an acquaintance, a member of the armed forces serving in a tank unit, that his unit had crossed the Czechoslovak frontier in May, entered Kosice and stayed there for over a month. I decided on the spot that if Soviet troops were taken into Czechoslovakia, I would protest.

Judge: Accused, all this is understandable. You made up your mind in advance – now tell us how you carried out your decision.

Dremlyuga: On 21 August, I learnt about the despatch of troops from the papers. Not from the radio – I do not listen to Soviet radio. I therefore went to the Square. Whether by agreement or without agreement is irrelevant to the case – it is not required for article 190. I wrote a two-sided banner, wrote it myself. 'Freedom for Dubcek!' on one side, 'Down with the occupiers!' on the other.

How it all happened has already been told here. Witness Dolgov, from Military Unit 1164, twice struck Litvinov with an attaché case, kicked him in the leg and swore. Litvinov went on sitting. The man standing next to Dolgov shouted at Litvinov: 'I've been after you a long time, Yid-face' and added: 'You. . . .' followed by a five-letter word beginning with 'b' which you will not allow to be spoken, followed by 'Anti-Soviets!'

Judge: Accused, I am reprimanding you and ask you to choose expressions which may be used in a courtroom.

Dremlyuga: On the way to the police station, I opened the car window and, as we were being driven along, kept shouting 'Freedom for Dubcek'. I repeated this five or ten times.

Prosecutor: Which of the accused do you know, and for how long?

Dremlyuga: I know all the accused, but none of them for long, a matter of three or four months. I only recently settled in Moscow, having previously lived in Leningrad. I was only registered on 27 March, after four months of red tape.

Prosecutor: On what grounds were you registered?

Dremlyuga: I married, and was registered at my wife's domicile.

Prosecutor: And so you have not known the accused long? What were your relations with them?

Dremlyuga: I have known them for three or four months. Excellent relations with all of them.

Prosecutor: Have you been to their homes?

Dremlyuga: Yes, sometimes.

Prosecutor: When did you last see the accused Bogoraz before the twenty-fifth?

Dremlyuga: On the twenty-second or, more accurately, on the night of 22/23 August – I spent the night at her place.

Prosecutor: And when did you see Litvinov?

Dremlyuga: On 21 August, at Anatoli Marchenko's trial.

Prosecutor: And when did you see Babitsky?

Dremlyuga: A month earlier.

Prosecutor: And when did you see Delone?

Dremlyuga: On 21 August.

Prosecutor: Had you already taken a decision that day or did you only discuss your forthcoming public gesture?

Dremlyuga: No, that day it was Anatoli Marchenko's personal fate which worried me most. Intellectually, of course, I realized that such an act – I wanted to use a word, but will refrain – committed by our government was a terrible crime and much more important than the sentencing of one man, but emotionally Marchenko's fate disturbed me more that day.

Judge: Accused, keep to the substance of the case.

Prosecutor: You are answering with great emotion, but not the questions put to you. Did you hold conversations with the other accused before the twenty-fifth?

Dremlyuga: Opinions were exchanged.

Prosecutor: Did that exchange of opinions include the preparation of your public gesture?

Dremlyuga: No, it did not.

Prosecutor: Where did you meet the accused Bogoraz on the twenty-fifth?

Dremlyuga: At the Execution Ground.

Prosecutor: When you arrived, who was there?

Dremlyuga: I will not enumerate them. They are all known to you.

Prosecutor: When exactly did you arrive in Red Square?

Dremlyuga: Seven or ten minutes before twelve.

Prosecutor: How do you explain that it was these people in particular who you approached on arriving in Red Square?

Dremlyuga: Because these people were acquaintances. I would not go up to comrades who were not known to me, would I?

Prosecutor: When did you sit down at the Execution Ground?

Dremlyuga: I sat down at exactly 12 o'clock.

Prosecutor: You said that you arrived at seven or ten minutes to twelve. What did you do during those seven or ten minutes?

Dremlyuga: I talked with my friends.

Prosecutor: With whom in particular?

Dremlyuga: With all of them.

Prosecutor: Quote the surnames.

Dremlyuga: What do you want – an enumeration of all the accused? Litvinov, Bogoraz, Feinberg, Gorbanevskaya, Delone, Babitsky, Dremlyuga. Or rather, Dremlyuga – that's me.

(*Animation in the courtroom*)

Prosecutor: What did you talk about?

Dremlyuga: About the fine weather.

(*Noise in the courtroom*)

Judge: The court again reprimands you. One should not speak in that tone of voice. The Prosecutor is questioning you politely, and about the substance of the case. You may refuse to answer, but in answering, you must speak politely.

Prosecutor: What size was the slogan you were holding?

Dremlyuga: 20 by 40 inches.

Prosecutor: What did it look like?

Dremlyuga: Just canvas, there were no slats.

Prosecutor: Did you know that the others also had slogans?

Dremlyuga: I did not know about the other banners.

Prosecutor: How do you explain that you chose Red Square in particular for your actions?

Dremlyuga: It has already been explained to you that there is no traffic in Red Square. I had been there several times beforehand, I even timed it – one car goes by every two hours.

Prosecutor: So you were looking for a quiet place – why then did you not go to say, the Alexandrovsky Gardens?

Dremlyuga: I don't know Moscow well – after all, I am a newcomer. Besides, there are no people in the gardens and these 'persons' as you call them, would have let themselves go even more.

Judge: One should say 'citizens' – here everybody is a citizen.

Dremlyuga: Yes, well, these citizens would have let themselves go even more.

Prosecutor: So, the only motive was absence of traffic?

Dremlyuga: Yes.

Prosecutor: Were you employed when you committed this crime?

Dremlyuga: I had not been employed for the last month. Before that I worked as a railway electrician.

Prosecutor: Where did you study?

Dremlyuga: I studied at Leningrad University, I was expelled.

Prosecutor: For what particular reason were you expelled?

Dremlyuga: For unlawful misappropriation of the name of a Soviet Chekist [Member of Security Police]. It's a long story. It was a joke at the expense of a former KGB member. I shared a flat with him. While I was away he was handed a letter at my instigation addressed to 'KGB Captain Vladimir Dremlyuga'. The neighbour, of course. . . .

Judge: Be brief – how was your expulsion worded?

Dremlyuga: For unworthy behaviour casting a slur on the good name of a Soviet student.

Prosecutor: Were you a member of the Komsomol?

Dremlyuga: Yes, from 1955 to 1958.

Prosecutor: Why did you leave?

Dremlyuga: I was expelled.

Prosecutor: What for?

Dremlyuga: For my moustache.

(*Laughter in the courtroom*)

Judge: Accused, I have reprimanded you before, What does that mean?

Dremlyuga: I am telling the truth, that's how it was put: 'For wrecking a Soviet family, non-payment of membership dues and for a moustache.'

Prosecutor: On what charges have you previously appeared in court?

Dremlyuga: Under article 174, for re-selling car tyres.

Prosecutor: Your note-book is on file with the names of forty-eight women of seventeen and above. What are these, all your acquaintances?

Dremlyuga: Yes, acquaintances.

Prosecutor: Does this list of your acquaintances touch on your intimate life?

Dremlyuga: One might say so, yes.

Advocate Monakhov: Do you mean 'my intimate life among other things'?

Dremlyuga: Yes, among other things.

Judge: The court will not go into this question at present.

Monakhov: Did you consider on 25 August that your slogans contained deliberately false information?

Dremlyuga: I see no deliberately false information in the text of the slogans. In particular, there was no slander in the slogan 'Freedom for Dubcek'. I knew that Dubcek had been interned – it was the truth.

Prosecutor: Where did you get it from that Dubcek was interned?

Dremlyuga: I listened to the Israeli radio. Even our own newspapers carried no information about Dubcek. They only wrote that he was a revisionist and a traitor. President Svoboda arrived in Moscow. . .

Judge: All is clear, you need not continue.

Dremlyuga: You shut me up when I want to explain the motives for my actions.

Monakhov: Did I understand correctly that you concluded from our papers that Dubcek had apparently been interned?

Dremlyuga: Yes, that is correct.

Advocate Kaminskaya: Did you or any of those near you offer resistance to the people who detained you?

Dremlyuga: Neither I nor anyone else offered resistance.

Kaminskaya: Did they proffer any form of official identification?

Dremlyuga: Nobody proffered any official identification of any kind.

Kaminskaya: Did they have arm-bands?

Dremlyuga: No, there was nothing.

Kaminskaya: Did any of them suggest that you should leave the Execution Ground?

Dremlyuga: On the contrary, they surrounded us because they were afraid that we might leave the place.

EXAMINATION OF WITNESSES

Examination of witness Strebkov, Ivan Vasilevich

Strebkov: It was on 25 August of this year. I was on duty in Red Square in a patrol car. At around 12 noon, I was ordered to go immediately to the Execution Ground part of Red Square. When I drove up I saw very many people, a crowd. I did not understand what had happened. I opened the door, got out and had just stopped when three citizens came up to me, one on either side and one in the middle. They held him by the arms. They ordered me to deliver the citizen urgently to police station No 50. At the station, I handed the citizen over to the man on duty, reported the situation to the town duty detail and returned to Red Square.

Judge: Can you recognize among the accused whom in particular you delivered to the police station?

Strebkov: Maybe not. Perhaps the one with a white shirt and glasses. Perhaps him (pointing at Babitsky).

Prosecutor: How would you describe the traffic at that place?

Strebkov: I don't understand.

Prosecutor (explains): Were cars passing there?

Strebkov: No, traffic is forbidden there, the Mausoleum was open at that time.

Prosecutor: And from the Spassky Gates? Did they have to go by the Execution Ground?

Strebkov: No, cars go straight from the Kremlin along Kuibyshev Street. Past the Execution Ground, but to the side.

Prosecutor: How did this citizen behave?

Strebkov: He behaved quietly, not a word.

Prosecutor: And those people who put him in the car?

Strebkov: I didn't see. They put him in and said to deliver him.

Prosecutor: Accused Babitsky, did this witness deliver you to the police station?

Babitsky: I assume that I was delivered to the police by this citizen.

(Babitsky had no questions for the witness)

Bogoraz: Who gave the instruction to drive up to the Execution Ground?

Strebkov: I received an order from the senior officer in the squad.

Bogoraz: And to deliver to the police station?

Strebkov: Unknown citizens gave me this order.

Bogoraz: There are two of your reports in the case. It is stated there that you saw a banner in the hands of a KGB member at the police station. Tell us about this in detail.

Strebkov: While I was telephoning in a neighbouring room, a citizen came in. A member of the KGB, it later turned out. He brought a slogan: 'Hands off Czechoslovakia!'

Advocate Kaminskaya: Did you see any cars leaving the Spassky Gates?

Strebkov: Government cars streak back and forth every minute.

Kaminskaya: But the crowd stood to one side?

Strebkov: Yes.

Kaminskaya: So, it was not interfering with the traffic?

Strebkov: No, it did not interfere. There is a man on point duty there.

Kaminskaya: How long were you at the Execution Ground?

Strebkov: One or two minutes – it's an efficient car.

Kaminskaya: How many cars left the Spassky Gates during that time?

Strebkov: I don't know. I paid no attention.

Advocate Kallistratova: From whom did you learn that it was a member of the KGB who brought the banner?

Strebkov: He identified himself.

Kallistratova: What did he say in this connection?

Strebkov: That he had taken away the banner during a search.

Kallistratova: You were given the order to take them to police station No 50. What citizens gave you the order?

Strebkov: Some kind of citizens.

Kallistratova: And you carried out the order of some kind of citizens?

Strebkov: Yes.

Judge (simultaneously with Strebkov's answer): The answer to this question has already been provided.

Advocate Pozdeev: Did the citizen detained offer resistance?

Strebkov: No, he did not resist.

Advocate Monakhov: For what purpose were you in Red Square?

Strebkov: To keep order.

Monahkov: Did cars stop?

Strebkov: I paid no attention.

Kaminskaya: Your preliminary evidence states that you took the last one. Explain.

Strebkov: I don't know whether anyone was left there. Yes, I'd say I drove away the last one. I think so because there were no other cars.

Babitsky: If two people leading a third come up to you tomorrow and order you to take him away, will you carry out their order?

Judge: The question is hypothetical, and is therefore struck out.

Babitsky: The citizens were known to you?

Strebkov: No.

Babitsky: What made you carry out an order from people you did not know?

Strebkov: As a member of the militia, I am obliged to detain at anyone's request.

Dremlyuga: Did they produce any documents?

Strebkov: No, they did not.

Dremlyuga: You said that the Traffic Control Department had closed Red Square to traffic in connection with the queue to the Mausoleum. On which side was the crowd?

Strebkov: On the cathedral side.

Dremlyuga: At what distance from the Execution Ground do cars pass?

Strebkov: I couldn't say.

Prosecutor (to Dremlyuga): On which side of the Execution Ground were you sitting?

Dremlyuga: Facing the Historical Museum.

The Judge consulted each of those involved in the case as to whether Strebkov should be allowed to absent himself for the rest of the proceedings as he had to attend a funeral.

The Prosecutor did not object to Strebkov being released.

The Advocates and *Accused* did not object, but asked the court to secure Strebkov's return to the proceedings after the funeral: 'Strebkov must be present at the examination of other witnesses since there were discrepancies between his statements and those of other witnesses at the preliminary investigation.'

The Court consulted without rising and ruled that Strebkov be released from the court proceedings.

Supplementary statement by Bogoraz

Now that the rest of the accused have spoken, I think I should state which banner I was holding, since this is in any case obvious by elimination – 'Hands off the CSSR!' The banner was done in black on white canvas. I repeat once again that I accept responsibility for all the banners.

Further to Dremlyuga's statements: I have remembered that I also heard the words addressed to Litvinov: 'At last I've got you, Yid-face!'

In reply to what the Professor said about collusion in connection with the question of coincidence or previous agreement: as Litvinov pointed out, a third possibility exists – information through some third persons.

Judge: Please elucidate this point.

Bogoraz: I did not conceal my intentions from anyone, even though I do not assert that I mentioned them specifically to the accused. To elaborate, I selected this particular form of protest because I had also protested in other ways, for example by submitting a statement at work, but had received no reply. And a form of protest such as a demonstration is also legal and safeguarded by the constitution.

Prosecutor (to Dremlyuga): Did you at the preliminary investigation refer to this sentence addressed to Litvinov?

Dremlyuga (proudly): At the preliminary investigation I gave no evidence whatsoever.

Litvinov (supplements): I now also remember this sentence – and remember who uttered it and when. It was spoken by the man who sat at the wheel when we were driven to the police station and could have been heard by Dremlyuga, Bogoraz and others.

Interrogation of the witness Yastreba, Yevgenia Nikolaevna

Yastreba: On 25 August of this year, at ten to twelve, I came to the Execution Ground to meet some girls I know. I saw a woman with a pram walk past me. At that moment a woman – Bogoraz – and three men – Litvinov, Delone and, I think, Feinberg – came up to her from the opposite direction. They talked for a few minutes. The woman with the child sat down by the Execution Ground and all the others followed her. They there and then raised their hands: they were holding banners. The woman with the child raised a flag – she said it was the Czech national flag. I tried to read the slogans, but was not able to. I only read the slogan: 'For your freedom and ours' – it was held by Litvinov. At that moment three men ran up, tore away the slogans and one of them broke the stick of the flag. A large crowd gathered. People said 'It's not right to behave like that' and asked for the police. Then a car was brought up. More people were put into it than I had seen earlier (five altogether). Feinberg shouted: 'Down with aggression.' Litvinov and Delone went quietly.

Prosecutor: Did you identify anyone during the preliminary investigation?

Yastreba: Yes, I identified Feinberg, Litvinov, Delone and Bogoraz. I did not recognize Dremlyuga and Babitsky.

Prosecutor: How did those citizens who gathered react to what was happening?

Yastreba: They were very indignant. Someone said: 'My father died for Czechoslovakia and look what you're doing', 'You've warmed yourselves, you've eaten our bread'.

Prosecutor: What did those sitting answer?

Yastreba: They were answering quietly. I did not hear. Something about the constitution, I think. Someone in the crowd replied: 'You know the constitution and you fix up this sort of thing!'

Prosecutor: What do you do? Do you work or study?

Yastreba: I am a fifth year student of the Cheliabinsk Polytechnic Institute.

Prosecutor: You are a Komsomol member?

Yastreba: Yes, I am a Young Communist.

Bogoraz: Did the people in the crowd commit any gross disorder?

Yastreba: They did. One man struck Delone twice with a brief-case about the head and shoulders. He only scratched him.

Bogoraz: Was Feinberg beaten?

Yastreba: I did not see, but I heard someone in the crowd saying that he had been hit. He was told, also from the crowd: 'He hit himself with his own fist.'

Bogoraz: Did any cars go by from the Spassky Gates? Did you see any traffic jams?

Yastreba: I was not watching the cars. They were moving on the side towards the Spassky Gates, but there were no jams.

Bogoraz: Did you take part in detaining us?

Yastreba: I personally did no detaining.

Advocate Kallistratova: Who struck Delone?

Yastreba: A man ran up, and hit Delone in the heat of the moment. The next man running shouted: 'Stop hitting.' Then the first man struck again.

Kallistratova: Did the one who struck him snatch the slogan?

Yastreba: Yes.

Kallistratova: When they were detaining Delone and leading him away, did he resist?

Yastreba: I did not see him resisting, but there was a row of people between him and me.

Kallistratova: What did the accused do while they were being beaten and their slogans were being snatched away and after-wards?

Yastreba: They sat quietly and did not attempt to resist: maybe they said something – I did not hear. Only the woman with the child said: 'What are you doing? Don't touch! It's the Czech national flag.'

Advocate Monakhov: How did Delone react to being hit twice?

Yastreba: Delone did not even get up and took no action what-soever. He used no physical force in reply to being beaten.

Bogoraz: Make it clear where we were sitting.

Yastreba: There is a little parapet and you sat on it facing the Historical Museum.

Litvinov: In which of our actions did you observe a violation of public order?

Judge: The court strikes out this question.

Litvinov: As you stated, the woman with the child was walking by herself and we came up later. Where did this happen?

Yastreba: You met a few metres from me.

Babitsky: Did you see any representatives of the police at the Execution Ground?

Yastreba: I think there were no policemen at the Execution Ground.

Delone: What did those who ran up to us have time to shout before they began to hit and tear away the slogans?

Yastreba: Someone shouted: 'How dare you?', 'What are you doing here?'

Delone: Did I understand you correctly – that the man struck me after he had snatched away the slogan?

Yastreba: I don't remember. Afterwards, I think.

Dremlyuga: You were looking at us from the back.

Yastreba: Yes.

Delone (explains): Yastreba stood at the back, and mistook one banner for two.

Bogoraz: I again draw the court's attention to the fact that our friends and some relatives have not been allowed into the courtroom. This is an infringement of the principle of open trial.

Judge: The court is not concerned with this question. That is within the competence of the court commandant.

Examination of witness Dolgov, N. I.

Dolgov: On 25 August I had arranged to meet my children near the Lenin Mausoleum. I watched the sentries marching and changing over. I looked round and, at the Execution Ground, with the church at the back, I saw a group of individuals – five men and a woman with a pram. The woman with the pram held a Czech national flag. Over the heads of the rest was a solid strip of banners, not less than four. Something was wrong, I felt, some sort of provocation was afoot. I quickly went up and removed two banners. A two-sided banner from Dremlyuga, with 'Freedom for Dubcek' on one side and something else on the other – 'Down with the occupiers', I think; from the man sitting next to him, 'For your freedom and ours'. A crowd gathered, I was surrounded. People stood about and said they should be taken to the police. Two or three minutes went by and cars drew up. They were loaded into the cars. I wanted to hand over the banners to a policeman. He said I should write a statement for police station No 50. I wrote it and handed it in. I made my way out of the crowd.

Prosecutor: Explain what these banners were like. Were they only pieces of cloth or anything else?

Dolgov: The banners were not written out like official ones – they were hand made, messily. Not large – Dremlyuga's banner 'For your freedom and ours' was a bit longer, on slats. When I seized the banner the slats broke.

Prosecutor: How did the surrounding citizens react to what was going on?

Dolgov: Very indignantly. There were shouts from the crowd: 'Parasites', 'You ought to be ashamed'.

Prosecutor: And how did those sitting down answer?

Dolgov: The woman with the child said something, sort of sharply. But I didn't hear properly.

Bogoraz: The witness has stated that he had been in Red Square for a long time. Were there many people at the Execution Ground before this?

Dolgov: I did not spend very long there. I saw no gathering before this. People were wandering about, looking around.

Bogoraz: Did you see any acquaintances or colleagues in the crowd?

Dolgov: No.

Advocate Kaminskaya: Where do you work?

Dolgov: In a military unit.

Kaminskaya: Which?

Judge: There is no need to give the number, it is correctly noted in the record.

Kaminskaya: How many people ran up at the same time as you did?

Dolgov: I think I ran up first. A second later, others came along too. People gathered very fast. They were coming from the Mausoleum and turned towards the Execution Ground.

Kaminskaya: How long was it until the cars arrived?

Dolgov: Some two to three minutes, it seemed to me.

Advocate Kallistratova: How did you remove the banners?

Dolgov: The first by its slat, the second by the material.

Kallistratova: To whom did you hand over the banners?

Dolgov: I handed them to a police sergeant in uniform.

Kallistratova: Do you know witnesses Bogatyrev, Veselov, Ivanov and Vasilev?

Dolgov: No, I do not.

Kallistratova: What – you don't know them at all?

Dolgov: I am not personally acquainted with them. Maybe I have seen them somewhere at a party conference.

Kallistratova: Did you see blows being struck at anyone in your presence.

Dolgov: No, I did not.

Kallistratova: And you did not aim any blows yourself?

Dolgov: I took no part myself.

Kallistratova: Did you proffer any official identification to those sitting down?

Dolgov: No.

Kallistratova: Did you suggest to those sitting down to fold up or surrender their banners?

Dolgov: No.

Advocate Pozdeev: Did anyone offer resistance?

Dolgov: To me, no.

Pozdeev: There were no cars apart from those taking away the demonstrators?

Dolgov: No, I saw no other transport.

Advocate Monakhov: And how did you deliver your statement? By post?

Dolgov: No, I wrote it out and handed it in at the room by the Spassky tower.

Delone: Were you holding anything in your hands?

Dolgov: No, there was nothing.

Delone: You don't remember my face?

Dolgov: No, I don't think so.

Delone: You maintain that neither you nor anyone else hit us?

Dolgov: I did not lay a finger on you and did not notice anybody else touching you.

Babitsky: Clarify where you were at 12 o'clock.

Dolgov: By GUM, nearer to the Historical Museum.

Babitsky: It was at that moment that you read the slogans?

Dolgov: I read the slogan in Czech. I do not understand it, but it has remained in my memory. I read another close to.

Dremlyuga: How large is your organization?

(Laughter in the hall)

Judge: The question is struck out.

Dremlyuga: Do you know many of your colleagues?

Dolgov: Yes.

Dremlyuga: And you did not see a single one of them there?

Dolgov: No, not one.

Delone: Why did you decide to snatch away the slogans without talking to us or showing documents?

Dolgov: I got indignant. I have seen a lot, I was in the war, I read the papers. I saw straight away that it was some sort of provocation.

Delone: Why did you act so wilfully?

Dolgov: I followed my conscience.

Delone: Why did you not approach the representatives of authority, the police?

Dolgov: Are you saying that if someone sticks a knife into me, I ought to approach the police?

Dremlyuga: At a great distance, and without seeing the text of the slogans, you made up your mind that some sort of provocation was afoot?

Judge: Witness Dolgov, exactly how far were you from the slogans when you read them?

Dolgov: I read the slogan 'Freedom for Dubcek' at 32 yards.

Dremlyuga: Why did you decide that the slogan 'Freedom for Dubcek' was a provocation and think it necessary to snatch it away?
Judge: The court strikes out this question.
Bogoraz: You saw the slogan 'Freedom for Dubcek'. How was it written?
Dolgov: In pencil.
Bogoraz: And you did not read the slogans written with paint?
Dolgov: No.
Litvinov: Did you walk or run to the Execution Ground?
Dolgov: I went at the double.

Examination of the witness Savelev, Platon Pavlovich

Savelev: On 25 August I came to Red Square with my family to visit the Mausoleum. I parked my car and set off towards GUM. I walked along and what did I see – persons with banners sitting in a half-circle on the Execution Ground. Suddenly, a comrade with a briefcase ran in that direction and snatched away a banner. I ran there the same way. Three people were sitting there, a man was standing and women were also standing. By the time I came close, the banners had already gone. One man stood and shouted: 'Soviet tanks in Czechoslovak streets', 'Freedom for Dubcek'. Someone else shouted: 'Red bastards'. Who was shouting, I don't know.
Prosecutor: Did you notice the texts of the banners?
Savelev: I never saw what was written there.
Prosecutor: How many people had gathered around?
Savelev: Difficult to say – getting on for fifty.
Prosecutor: Did you see women with children there?
Savelev: I saw one woman. She was put in the car. She shouted: 'Long live free and independent Czechoslovakia.'
Prosecutor: What are you by trade?
Savelev: I'm a driver.
Bogoraz: Did the witness see me in Red Square? Was I shouting anything?
Savelev: No, but there was something of the kind. There was a woman with a child I saw – she shouted.

Bogoraz: The dossier contains two statements by witness Savelev: the first, that he heard a woman shouting something; in the second, that he heard no shouts at all. (She indicated the folio and page of the dossier.)

The Judge checked this.

Bogoraz: How can one explain the discrepancy between your statements?

Savelev was silent.

Judge: Witness Savelev's second statement was made at the confrontation with Dremlyuga and concerns Dremlyuga only.

Advocate Kaminskaya: Did you personally take a part in detaining these people?

Savelev: No.

Kaminskaya: Did you drive to the police station?

Savelev: No.

Kaminskaya: How did you come to be called to the investigation?

Savelev: My name was taken on the spot. I was summoned as a witness.

Kaminskaya: How long did all this take?

Savelev: About fifteen to twenty minutes.

Kaminskaya: Afterwards did you stay there for a long time?

Savelev: For a long time.

Kaminskaya: The record of the interrogation states that the witness arrived in a car so that his children could visit the Mausoleum. But they did not get into the Mausoleum. Why?

Savelev: There was a queue for the Mausoleum.

Kaminskaya: The dossier contains a statement by you that the Mausoleum was closed.

Savelev: No, it was open, but there was a queue.

Advocate Kallistratova: Did you see who it was that first ran up to those sitting down?

Savelev: I did. The first to run up was a man with a briefcase. There was nobody around them before that.

At *Kallistratova's* request witness Dolgov was recalled.

Kallistratova (to Dolgov): You are sure that you were the first to run up to the Execution Ground?

Dolgov (hesitating): Yes.

Kallistratova: Were you holding anything?

Dolgov: No.

Kallistratova (to Savelev): Do you recognize this man. Did he have a briefcase?

Savelev (hesitating): The other one was sort of taller.

Kallistratova: Did you hear any shouts from anybody else apart from the woman?

Savelev: I heard no shouts from those who were sitting there. One man I did hear – he isn't here.

Advocate Pozdeev: Did you see any cars in the Square?

Savelev: The cars which came to fetch them were there, no others.

Judge: Did you actually see this or can you not say for certain?

Savelev: I cannot say for certain.

Advocate Monakhov: Did you happen to notice any traffic jams?

Savelev: The crowd was thick, a traffic jam could have happened.

Monakhov: Did you or did you not see a traffic jam?

Savelev: I didn't.

Bogoraz: Did you yourself remove any slogans?

Savelev: No.

Litvinov: Do you recognize me?

Savelev: No.

Litvinov: Did you see me in the Square?

Savelev: No, I didn't see you. At the identification I didn't identify you.

Babitsky: How far were you from the banners when you saw them?

Savelev: About 26–30 yards.

Delone: Do you recognize me?

Savelev: No.

Delone: Did the man with the briefcase who ran up to us first grab a slogan or did he not?

Savelev: He tugged.

Delone: Did you see anything else he did?

Savelev: No, I didn't, people got in the way.

Bogoraz: What was your purpose in running along?

Savelev: To find out what was up, out of curiosity.

Examination of witness Ivanov, I. G.

Ivanov: On 25 August of this year, I was taking a walk in Red Square before going to work. The guard was changing. I was on the corner of GUM. Suddenly, I heard a noise at the Execution Ground. I went there at the double. Police were on the spot. I helped to put Dremlyuga in the car. I heard shouts from the car: 'Freedom for Dubcek!', 'Freedom for Czechoslovakia!'

Judge: Was he resisting?

Ivanov: Yes.

Judge: Did you use force on him?

Ivanov: No.

Prosecutor: You did not recognize anyone apart from Dremlyuga?

Ivanov: No one.

Prosecutor: How many people had assembled?

Ivanov: A great many people assembled.

Prosecutor: How did citizens react to what was going on?

Ivanov: The eye-witnesses were terribly indignant. The others had already gone.

Bogoraz: Your statements contain an estimate of numbers in the crowd. How many people were there?

Ivanov: I cannot say exactly. About 250–300.

Bogoraz: I ask the court to read out the appropriate statement by Ivanov at the preliminary investigation.

(*The Judge* read it aloud. It became clear that, at the preliminary investigation, Ivanov estimated the crowd at about 25–30 people.)

Judge (to Ivanov): About 30 people – had you in mind numbers before the demonstrators were taken away?

Ivanov: Yes.

Bogoraz: Did you personally remove any banners while we were being detained?

Ivanov: No.

Bogoraz: Where does witness Ivanov work?

Ivanov: In Military Unit 1164.

Bogoraz: Do you know witness Dolgov?

Ivanov: Well, of course – we work together.

Bogoraz: Had you an agreement to meet?

Ivanov: No.

Bogoraz: Did you see him on the twenty-fifth in Red Square?

Ivanov: No.

Bogoraz: You did not see any of your other colleagues?

Ivanov: No.

Litvinov: For what purpose did you go to Red Square?

Ivanov: I was going to work.

Litvinov: Do you know Vasilev?

Ivanov: Yes.

Litvinov: Bogatyrev?

Ivanov: Maybe.

Litvinov: Dolgov?

Ivanov: Yes.

Litvinov: Veselov?

Ivanov: No.

Delone: Does Dolgov know you?

Ivanov (with a smile): Yes.

Delone: What was your motivation in lending a hand when Dremlyuga was put into the car?

Ivanov: I saw he was being put into a car, so I helped.

Delone: Were you asked to?

Ivanov: No, I helped the comrades on my own initiative. I helped because the comrades were very indignant. I was told that he was a citizen belonging to this group.

Dremlyuga: Who in fact marched me along?

Ivanov: I don't know.

Dremlyuga: What resistance did I offer?

Ivanov: You would not go. You stood fast.

Dremlyuga: How did I stand fast?

The Judge struck out the question.

Dremlyuga: And did you use force on me?

Ivanov: Yes, I did use it.

Dremlyuga: In what way?

Ivanov: I twisted your arm when I put you into the car.

Dremlyuga: How much force did you use?

Ivanov: I forcibly helped you to sit down.

(Laughter in the court)

Examination of witness Fedoseev, B. I.

Fedoseev: On 25 August I was coming into Red Square from Kuibyshev Street. I checked my watch at the building on the corner – it was exactly 12 o'clock. I spotted men running to the Execution Ground. I looked, two men and a woman with a pram were sitting down. They said, addressing the crowd: 'We are ashamed of our government. You still have not understood the situation. When you do understand, you too will be ashamed.' A car drew up. They were led to the car. I saw a third man, his face was covered in blood. He shouted: 'Down with the tyrants' government.' He was put into the car. The woman with the pram was left. She was told from the crowd: 'What do you go on sitting for? Get away, or they'll scoop you up, too.' She said: 'We have declared a sit-down strike. I won't go away anywhere. They can only take me away by force.' Cars did arrive, the woman with a child was put in a car and taken away in it and the pram in another.

Judge: Did you see banners?

Fedoseev: When I was still a long way off, at the corner of Kuibyshev Street, I saw something white being snatched from them. When I got close I saw a rolled up canvas in one man's hands.

Prosecutor: Are you from Moscow?

Fedoseev: No, I'm a stranger from Dzerzhinsk, Gorky district.

Prosecutor: What is your trade?

Fedoseev: I'm a mechanic.

Prosecutor: Education?

Fedoseev: Secondary technical.

Prosecutor: Do you recognize any of the accused?

Fedoseev: Yes (pointed to Litvinov).

Prosecutor: Were you shown anyone for identification?

Fedoseev: Yes.

Prosecutor: Did you identify anyone?

Fedoseev: Yes. I recognized the man whose mouth was pouring blood.

Prosecutor: How many people were around?

Fedoseev: Very many; about 50, perhaps more.

Prosecutor: How did those who had gathered react to what was going on?

Fedoseev: The man next to me said to those sitting down: 'My father died on Czechoslovak soil and here you are holding meetings!'

Prosecutor: Did they reply in any way?

Fedoseev: No, they didn't reply.

Prosecutor: What else was said?

Fedoseev: Well: 'You've stuffed your gobs . . .' (*The Judge* stopped the witness)

Prosecutor: Did they answer?

Fedoseev: They bowed their heads and made no reply.

Bogoraz: Did you confiscate any banners yourself or help detain us?

Fedoseev: No.

Bogoraz: Did you want to detain us?

Fedoseev: No, I did not.

Bogoraz: Why did you make for the Execution Ground?

Fedoseev: I saw people going there.

Bogoraz: Did cars go by the Kremlin?

Fedoseev: Yes, they did.

Bogoraz: Were there traffic jams?

Fedoseev: No, the police cleared a passage.

Advocate Kaminskaya: Where were you when you checked your watch?

Fedoseev: At 12 – on the corner.

Kaminskaya: How long did you spend walking to the Execution Ground?

Fedoseev: I walked for about a minute; when I got there, the slogans had already gone.

Kaminskaya: How long did they sit on after this?

Fedoseev: Less than five minutes.

Advocate Kallistratova: Can you describe in greater detail anything done by the accused?

Fedoseev: They just sat and said they were ashamed of our government. I saw nothing else they did.

Advocate Pozdeev: When you say 'they', whom have you in mind?

Fedoseev: Three men and a woman.

Pozdeev: Do you recognize Babitsky?

Fedoseev: No.

Advocate Monakhov: Did policemen in uniform approach the citizens sitting down?

Fedoseev: The police were clearing a passage from the Kremlin. There were no other uniformed policemen about.

Litvinov: You identified me. What, factually, can you say about my actions?

Fedoseev: You were sitting and also saying that you 'were ashamed of our government'.

Delone: Would you describe the exclamations from the crowd as exceedingly indignant, insulting or verging on obscenity?

Fedoseev: No, I noticed nothing like that.

Delone: You were quoting certain words which the presiding judge interrupted. Were there other insulting remarks from the crowd?

Fedoseev: Apart from this, nothing insulting was said.

Dremlyuga: Which Ministry is served by the organization in which you work?

Judge: The court strikes out this question.

Examination of witness Davidovich, Oleg Konstantinovich

Davidovich: I saw all the accused in Red Square on 25 August. They had anti-Soviet banners: 'Freedom for Socialist Czechoslovakia', 'Hands off Czechoslovakia'. They made speeches of an anti-Soviet nature condemning the government and the party in connection with Czechoslovakia and shouted out sentences.

Judge: Who had slogans?

Davidovich: I don't remember exactly.

Judge: Who shouted out these sentences?

Davidovich: The citizeness on the right (Bogoraz), Litvinov and Dremlyuga.

Prosecutor: Are you from Moscow or a stranger?

Davidovich: I am permanently domiciled outside Moscow.

Prosecutor: When were you in Red Square?

Davidovich: At about 12.30.

Prosecutor: Do you remember that exactly?

Davidovich: I may be fifteen to twenty minutes out.

Prosecutor: What occurrences first attracted your attention?

Davidovich: Citizens were sitting down and unfolding banners.

Prosecutor: Where did they come from?

Davidovich: I came from G U M and they came towards me.

Prosecutor: Whom do you remember?

Davidovich: There were seven or eight people in the group, men and women.

Prosecutor: Did you notice the pram?

Davidovich: Gorbanevskaya had the pram, she took the slogans from it.

Prosecutor: What did she do with these banners?

Davidovich: She kept one and gave the other to a man. Dremlyuga, I think.

Prosecutor: You saw this exactly?

Davidovich: Exactly, I think.

Prosecutor: Did you read the texts of the banners?

Davidovich: One banner had 'Freedom for Socialist Czechoslovakia', in Czech, the other 'Hands off Czechoslovakia'.

Prosecutor: Do you know Czech?

Davidovich: I don't know the language, but I guessed the sense. About five minutes went by before the others appeared. I was right next to them, about three yards away.

Prosecutor: How many people were round them?

Davidovich: About forty.

Prosecutor: How did the citizens react to this group?

Davidovich: Those round them were indignant, demanded that they should clear out of Red Square and called for the police.

There were shouts of indignation demanding that they be detained.

Prosecutor: Did you help to detain anyone?

Davidovich: Yes, at the request of members of the police.

Prosecutor: Whom?

Davidovich: I helped to detain the citizen on the left (he pointed to Delone).

Delone: So it was you who twisted my arms?

Prosecutor: How did he behave?

Davidovich: He resisted passively – he did not comply with the requests of the members of the police and refused to get into the car.

Prosecutor: Did he say anything at this time?

Davidovich: I do not remember.

Prosecutor: Did the others say anything?

Davidovich: The others were asserting the injustice of introducing troops into Czechoslovakia and saying that this constituted aggression.

Prosecutor: Were you in uniform?

Davidovich: No, in plain clothes.

Bogoraz: Describe my actions. What did I say, did I resist and so on?

Davidovich: You were not holding a banner. I don't know whether you offered resistance – I did not see. You made a speech to the crowd. You said that the request by a group of Czechoslovak Communist Party Central Committee members for the despatch of troops was an invention, a forgery, because their names had not been published and that injustice and aggression had been committed.

Bogoraz: Do you maintain that I was not holding a banner?

Davidovich: I think you were not holding one.

Bogoraz: According to your statements at the preliminary investigation the demonstrators were detained by men in plain clothes aided by members of the police. At the confrontation you maintained you did not know whether the police were there or not. How do you explain these contradictions?

Davidovich: On the contrary, the police were doing the detaining, helped by citizens in plain clothes.

Bogoraz: That is an even stronger assertion.

The Judge read out both statements; they contradicted each other, as Bogoraz had said.

Advocate Kaminskaya: You said that you were about three yards from the people sitting down. You were there before the slogans were raised. Did you take away any slogans?

Davidovich: No, but I was present when the slogans were taken away. I was not in the immediate vicinity of the people sitting down.

Advocate Kallistratova: How much time elapsed between the moment when they sat down at the Execution Ground and the moment when they were put into the cars?

Davidovich: Very little, about three minutes.

Kallistratova: Are you sure that you arrived in the Square at half past twelve?

Davidovich: Yes, at 12.30, or perhaps at 12.40.

Kallistratova: You maintain that the accused were making speeches. What was their length? What sort of speeches were they? How loud?

Davidovich: The speeches were like those at a public meeting. They lasted two or three minutes. Several people spoke at once, quite loudly.

Kallistratova: You say that Delone resisted passively. Did you put only him into a car, or several people?

Davidovich: Several people.

Kallistratova: Did the others also resist?

Davidovich: They resisted.

Kallistratova: Delone's resistance had to be overcome by force?

Davidovich: Yes.

Kallistratova: How was force applied?

Davidovich: So that, despite resistance, he finished up in the car.

Kallistratova asked the court to recall Yastreba.

The Court carried out her request.

Kallistratova (to Yastreba): You saw Delone being led to the car. In your statements you said that he went quietly and did not resist. Do you confirm your statement?

Yastreba: As far as I could see, yes.

Kallistratova (to Delone): Do you identify Davidovich?

Delone: I do not identify this man. I cannot be categorical, but as far as I remember he did not come near me.

Advocate Pozdeev: Elucidate where the banner in Czech appeared from.

Davidovich: Gorbanevskaya fetched both banners from the pram.

Pozdeev: Do you remember Babitsky?

Davidovich: Yes.

Pozdeev: Describe his actual behaviour.

Davidovich: I could not say.

Pozdeev: It was Gorbanevskaya who handed him the banner?

Davidovich: Yes.

Pozdeev (to Babitsky): Babitsky, do you confirm this?

Babitsky: I refuse to answer that question.

Advocate Monakhov: You have appeared in court in uniform. To which branch of the forces do you belong?

Judge: The court strikes out that question.

Monakhov: I wish to address the court. I ask the court to certify that witness Davidovich's uniform is either the KGB uniform or the uniform of troops of the Ministry for the Protection of Public Order.

Judge: The court cannot answer the question. The court does not distinguish between uniforms.

Kallistratova: How do you know Gorbanevskya's name?

Davidovich: From the confrontation in the course of the investigation.

Monakhov asked the court to recall Yastreba. (Turning to her): Were there meeting-style speeches?

Yastreba: I did not hear. A row of people stood between me and those sitting down and there was noise and I could not make things out.

Monakhov: How far were you from the people sitting down?

Yastreba: About a yard.

Monakhov: And at a distance of one yard you could not make out whether there were speeches?

Yastreba: No, I could not.

Monakhov: Do you confirm your statement that nobody in uniform approached the Execution Ground?

Yastreba: I cannot be definite, but I do not think so.

Monakhov asked the court to recall witness Fedoseev. (To Fedoseev): Do you confirm your statements that in answer to insults and shouts, and in particular to the words: 'My father died for Czechoslovakia, and here you are . . .' the accused bowed their heads and did not answer?

Fedoseev confirmed this.

Litvinov (to Davidovich): Witness Davidovich, for what purpose did you come to Red Square?

Davidovich: No purpose.

Litvinov: Did you first see us at the Execution Ground or earlier?

Davidovich: I saw you earlier, paid no attention and remembered it later. You were all together.

Litvinov: Where?

Davidovich: To the left of GUM.

Litvinov: And Gorbanevskaya was with us?

Davidovich: Yes.

Litvinov asked the court to recall Yastreba. (To Yastreba): Do you confirm that we only met Gorbanevskaya at the Execution Ground?

Yastreba: I think so, yes.

Litvinov (to Davidovich): At the preliminary investigation you said that you emerged from GUM. GUM is closed on Sundays. How do you explain that?

Davidovich (defiantly): That has no importance. I am talking about what I saw.

Litvinov: Was Gorbanevskaya holding a banner or a small flag?

Davidovich: A small flag.

Litvinov: At the preliminary enquiry you asserted that she was holding a banner. What are you by training?

Davidovich: A lawyer.

Babitsky: Where were the uniformed members of the police?

Davidovich: At the same place.

Babitsky: Were members of the police among those who led away the detainees?

Davidovich: Yes, they took part in the detention.

Babitsky: Those who were leading us away were in uniform?

Davidovich: Yes.

Babitsky: You saw this?

Davidovich: Yes.

Babitsky: Did you see the banners being taken away?

Davidovich: No, I did not.

Babitsky: Where were you at that time?

Davidovich: Nearer the Spassky Gates.

Babitsky: Did you see Feinberg being hit?

Davidovich: No.

Delone: You identified me. Enumerate my actions.

Davidovich: You were making speeches of a political nature.

Delone: What was the general drift of these 'speeches'?

Davidovich: Well, you shared the point of view of your group. You argued with the citizens and said the government's actions involving the introduction of troops were wrong.

Delone: Any other specific actions of mine?

Davidovich: I saw no others.

Delone: Are you sure you took part in detaining me?

Davidovich: Yes.

Delone: Did you present an official identification at this time?

Davidovich: No, a member of the operational group produced his identification.

Delone (surprised): What member?

Davidovich: In plain clothes.

Delone: What was I doing when I was being led to the car?

Davidovich: You were resisting, digging your heels in, trying to break loose.

Delone: Did they twist my arms?

Davidovich: I don't think so.

Delone: Did I say anything as I walked from the Execution Ground to the car?

Davidovich: You did say something – 'shame', I think – but I don't remember.

Delone: My further actions?

Davidovich: I don't know. I did not travel with you.

Delone: Did you later see the man who was supposed to have shown his papers?

Davidovich: Yes, at the police station.

Advocate Kaminskaya: Did you see anybody with bodily injuries?

Davidovich: Yes, Feinberg had some at the confrontation.

Kaminskaya: Did you see anyone strike blows?

Davidovich: No, I didn't.

Kaminskaya: Did the man who showed his papers when detaining Delone write an explanation at the police station?

Davidovich: I know nothing about that.

Kaminskaya: Do you know anything about this man?

Davidovich: No, I know nothing about him.

Bogoraz: As to the police, does this refer only to Delone or to all?

Davidovich: No, to all. The crowd was large. Everybody was indignant. People in plain clothes were also doing some detaining.

Bogoraz: Roughly how many policemen were there in uniform?

Davidovich: About five or six.

Bogoraz: They have not been interrogated. Where have they got to?

Davidovich: I don't know.

Bogoraz: Everything happened in five minutes. According to witness Davidovich's statement the speeches lasted two or three minutes, so that we could only have spoken simultaneously. How could the witness have made out who said what?

Davidovich: Well, I did make them out.

Bogoraz: All of them?

Davidovich: All of them.

Advocate Kallistratova: Were you interrogated the same day?

Davidovich: Yes.

Kallistratova: You said then that you had emerged from GUM. How do you explain this assertion?

Davidovich: I am sure that I did not tell that to the investigator.

Dremlyuga asked that witness Dolgov should be recalled. (To Dolgov): Did you see Davidovich?

Dolgov: No.

Dremlyuga (To Davidovich): Did you see the first man to run up to the Execution Ground?

Davidovich: No, I paid more attention to the demonstrators.

Litvinov: Can you say in what order we were sitting?

Davidovich: I stood facing the demonstrators. Gorbanevskaya was on the extreme right, then Bogoraz, Feinberg, Babitsky.

Litvinov: Were they all taken away together?

Davidovich: No, Gorbanevskaya was taken away after the others.

Delone: Only two people led me away, you and the citizen in plain clothes who produced an identification?

Davidovich: Yes.

Delone: On what grounds did you decide to detain me?

Davidovich: At the request of the second comrade.

Delone: Did you hear shouts from the crowd addressed to the demonstrators?

Davidovich: Yes, indignant shouts.

19.25 End of the first day.

10 *October* 1968 – 10.00

Bogoraz (making a statement): I do not see two of my relatives, Alexeeva and Buras, in court.

Judge: All relatives cannot be admitted – the hall is over-crowded.

Litvinov: I do not see my wife and her father in court. I have a petition concerning the substance of the case.

Dremlyuga: May we talk among ourselves?

Judge: No. Conversation is only permitted with an advocate.

Dremlyuga: As I have no relatives in Moscow, I ask that two or three of my friends be admitted.

Judge: Give the names of your friends to the Court Commandant. He will decide this question.

Dremlyuga: Piotr Ionovich Yakir, Yuli Kim and Ilya Gabai.

Delone: As we have made our statements I ask that conversation between the accused be permitted during recesses.

Judge: No, the hearing has not been completed and I will therefore not permit any conversation. What petitions are there concerning the substance of the case?

Litvinov: I ask that the case be sent for further examination, since the investigation did not wish to produce certain direct participants – those individuals who broke up the demonstration – although it was fully in a position to do so; the identity of one KGB member could have been established from Strebkov's statement, witness Davidovich referred to the actions of another and of policemen. Witnesses Panova and Baeva should be called, the more so because Baeva was frequently called for interrogation during the preliminary investigation and the case against her was only dropped after three weeks.

Delone: I fully support Litvinov's petition.

Advocate Kaminskaya: I support Litvinov's petition. The defence intended to petition that members of Police station No 50 be asked which KGB members and policemen detained and delivered the accused. I consider that this can be done without further investigation, as part of the court hearing.

Advocate Kallistratova: I support Kaminskaya's petition. All the more so because members of the police always prepare a report on detentions stating who delivered offenders to the police station. For example, Davidovich testified that Delone offered resistance. This contradicts his own statements and those of other witnesses. I therefore consider it essential to call individuals in official positions – those members of the KGB and police who took part in the process of detention.

Advocates Pozdeev and Monakhov supported the petition.

Bogoraz: I support those petitions by the advocates and Litvinov which concern me personally. A banner I had held was later seen at the police station in the possession of KGB members. It is not known who brought the banners and the small flag to the police. It is not known who broke the small flag: this is important because an insult to the national flag, at least insofar as our own flag is concerned, is penalized under article 190/2.

Babitsky: I fully support this.

Delone: I insist on the identification of the KGB member

mentioned by Davidovich, as I did not resist detention and nobody presented any official identification.

Prosecutor: I consider that Litvinov's petition to send the case for further investigation is insubstantial since the court has all the necessary evidence on file and is fully able to adjudicate on the strength of it. The petition to summon additional witnesses has been satisfied in part: three further witnesses have been called, but not yet examined. Kaminskaya's petition should not be satisfied, because she wrongly quoted Strebkov's statements. He did not say that a KGB member took part in the process of detention – his statements only referred to the banner held by a KGB member at the police station. As to an enquiry at the Directorate for the protection of public order about the individuals who detained the accused, all names are on the file. As regards Kallistratova's petition concerning contradictions between the statements of witness Davidovich and those of other witnesses, Davidovich could be recalled. The court will take account of all contradictions in delivering judgement.

The Court declined all the petitions on the strength of articles 331 and 276 of the Code of Criminal Procedure.

Examination of witness Udartsev, Vladimir Alexandrovich

Judge: What are your relations with the accused?

Udartsev: I do not know any of them. I come from Rostov, I am a metal worker.

Judge: Tell the court briefly what you know about this case.

Udartsev: At about 12 noon on 25 August, I visited the Lenin Mausoleum and then went into St Basil's Cathedral near the Execution Ground. I saw many people. I thought somebody had been taken ill. I went up. Six or seven people were sitting near the Execution Ground. Among them I noticed a woman with a child. They were shouting slogans: 'Down with Soviet aggression', 'Down with Soviet tanks' and so on. I don't remember exactly. People were getting indignant, of course.

Judge: At what time was this?

Udartsev: At about twelve.

Judge: How many people stood around?

Udartsev: About 30–40.

Judge: Did you see the accused? (indicates them)

Udartsev: I saw them from the back. I only noticed the woman with a child.

Judge: What were they holding?

Udartsev: I saw a stick with something tattered hanging from it.

Judge: What were they doing?

Udartsev: They were shouting slogans: 'Down with escalation in Czechoslovakia.'

Prosecutor: Could you not specify how many men and women were sitting?

Udartsev: Five men and two women, I think.

Prosecutor: What were they holding?

Udartsev: Shreds of banners.

Prosecutor: How many?

Udartsev: Several, I don't remember exactly.

Prosecutor: How were the surrounding citizens behaving?

Udartsev: They were very indignant.

Judge: So, the citizens were very indignant.

Prosecutor: Did you see them being detained?

Udartsev: I did. First they took the lot, only the woman with a child was left. Then she was also taken.

Prosecutor: How did the accused behave?

Udartsev: They resisted, kept trying to break away.

Prosecutor: Did you see anyone being beaten up?

Udartsev: I did not.

Prosecutor: You said something else at the preliminary investigation.

Udartsev: Yes. When the woman was being taken she broke a young man's glasses.

The Prosecutor reminded Udartsev of his statement about Feinberg striking himself.

Udartsev: People said that one of them struck himself on the nose with his fist or a stick and that blood flowed.

Judge: Did you see this yourself?

Udartsev: No, people said so.

Prosecutor: How did the woman with a child behave?

Udartsev: When they were putting her into the car, she shouted slogans and clutched the child.

Prosecutor: Intending to harm it?

Udartsev: No, she wanted to clutch it.

Bogoraz: Did you see me in the Square?

Udartsev: Yes.

Bogoraz: Was I resisting?

Udartsev: No.

Bogoraz: You asserted in your evidence on 26 August that three men wore glasses. Do you confirm this? Is the witness certain that it was we who shouted slogans or does he, perhaps, mean other people?

Udartsev: The shouts I heard were from those sitting down. One man shouted: 'Down with aggression.' Who it was I don't remember.

Bogoraz: Where were we sitting?

Udartsev: On the pavement, leaning back against the railing of the Execution Ground.

Advocate Kaminskaya: Did you see the banners for yourself and are you aware of the inscriptions?

Udartsev: No, they had already gone when I came up.

Advocate Pozdeev: Whom did you identify?

Udartsev: The woman with a child.

Pozdeev: How many men did you see? At the interrogation, you said that the slogans 'Down with escalation!' and something else were shouted out only by the woman with a child. How did the others behave?

Udartsev: About the others there's nothing I can say.

Advocate Monakhov: Were there any traffic jams? Did you see any cars?

Udartsev: I did not.

Bogoraz: Did you take part in detaining us?

Udartsev: No.

Bogoraz: Did you see who detained us?

Udartsev: No.

Delone: What was being shouted at us?

Udartsev: 'You are anti-Soviet people.'

Advocate Kallistratova: At the actual moment of detention was anybody in uniform present?

Udartsev: No, I saw nobody in police uniform.

Examination of witness Savilov, A. T.

Savilov: I work at the Likhachev factory as a senior engineer-technologist. On 24 August my brother came from Lipetsk with an excursion. The coach arrived in Red Square. It stopped by the Spassky Tower. The guide was giving a commentary. The guard was being changed. A comrade was taking photographs nearby. We saw a crowd of people and thought it might be a fight. People started running. Whistles sounded. Some two or three minutes later a car came out of the Spassky Gates. One, two or three cars. I saw people sitting in them. A lot, about eight. One woman was stopping the mouth of another who shouted: 'Freedom for Dubcek.'

Prosecutor: The crowd was large?

Savilov: About 100 people, many indignant.

Bogoraz: Did you try to take part in detaining these people?

Savilov: What for? They were already sitting in the car.

Bogoraz: Was it in the same cars which had come from the Kremlin that the people were put?

Savilov: I do not remember the numbers. But they were being put into those very Volgas.

Advocate Pozdeev: When did you see a crowd of people?

Savilov: The crowd gathered when the people were already in the cars.

Litvinov: How did you come to be a witness?

Savilov: The citizen with the camera was collecting witnesses, so I gave my name.

(The next witness called was Vasilev, but for reasons unknown he was not present.)

Examination of witness Kuklin, E. E.

Kuklin: On 25 August I was at my post at the crossing of Kuibyshev

Street and Sapunov Drive. At about 12 noon I noticed a group of people at the Execution Ground. They had banners. People began to congregate and interfered with the traffic. I told them: 'Citizens, make way for the traffic.' This is when I heard shouts of 'Withdraw troops from Czechoslovakia', 'Freedom for Dubcek'. People were indignant. They asked me to remove the banners. My colleague at the crossing at Red Square went off to telephone. I therefore went to the other place. I had to clear a taxi to put the people in. Citizens started to put these people into cars. They started to put some into cars and some resisted. I was asking the crowd: 'Citizens, make way, disperse, don't interfere with the traffic.'

Judge: Who was shouting slogans?

Kuklin: Those with the banners and those in the car. They even shouted them from the car.

Judge: Where were these people? Were they sitting or standing?

Kuklin: They were sitting facing the Historical Museum, about six of them. The rest were standing. The citizens who had run up were taking away the slogans. They took them by the arm and as they were put into the cars they shouted: 'Freedom for Dubcek', 'Withdraw troops from Czechoslovakia'. Dremlyuga was shouting.

Prosecutor: Where is your post? You now say at the junction of Kuibyshev Street and Sapunov Drive. But at the preliminary investigation, you said Kuibyshev Street and Red Square.

Kuklin: It's the same post.

Prosecutor: Explain exactly where you were standing.

Kuklin: It's a nearby crossing. My colleague went to the telephone and I could not leave the post.

Prosecutor: Which of the accused do you remember?

Kuklin: Accused Dremlyuga and Litvinov.

Prosecutor: How did Dremlyuga behave?

Kuklin: He would not go to the car. He was taken by the arm and led away. I did not see any more.

Prosecutor: You stated at the preliminary investigation that he was shouting: 'Freedom for Dubcek', 'Withdraw the troops from Czechoslovakia'.

Kuklin: As he was put in the car, he shouted.

Prosecutor: Were there cars which had come from the Kremlin among those into which the people were put?

Kuklin: No, there were not. These cars happened to be around.

Bogoraz: You testified at the preliminary investigation that, being at your post, you saw a group of citizens walking to the Execution Ground and ran there. Could you have thought that a group of six to eight people would disrupt the traffic?

Kuklin: Policeman Rozanov was not there and the post must not be left unattended. People were beginning to congregate. If they had walked about like all other citizens in the Soviet Union – sometimes there are excursion groups, much larger ones – there would have been no question at all. But when this group of six walked along people began to gather round them.

Bogoraz: To whom did you address a request to disperse?

Kuklin: To everybody. I asked the crowd to disperse.

Advocate Kaminskaya: You wrote your report on 25 August. After what?

Kuklin: After my turn of duty was finished.

Kaminskaya (indicating a page in the file): How do you explain that the report is dated 3 September.

Kuklin (after a pause): I wrote my report at the end of the working day but left out the actual mention of traffic disruption.

Kaminskaya: Why did you write a second report? To whom did you write the first? To your chief?

Kuklin: Yes.

Kaminskaya: Do you know where it is?

Kuklin: No.

Kaminskaya: What was it you omitted in your first report?

Kuklin: That a traffic jam is the worst trouble in our business.

Kaminskaya: When you reached Rozanov's post, was it empty?

Kuklin: Yes.

Kaminskaya: Was it you who told Rozanov to go and ring up?

Kuklin: No.

Kaminskaya: In the preliminary investigation you stated that you did not go close to the Execution Ground and did not see the slogans. Do you confirm this?

Kuklin: Yes, I saw nothing.

Advocate Kallistratova: Who did not comply with the request to leave the roadway?

Kuklin: Some moved along and some would not go away.

Kallistratova: Was the Execution Ground visible from your post?

Kuklin: Yes, that part which faces Historical Drive.

Kallistratova: Where did you notice this group?

Kuklin: I saw the group on the pedestrian crossing from GUM to the Execution Ground.

Kallistratova: Who asked you to obtain transport? Citizens?

Kuklin: Yes.

Kallistratova: At the preliminary investigation, you stated that a man spoke to you.

Kuklin: Well, that man was a citizen too.

Kallistratova: Did the man approach you before or after Rozanov returned?

Kuklin: I can't say exactly.

Kallistratova: Did you personally detain anybody?

Kuklin: No.

Kallistratova: Did you see any members of the police?

Kuklin: Apart from Rozanov at his post, I did not.

Kallistratova: Did the police detain anybody?

Kuklin: No.

Advocate Monakhov: You said at the preliminary investigation that you had not been near and had heard no shouts. (Reading out the statement: 'Rozanov went to ring up and I took his place at the post. Then a man came up and started to demand that I should produce a car. I heard no shouts.') Did you make this statement?

Judge: Specify when you heard and when you did not hear shouts.

Kuklin: When they were being put into the car, that's when they shouted.

Litvinov: You wrote a report on the twenty-fifth, at the end of your shift?

Kuklin: Yes.

Litvinov: And on 3 September you decided to supplement it?

Kuklin: Yes.

Litvinov: Were you summoned for interrogation between these two occasions?

Kuklin: I do not remember.

Litvinov: And why was it on the third in particular that you decided to supplement your report?

Kuklin: My chief told me that the report must be supplemented.

Litvinov: And did he tell you what needed adding?

Kuklin: I know what needs adding without being told.

Litvinov: Why did you decide that Rozanov had gone to ring up?

Kuklin: It would have to be a man's very first day on duty for him not to know.

Litvinov: How could you have addressed the citizens if you were not near the Execution Ground?

Judge: Specify the distance.

Kuklin: About 11 yards.

Litvinov: On the one hand, you did not go close, on the other, you spoke to the citizens. So you could not have spoken to those who were sitting down?

Kuklin: No. I did not ask those who were sitting down to disperse. The six people sitting down were not interfering with the traffic.

Dremlyuga: If people sit on the parapet do they interfere with traffic?

Kuklin: No, they don't, they interfere with pedestrians.

Bogoraz: I ask the court to certify that witness Kuklin was interrogated in the interval between the two reports. The first report contained nothing about traffic jams.

(*The Judge* examined the record and gave a certification.)

Bogoraz: As a member of the traffic control department the primary duty of which is to control traffic why did you not note in the first report that there had been jams?

Kuklin: It was a Sunday, I was in a hurry and probably left out what needed reporting.

The Prosecutor admonished Advocate Monakhov: You are laughing and it is unethical to laugh in court.

Monakhov: You are wrong – I am smiling, not laughing. And even advocates are not forbidden to show their emotions.

Judge (to Monakhov): The court asks you to pay attention.

Delone: What have you in mind when speaking of a traffic jam? Did any cars stop? Did you actually see any cars? How many were there? Did you note their numbers?

Kuklin: There was no need to note them.

Litvinov: Was there any interference with cars travelling from the Moskva River to Kuibyshev Street?

Kuklin: There was.

Litvinov: How far is it from the Execution Ground to this section of the road?

Kuklin: About 23 yards.

Advocate Kaminskaya: To whom was your first report addressed?

Kuklin: To the chief of Section 4, Traffic Control Department.

Prosecutor: Oh, was this report for internal circulation only?

Kuklin: How do I know? They don't report to us.

Kaminskaya petitioned that witness Kuklin's first report be put at the court's disposal.

Advocate Kallistratova: I consider it extremely important for the hearing of this case that this original document be placed on the file.

(All the Advocates and accused supported this petition.)

Prosecutor: I consider that there would be no point in requesting this document, since the witness has made exhaustive statements about the contents of this report.

Court ruling: Kaminskaya's petition not to be granted as not being essential to the case.

Examination of witness Besedin, Edward Mikhailovich

Besedin: On 25 August I was walking in Red Square. A crowd attracted my attention. Two cars drove off. From one of them a woman in a blue dress shouted 'Freedom for Czechoslovakia'. In the crowd a man caught my eye because he was behaving in a violent way and telling the crowd something. He was detained and put in the second car by people in plain clothes. He was handed over to the militia two to three yards from the car.

Prosecutor: How did the people around react?

Besedin: The people in the crowd were very indignant: 'They live here, eat our bread and then do this sort of thing.'

Prosecutor: Could you identify the man who was behaving violently? What did he look like?

Besedin: I saw his face looking out of the car, but not his clothes.

Prosecutor: Was he put before you for identification at the preliminary investigation?

Besedin: Yes, he was. It was citizen Babitsky. But he says he was sitting and this man was standing.

Prosecutor: Does this confuse you?

Besedin: Yes.

Prosecutor: Where do you work?

Besedin: I am a student at the Moscow Energetics Institute.

Advocate Pozdeev: You have stated that the man you spoke of was dressed in a dirty pink shirt and brown trousers, while you now say that you do not remember the clothes, only the face.

Besedin: I am talking about two different people. I saw Babitsky for the first time in the car. It was someone else who behaved violently.

Litvinov: Did you see me in the Square?

Besedin: No.

Delone: And did you see me?

Besedin: No.

Dremlyuga: And me?

Besedin: No.

Dremlyuga: How do you explain that you found yourself behind a glass door at the identification?

Judge: The court strikes out that question.

Dremlyuga: Why?

Judge: The court offers no explanations.

Litvinov petitioned that his wife Maya Rusakovskaya be admitted to the court, together with his friends and friends of the other accused since, under article 18 of the Code of Criminal Procedure, the court must ensure that justice is administered in public. Instead, a mass of outsiders who had got in with passes of unknown origin were attending the hearing. He asked that this be entered in the record and that the petition be considered.

Judge: Your statement will be entered in the record. There has not yet been a recess and we will be considering your statement.

Delone: I support Litvinov's petition, and address a complaint to the court against the Commandant. For the second day running outsiders have entered the courtroom before anyone else, while my friends are not admitted.

The Judge did not accept the statement concerning the Commandant and authorized statements similar to that of Litvinov.

Examination of witness Rozanov, Ivan Timofeevich

Rozanov: On 25 August, I was on point duty at a crossing from 8 a.m. to 9.30 p.m. I noticed a group of five to six people. I paid no attention to them at first because they were not disrupting the traffic. An excursion, so I thought. About five minutes went by. Then I saw folk starting to run from the Mausoleum to the Execution Ground. I saw people who had sat down, canvasses above them, but as I ran up to them some citizens were already taking away the canvasses. I ran and rang up the duty officer. Cars came out of the Spassky Gates. I cleared a way for them and then went back to my post.

Prosecutor: How many people were around the Execution Ground?

Rozanov: About three hundred.

Prosecutor: What was the text of the slogans?

Rozanov: I didn't see.

Prosecutor: Did you take part in the detaining?

Rozanov: I couldn't have – I was reporting to the duty officer.

Prosecutor: How did the surrounding citizens react?

Rozanov: I can't say. I didn't see.

Bogoraz: Was traffic actually disrupted?

Rozanov: Yes, it was. I had to clear the roadway.

Bogoraz: Did those sitting down interfere with the traffic?

Rozanov: Not as such, but a crowd gathered round them.

Bogoraz: Were you away for long, ringing up?

Rozanov: No, just for a second.

Bogoraz: Did the man who relieved you arrive after the banners were raised?

Rozanov: The man who relieved me ran up after the banners had been removed.

Advocate Kaminskaya: Did anyone grab the banners?

Rozanov: Yes, citizens grabbed them.

Advocate Kallistratova: Did you see the accused being detained?

Rozanov: No.

Kallistratova: Were there police at the Execution Ground?

Rozanov: No. Members of the police formed a cordon to regulate people's access to the Mausoleum.

Delone: Did any cars coming from the Spassky Gates stop at the Execution Ground?

Rozanov: None stopped.

Examination of the witness Korkhova, Inna Vladimirovna

Korkhova: On the evening of 24 August, Pavel Litvinov rang me and asked whether I would be free on the twenty-fifth. We agreed to meet at the Prospekt Marxa metro. Pavel suggested that we walk to Red Square. There I saw Bogoraz and several people unknown to me. Later, I saw Natasha Gorbanevskaya. Pavel said: 'Don't get mixed up with anything, just watch.' They then sat down by the Execution Ground and unfolded banners. They sat quietly and I heard no shouts. After a minute I saw people come running from everywhere and heard militia whistles. People ran up behind some men in plain clothes and a crowd formed. For a while I saw nothing beyond this crowd. When I came closer, I saw a Volga being driven up. Litvinov was pushed into it. I saw a man with a blood-smeared face. I saw him holding his teeth in his hand. At the police station I found out that it was Feinberg. Gorbanevskaya remained in the Square for some time. She and her pram were then taken away. I stayed in the Square for some time after this. I heard a policeman say as he was breaking up the crowd: 'Well, didn't you see any drunks, didn't you see any madmen?' A man came up to me and demanded that I should go to the police station with him. I was kept there until ten-thirty that night.

Judge: Which of the accused do you know and what are your relations with them?

Korkhova: I've known Litvinov a year or two, we are on comradely terms; I also know Bogoraz, but not very closely; Gorbanevskaya I have known for a long time, but not closely. The others I don't know at all.

Prosecutor: During your acquaintance with Litvinov, have there been occasions when he has arranged to meet you in town?

Korkhova: There may have been, but I do not remember any.

Prosecutor: Who suggested that you should go to Red Square?

Korkhova: Litvinov.

Prosecutor: Were you not surprised at Litvinov's invitation?

Korkhova: I was.

Prosecutor: What did you talk about when you met?

Korkhova: He said nothing special, just: 'You'll see for yourself.'

Prosecutor: Did you meet other individuals on the twenty-fifth?

Korkhova: No. As I approached Red Square at ten to twelve on the twenty-fifth, I saw Bogoraz standing with several men by Kuibyshev Drive. We exchanged greetings; they were talking among themselves, but I did not try to hear what they were saying.

Prosecutor: How was Litvinov dressed?

Korkhova: In a white shirt and grey trousers.

Prosecutor: Did he have anything with him?

Korkhova: No, his hands were empty and there was nothing sticking out of his pockets.

Prosecutor: Did you mention the meeting with Litvinov to anyone?

Korkhova: I talked to my friend Irina Zholkovskaya on the twenty-fourth in the evening and said that Pavel had rung and asked me to meet him.

Prosecutor: Do you remember any conversation between Bogoraz and Litvinov?

Korkhova: I do not.

The Prosecutor asked the court to certify that she had stated at her confrontation with Litvinov that Bogoraz and Litvinov had briefly spoken to each other, including the words: 'Let's go.'

Korkhova: Yes, I made these statements, but cannot tell who exactly said this.

Prosecutor: How far were you from the Execution Ground?

Korkhova: Forty-five yards at the start. I then walked towards the Execution Ground.

Prosecutor: Did you hear any conversations or shouts?

Korkhova: I heard no conversations between those sitting down and the crowd.

Prosecutor: Where do you work?

Korkhova: As a junior scientific assistant in the World Economics and International Relations Institute.

Advocate Kaminskaya: Do you confirm your statements at the confrontation that the accused sat quietly?

Korkhova: Yes, I confirm that.

Advocate Monakhov: Nothing happened to any glasses?

Korkhova: Nothing.

Advocate Monakhov: Was the traffic held up?

Korkhova: There was no traffic at all.

Litvinov: How did the citizens behave, did they tear away the banners?

Korkhova: I saw a group run up. I saw people pushed with great roughness into a car. At the police station I heard that those detained were asking for a medical examination in connection with Feinberg's broken teeth.

Litvinov: Do you consider, as stated in the indictment, that actions took place which grossly violated public order?

Korkhova: No, I do not.

Delone: Do you know any of the witnesses?

Korkhova: I became acquainted with witness Leman at the police station. In the witnesses' room I became acquainted with Velikanova. Other witnesses, however, were already acquainted with each other. I heard one witness ask as he came into the witnesses' room: 'Are many of ours here?' and another reply: 'About eight.'

Dremlyuga: Were any documents produced when you were detained?

Korkhova: The man who put me into a car showed me no

documents, and the same at the police station. No members of the police were present while the accused were being detained.

Examination of witness Velikanova, Tatiana Mikhailovna

Velikanova: I found out about the demonstration on the morning of 25 August, at 11 o'clock. My husband told me that he was going to protest against the introduction of troops into Czechoslovakia. He then left. I was very worried. I rang some acquaintances and we arranged to meet. When we reached Red Square I saw my husband and, next to him, Feinberg and a woman with a pram. I did not notice the others. People rushed at them. I heard a whistle. They set about taking away the slogans and kicking. I particularly noticed the man who beat up Feinberg. Another was kicking my husband in the abdomen. I then spotted Larissa Bogoraz on the left. I heard remarks by the people in plain clothes who had run up and were operating in a very active and concerted way. I well remember the remark of one of the attackers who had been hitting out and helping to get the demonstrators into the car: 'You hooligans, what are you sitting here for?' I heard Gorbanevskaya reply: 'In twenty years or so you too will understand and then you'll be ashamed.' I heard my husband's remark: 'We are losing our best friends – the Czechs and Slovaks.' After the demonstration, I saw somebody's film being exposed. I did not see the others being piled into the car – I had eyes only for my husband and those sitting next to him. I wish to inform the court that my friend Panova, who was with me in Red Square, yesterday recognized among the plain clothes agents surrounding the court building the man who beat up Feinberg. When she came up to him, he quickly made off. . . .

The Judge silenced the witness.

Advocate Pozdeev: Do you know whether your husband made arrangements with anyone in advance?

Velikanova: No, I do not know.

Advocate Pozdeev: How was your husband dressed?

Velikanova: He wore green trousers and a white shirt. We were planning to visit our grandmother on her saint's day. The children left that morning. He asked them to take his guitar. He was holding nothing in his hands.

Advocate Pozdeev: Do you know anything about the preparation of the banners?

Velikanova: I saw a board with some writing on it during the search.

Advocate Pozdeev: Were cars coming from the Kremlin?

Velikanova: No, the cars from the Kremlin went by much later. I was there for about 20 minutes.

Advocate Pozdeev: How long have you been married?

Velikanova: 18 years. We have three children: 10, 12 and 15.

Advocate Pozdeev: Were you asked at the preliminary investigation how your husband and the other accused reacted to the actions of those who detained them?

Velikanova: I was amazed by their refusal to resist. They were being kicked and did not react, as though they were not of this world.

Prosecutor: Did you try to dissuade your husband?

Velikanova: I did not think I had the right to dissuade him, if this was what he believed and his conscience told him to do it. Besides, as I said at the investigation, it would have been pointless to try to dissuade him, because he is very stubborn.

Advocate Monakhov: Has anyone identified the man who beat up Feinberg?

Velikanova: Panova identified him yesterday near the court but he made off very quickly.

Prosecutor: Clarify the substance of the conversation with your husband on the morning of 25 August.

Velikanova: My husband said that he intended to protest near St Basil's. I asked whether he would be alone. He said that there might possibly be other people.

Prosecutor: You stated at the preliminary investigation that 'my husband said that he could not keep silent', and that he was going to Red Square where 'they will be protesting'.

Velikanova: The inaccuracy is mine. I went to Red Square, where my husband said he intended to protest. I simply took it that he would not be alone and therefore said 'they'. I went there because I had to see what it would all be like. I rang my friend Medvedovskaya and asked her to come with me. Meanwhile, another friend, Panova, rang me. She wanted to see me and I also invited her to Red Square. I met Medvedovskaya at the metro, but saw Panova only in Red Square.

Prosecutor: What was written on the board found during the search?

Velikanova: One could make out: 'Stop intervention in the CSSR.'

Examination of witness Medvedovskaya, Irina Feodorovna

Medvedovskaya: I only know Babitsky. He is the husband of Velikanova my fellow student, now a colleague with whom I work in the computer centre of the Moscow Auto Transport Chief Directorate. I do not know the other accused. On 25 August I was in Red Square with Tatiana Velikanova and saw a group of people stating their protest about events in Czechoslovakia. They sat down with their back to the Execution Ground. They unfolded slogans. Almost immediately a whistle blew and two groups of men rushed at them and began to hit them. They neither stood up, nor reacted. I saw one policeman – first he started to run towards the demonstrators and then immediately ran back to the Spassky Gates and began to push a button.

Advocate Pozdeev: What was your conversation with Velikanova?

Medvedovskaya: She told me that her husband intended to state his protest against the introduction of troops into Czechoslovakia.

Advocate Pozdeev: Did she mention that some others would be there?

Medvedovskaya: No, she only mentioned him.

Advocate Pozdeev: Did the accused offer resistance; did you hear any shouts from them?

Medvedovskaya: Nobody offered resistance; I heard no shouts.

Advocate Pozdeev: How many people were around at the Execution Ground?

Medvedovskaya: Not very many.

Advocate Monakhov: Did traffic hold-ups not occur?

Medvedovskaya: There were no traffic hold-ups – there was simply no traffic.

Babitsky: How close to us did the policeman come?

Medvedovskaya: The policeman only started off towards the demonstrators and then turned back on the spot towards the Spassky Gates. I find it difficult to say how close he came.

Prosecutor: What was the purpose of your journey and did her request not seem strange to you?

Medvedovskaya: My friend asked me to go. She apparently found it hard to go by herself. Her request did not seem strange.

Prosecutor: Did the actions of your acquaintance's husband not seem strange to you?

Medvedovskaya: Strange – no, out of the ordinary – yes.

Examination of witness Leman, Mikhail Vladimirovich

Leman: Personally, I know none of the accused. I went out of the house and walked across Red Square. This was about 12.03–04. Near the Execution Ground, I saw a crowd. I became interested and went nearer. I saw some sort of fuss. I wanted to call policemen, but there was no policeman nearby. I saw two cars, official Volgas. A man in a white shirt was dragged past me to a car. I thought I had no business there and decided to go. I took two steps away. Then I was seized, my arm was twisted and I was twice struck on the neck. During this time, I heard words exchanged: 'This one?' 'No, not him.' 'No, this one.' Whereupon I was pushed into a car and driven to the police station.

Advocate Monakhov: In what particular way were you struck on the neck?

Leman: I don't know – I was struck with the edge of the hand.

Advocate Monakhov: What made you think they were official cars?

Leman: I live near Red Square and know there is no traffic in that place. Only official cars are allowed through.

Bogoraz: Recall the request I made to you in the militia station.

Leman: 'Ring Yakir and tell my son not to worry.'

Bogoraz: Are you acquainted with Yakir?

Leman: I had never heard the surname Yakir before.

Bogoraz: How was I dressed?

Leman: Trousers. I don't remember what you had on top.

Bogoraz: What did we all ask for at the police station?

Leman: For a medical examination of Feinberg. I was called for interrogation and do not know whether this request was met.

Litvinov: Where do you live?

Leman: I live in Kuibyshev Street.

Litvinov: Do you confirm your statement that someone struck the man wearing a green shirt?

Leman: I saw someone fetch out and strike with full force; then I saw a blood covered face.

Dremlyuga: Was Feinberg struck by hand?

Leman: He was struck by hand, but I did not see whether he was kicked.

Prosecutor: Specify when it was you entered Red Square: at the preliminary investigation, you said that it was at 12.15.

Leman: I left the house as the clock struck and I later made a point of checking how long it took – it was about 2–3 minutes.

Prosecutor: When you called on Yakir that evening did you notice any of the individuals whom you had seen in the Square?

Leman: Nobody. It was raining. I arrived, spent a couple of minutes wiping my glasses, passed on the request and left.

Prosecutor: You stated at the preliminary inquiry that you caught a glimpse of Tatiana Baeva in the corridor.

Leman: I said that it might possibly have been Baeva.

Prosecutor (to Bogoraz): Why did you make this request to Leman in particular?

Bogoraz: Because Leman was there by chance and I was not sure that the others would be released.

Prosecutor: Why did you ask him to inform Yakir and not one of your relatives?

Bogoraz: None of my relatives were in Moscow at that time.

Prosecutor: Why did you not mention this errand at the interrogation on 25 August?

Leman: I did not think that it was important.

The Judge informed the parties that witness Veselov had left Moscow on duty, witness Kuznetsov was in hospital, witness Bogatyrev had left Moscow and witness Vasilev was absent for unknown reasons.

SUPPLEMENTARY QUESTIONS TO THE ACCUSED

Advocate Monakhov (To Dremyluga): What is the state of health of your mother and brother?

Dremlyuga: She is very ill and will hardly live to see my return. My brother has been mentally ill since he was beaten up at a police station.

Monakhov: For what reason were you expelled from the institute?

Dremlyuga: First, for a protest letter to Ilichev. Secondly, because of a joke: I was brought a parcel addressed as though I were a member of State Security and was then accused of 'deriding the calling of Soviet Chekist'.

Prosecutor: When were you sentenced and when were you expelled from the institute?

Dremlyuga: I was expelled a year after the sentence.

The material evidence was produced – banners, the flag with its stick broken, the stick, a brush, Indian ink, watercolours.

Advocate Pozdeev (To Babitsky): Could this banner in Czech have fitted in your pocket?

Babitsky: Probably not.

Petition by Bogoraz

1. Insofar as the Prosecutor has raised the question of my employment report I ask the court to request from my place of work documents concerning my dismissal: who requisitioned my report, the date of the dismissal order, whether I was notified and asked to countersign the notice.

2. The witnesses' statements concerning interference with traffic are contradictory, above all as regards traffic in Red Square. Cars passing through the Spassky Gates are all registered: it can therefore be established whether there were any at this

time and the drivers can be asked whether any traffic obstructions existed.

3. I repeat my petition for the interrogation of members of Police station No 50 as to who detained us. The Prosecutor has said that this is on file; I have not seen it on the file. There is nothing at all about my actions in the file. I am interested, not in the actions of the individual who detained me, but in his description of my actions.

Petition by *Litvinov*: In the light of the statements by Leman, Velikanova and Medvedovskaya I once again insist, in implementation of our right to defend ourselves, that witnesses Baeva and Panova be called. I associate myself with Bogoraz's petition and submit a similar petition on my own behalf. I can identify the people who detained me.

Petition by *Delone*: I regard as false the statements by witness Davidovich. I request that the KGB representative who detained me and showed his documents to me according to Davidovich's statements be traced and called.

Petition by *Dremlyuga*: I fully associate myself with the petitions by Bogoraz and Litvinov. Since I am accused of disseminating slanderous fabrications, I demand the production of proof that Dubcek was free from 21 to 25 August.

(Noise in the hall)

Advocate Kaminskaya: I support the petitions by Bogoraz, Litvinov and Delone. I consider a query to Police station No 50 essential. Although the Prosecutor says that sufficient facts about the detentions of the accused are on file, I have acquainted myself with the file in detail and have not found them.

Advocate Kallistratova: I support the petition by Delone. The record of Delone's detention is dated 25 August at 23.50. This document is clearly irrelevant in so far as the circumstances of the case are concerned since it is established that Delone was detained at about 12 noon. No other facts about the process of detention are on file. I ask the court to review the petition to call witnesses Panova and Baeva.

Advocate Pozdeev: In connection with the question concerning cars leaving the Spassky Gates (Bogoraz's petition) it is most expedient to discover whether cars are indeed registered there. I leave this to the Court for consideration.

Advocate Monakhov: I support the petition concerning the interrogation of Panova and Baeva.

Prosecutor: I consider that the petition by Bogoraz concerning an enquiry at her place of work is unfounded. The file contains a reference to disciplinary action for absenteeism. I can add that the reference was supplied in answer to an enquiry by the Moscow Prosecutor's office. It is not necessary to establish car numbers – this is irrelevant to the case. Sufficient evidence is available from witnesses as to cars leaving the Kremlin. As to the identity of those who delivered the accused to Police station No 50, the names of those carrying out detentions are only recorded if they are members of the police. Their names are not registered if they are private citizens. Concerning Delone's request, it does not follow from witness Davidovich's statements that Delone was detained by a member of the KGB since it was only said that a person taking part in the detaining presented some sort of booklet. The nature of the booklet is not known. It is, therefore, not possible to trace him. In any case, all the circumstances of the detention of Delone are on file. As far as Dremlyuga's petition is concerned, the prosecution will be able to prove his guilt in its speech. As to calling witnesses Baeva and Panova, the court has examined numerous witnesses during the hearing and I consider it pointless to call any further witnesses.

The Court, after consulting, and without rising, delivered a ruling to refuse all petitions, since it considered the evidence in the case sufficient.

Supplementary petition by *Advocate Kallistratova*: Since the statements of various groups of witnesses conflict, I consider it necessary to call Krysin as an additional witness. I ask that papers indirectly showing that Delone was looking for work be included in the file. Direct proof of a search for work are difficult to produce since it usually consists of conversations and documents and no record survives. Delone said that he regards himself as a poet. None of his works has been published, but I ask that the diploma awarding him the second prize in a poetry competition for the fiftieth anniversary of Soviet power be included in the file. I also ask for the inclusion of a testimonial by the well-known Soviet writer Kornei Chukovsky in which he describes Delone as a young and gifted poet. Chukovsky writes that Delone is 'on the right road and, if he works hard at his talent, Soviet readers will acquire in him a powerfully great poet'.

Advocate Pozdeev: I was able to obtain only nine of Babitsky's scientific works. I ask for their inclusion in the file. A 12-page monograph is due to appear shortly. Please note that Babitsky has been successfully at work in the forefront of science. I also ask for the inclusion of a Housing Office certificate stating that Babitsky has three dependent children under age. Please note that, according to the evidence of the forensic experts, the piece of cloth found at Babitsky's home does not tally with the weave of any of the banners and that the text off-printed on the plastic board does not tally with that of any of the banners.

Prosecutor: I do not object to the inclusion in the file of the certificate concerning Babitsky's children and of Babitsky's scientific works. I do not object to Delone's diploma or to Chukovsky's reference to Delone's poems. As to the scraps of paper submitted by Kallistratova, I consider the petition for their inclusion groundless.

The Court ruled that it would grant the petitions concerning the inclusion of the diploma, Chukovsky's reference, the certificates about the children and the scientific works and would reject all other petitions. The court passed over Dremlyuga's petition without referring to it.

Judge: Are there any objections to concluding the hearing in the absence of other witnesses called: Bogatyrev and Veselov are away on duty, Vasilev is absent for unknown reasons, Kuznetsov is ill.

Prosecutor: The witnesses are absent for valid reasons. The circumstances of the case have been explored sufficiently clearly. I consider that the hearing may be concluded.

Bogoraz: I object to concluding the hearing in the absence of witnesses Vasilev, Bogatyrev and Veselov. According to statements by Bogatyrev and Veselov they took part in detaining the accused. Bogatyrev and Veselov put a woman into a car. Perhaps I was that woman?

Litvinov: For the same reasons as Bogoraz I object to concluding the hearing.

Babitsky: I object to concluding the hearing in the absence of witnesses Bogatyrev, Vasilev and Veselov. I do not object to the non-appearance of Kuznetsov.

Delone: I also object. All these people, except Kuznetsov, are members of military unit 1164.

Dremlyuga: I also object. Moreover, I demand a reply to my petition.

Advocate Kaminskaya: I object to concluding the hearing in the absence of these witnesses. Could an enquiry be made about the length of their absence on duty?

Advocate Kallistratova: I do not object to Kuznetsov's absence but I categorically object to concluding the hearing in the absence of the remaining witnesses who took part in detaining the accused.

Advocates Pozdeev and Monakhov also objected to concluding the hearing.

The Court ruled to conclude the hearing in the absence of the witnesses.

Judge: I declare the court hearing concluded. I declare a recess of an hour and a half for the preparation of speeches by the Prosecutor and advocates.

Kallistratova, on behalf of all the advocates, stated that this did not leave enough time and asked that the speeches be deferred to the following day.

The Judge announced a two and a half hour recess. The speeches then followed.

PROSECUTOR V. E. DREL'S SPEECH

Comrade Judges, as part of your task of administering justice, you must take cognisance of various violations of the law. Any criminal offence is abhorrent to Soviet people, in as much as it impugns lawfulness and the order of government.

The crime committed by Bogoraz, Litvinov, Babitsky, Delone and Dremlyuga on 25 August in Red Square in the city of Moscow aroused special indignation and execration among Muscovites and visitors to our Capital.

By appearing in Red Square with crudely painted banners, Bogoraz, Babitsky, Litvinov, Delone and Dremlyuga not only grossly violated public order, but permitted themselves malicious slander of the government's policy for rendering fraternal aid to the Czechoslovak people.

In the years of the war more than twenty million Soviet people gave their lives in the struggle against fascism and we know that over one hundred thousand perished in rescuing Czechoslovakia from the brown plague. Even now many of our people still mourn those near to them.

Without the Soviet Army there would not have been a free Czechoslovakia. Soviet people have always treated the Czechs as brothers.

We can all see how international imperialism, and American imperialism first and foremost, has recently been directing ever increasing efforts towards subversion. Faced by a sharp intensification of imperialist wars the whole vast anti-communist propaganda machine is directed at the attempt to undermine the socialist movement from within.

Events twelve years ago in Hungary are still fresh in the memory of the nation when a counter-revolutionary riot was organized and in the course of it some of the best sons of our Motherland died.

The same criminal hand is to be seen in the organization of counter-revolution in Czechoslovakia. Facts widely publicised in the pages of our newspapers prove that these counter-revolutionary activities were certainly not a matter of chance. Counter-revolution was making ready to seize power by all available means. There loomed the threat of forfeiting the conquests of socialism. In these circumstances, faithful to its international and treaty obligations, the USSR took the decision to render fraternal aid to the Czechoslovak people, a decision which fully accords with the right to individual and collective defence of Warsaw Pact member states. The fraternal countries proceeded, and proceed, from the position that nobody shall be permitted to wrench the CSSR from the socialist camp.

The Moscow talks proved a new blow against the forces of counter-revolution. The documents published in the press bear witness that complete agreement has been reached with the leaders of the CSSR. The entire Soviet people, our working class, the peasants and the intelligentsia, fully and entirely approved the measures taken by the Soviet government. At numerous meetings, the workers of our country have expressed their support for the actions of the government. One cannot overlook the fact that international imperialism has mounted an unbridled campaign of anti-Soviet propaganda. Using all possible channels, bourgeois propaganda is inventing and disseminating the most absurd fabrications and slander to discredit the actions of the fraternal countries. Soviet people understand the situation correctly and are giving a fitting rebuff to bourgeois propaganda.

Unfortunately there are, however, among our population of 240 millions certain morally unstable people – they come singly – who have swallowed the bait of bourgeois propaganda. They are not only wrongheaded, but also disseminate deliberately false fabrications and commit serious crimes. The present trial is an example of this.

As has been established, on 25 August of this year, at about 12 noon, the accused appeared in Red Square. They had previously prepared banners with deliberately false fabrications: 'Long live free and independent Czechoslovakia' (in Czech), 'For your freedom and ours', 'Hands off the CSSR', 'Down with the occupiers', 'Freedom for Dubcek'.

It was not by chance that these people chose for their disorderly assembly Red Square where many people – Muscovites and visitors – are always about. Red Square is infinitely precious to Soviet people, to all of us, – the place where our leaders' ashes rest, where the best of our land are buried. Whoever comes to Moscow regards it as his civic duty to visit Red Square.

We have tried to establish the reason why the accused chose Red Square in particular. At the preliminary investigation, the accused completely refused to discuss this point, while in court they tried, very insincerely, to convince us that they had chosen the place with the least traffic. We have quite a few places where there is no traffic at all. In fact, in answer to why they had not chosen Alexandrov Square for example, Dremlyuga admitted that they wanted to attract as much attention as possible to their criminal act. And this is precisely why they chose Red Square, thereby openly defiling the people's memories of the past.

When they reached Red Square the accused sat down on the pavement and unfolded banners taken from Gorbanevskaya's pram (Gorbanevskaya has been certified as insane in the course of the investigation). The accused refused to answer the question as to how the banners had been conveyed to Red Square. It follows from Davidovich's statements that they were conveyed in the pram. The accused were well aware that they would have been stopped earlier if they had carried the banners. Knowing that their actions would not meet with approval they invited their friends and relatives beforehand so that these might perform as extras to approve their actions. Litvinov invited Korkhova and Rusakovskaya, and Babitsky – Velikanova, while the latter called in two of her friends. Others were allegedly in the Square by chance. These circumstances all show that everything had been thought out and organized in advance. The question whether there was previous agreement has been examined. At the preliminary investigation the accused refused to answer this question, while in court they tried to represent it as a coincidence. True, Litvinov said that it might not have been a coincidence, but something else. Velikanova said that on the twenty-fifth she had learnt from a conversation with her husband that he intended to go to Red Square. Korkhova's statement also confirms this: she said she had seen Bogoraz approaching with several men who later sat down at the Execution Ground.

The existence of an agreement is confirmed by the fact that banners had been prepared.

The accused Dremlyuga held the banner 'Down with the occupiers' with 'Freedom for Dubcek' on the other side, Litvinov and Delone held 'For your freedom and ours', Babitsky – 'For a free and independent Czechoslovakia' (in Czech), Bogoraz – 'Hands off the CSSR'.

It is unnecessary to analyse the banners and demonstrate their deliberately false and slanderous nature. But since the accused deny their guilt, I shall touch on the content of the slogans. In particular, accused Dremlyuga held the two-sided slogan: 'Down with the occupiers' and 'Freedom for Dubcek'. As the statements of the accused show, they all express their solidarity with the content of all the slogans. All of us clearly remember what occupation means. The word 'occupiers' reminds us of Babi Yar, Lidice, Kosice, Auschwitz, Maydenek. Our press and radio gave exhaustive explanations of the need to introduce troops and it is impossible not to understand this. As to the other slogan – 'Freedom for Dubcek' – Dremlyuga referred to a broadcast of Israel radio. Yet it is known that while the accused was holding this banner the First Secretary of the Czechoslovak Communist Party Central Committee, Comrade Dubcek, was taking part in talks in the Kremlin and returned to his own country on 26 August.

(*The Judge* warned Dremlyuga not to smile and to listen.)

The fact that on 26 August Comrade Dubcek returned to Czechoslovakia was also broadcast by Israel radio.

Bogoraz held the banner 'Hands off the CSSR'. Might one ask what hands she had in mind? Those of the revanchists? Those of the fascists? No, Bogoraz meant the hands of our Soviet soldiers, of the army which had saved the fraternal people of Czechoslovakia from fascist slavery.

The accused Litvinov and Delone were holding the banner 'For your freedom and ours'. But what sort of freedom is intended in this case? If it is the freedom to hold such disorderly assemblies, the freedom to slander, then such a freedom does not and shall not exist.

The slogan – 'For a free and independent Czechoslovakia'. Should Babitsky not have known that it was just so that

Czechoslovakia might be free and independent that troops of the socialist countries were sent there?

All the banners were of a deliberately false and slanderous nature and it is entirely understandable that the citizens then in Red Square should have demanded their instant removal, begun to take them away without waiting for the agents of authority and despatched them to the police.

At this point the accused sedulously enquired by what right these citizens detained them. Yes, they all had this right and authority imparted to them by our Soviet law. Article 13 of the RSFSR Criminal Code binds Soviet citizens to suppress the violation of order. The decree of the Presidium of the RSFSR Supreme Soviet dated 26 July 1966 also deals with this: 'Actions of citizens aimed at suppressing attempts at crime and the detention of a criminal are lawful in accordance with the legislation of the USSR and allied republics and will not involve criminal or other liability, even if damage is inevitably inflicted on the offender by these actions.' The actions of these citizens were not only morally correct, but legally justified. The accused said that certain citizens insulted them. It may be that certain citizens did indeed insult them. But can a man who lost his father at the age of four remain calm? Can a man remain calm who sees the Party and government being grossly slandered? It may be that but for the timely intervention of some individuals who were keeping order in Red Square things might have ended more sadly for the accused.

Even when citizens and members of the police had come on the scene and removed the slogans the accused did not leave off their acts and shouts of provocation. This was described by witnesses Udartsev, Fedoseev and Savilov. Accused Babitsky does not even attempt to deny that he tried to talk the crowd round, by saying: 'Friends, we are losing our best friends . . .' One might well ask what friends he was talking about. Svitak, perhaps, and Brodsky, who fled to the USA? Yet these are sworn enemies of the Czech people. The Czech and Slovak peoples know and understand full well that their true friends are Soviet citizens and the Soviet Union. The introduction of troops has contributed to the strengthening of our friendship.

The accused Bogoraz, Litvinov, Babitsky, Delone and Dremlyuga, having organized a disorderly assembly, violated public order and disrupted traffic by their actions and prevented visitors to Red Square from acquainting themselves with the sights.

The guilt of the accused is, I take it, fully proved by the evidence in the case. Bogoraz's guilt, in particular, is attested by witnesses Yastreba, Davidovich, and Vasilev. Witness Korkhova equally confirms that she saw Bogoraz among those holding placards. Accused Bogoraz-Bruchman does not deny that she was in Red Square at 12 o'clock and held the banner: 'Hands off the cssr'.

Litvinov's guilt is confirmed by Yastreba and Fedoseev. Witness Korkhova testifies in the same sense. And Litvinov himself does not deny that he took part in these actions.

Babitsky's guilt is proved by witnesses Velikanova and Medvedovskaya. Babitsky himself does not deny that he was in Red Square and held a banner. It must be noted that the table-top on which he manufactured a slogan was discovered at his home.

Delone's guilt is also attested by the evidence of witness Yastreba. Nor does he deny that he took part.

Dremlyuga's guilt is attested by witnesses Dolgov, Ivanov, Savelev and Kuklin who saw him and testified that he was holding a banner. Nor does Dremlyuga deny these circumstances.

The banners have been placed on the record as exhibits and also represent proof of guilt.

All the witnesses, people who did not know the accused before 25 August, made honest and truthful statements. Some contradictions occur between their statements, but these cannot in any way controvert their reliability. Contradictions between the statements of these witnesses are explained by the fact that they saw things from different positions and at different times. They were also extremely agitated. These are people of different ages, professions and domiciles. Among them is a student, a worker from Noginsk, an engineer, a metal-worker, in other words they were, essentially, not concerned in the slightest to discredit the accused. They made it plain whom they could and whom they could not identify. This shows their truthfulness. The witnesses' statements cast no doubts on their reliability.

The guilt of the accused consists in having participated in collective actions, grossly violated public order and disrupted traffic. This is attested by witnesses Savilov, Kuklin, Strebkov and Davidovich, as well as by a certificate from Section 4 of the traffic control police.

The court's attention must be drawn to the fact that the accused do not deny that they were in Red Square on 25 August and were holding banners. They say, however, that their actions were lawful on the strength of article 125 of the Constitution which guarantees, in particular, freedom to demonstrate. Yes, that article does indeed provide for freedom to demonstrate. Yet what the accused committed can in no sense be called a demonstration. A demonstration, as we see it, is organized action. The accused demagogically drew on one part of the article of the Constitution while forgetting about the second part which describes a demonstration as an organized procession in the workers' interests and to strengthen the socialist order. As to the disorderly assembly on 25 August, it can not be described as a demonstration either in its nature or its tenor.

The accused have made a thorough study of their rights while forgetting about their duties. Some of the accused have made generous use of the right to education. Babitsky has completed two higher educational courses. Bogoraz has even defended her thesis and ranks as a candidate of science. If Delone and Dremlyuga were not given a higher education, the reasons for this were of their own making. The state gave them every opportunity.

As to the legal description of their actions, their crime is classified under articles 190/1 and 190/3 of the RSFSR Criminal Code. The evidence at the court hearing has confirmed the correctness of the charge and fully shown the guilt of the accused under these articles.

The accused Bogoraz, Litvinov, Babitsky, Delone and Dremlyuga prepared banners in advance with texts containing deliberately false fabrications and also shouted out slogans. These actions are fully covered by article 190/1 of the RSFSR Criminal Code.

They grossly violated public order and disrupted traffic in Red Square. These actions are fully covered by article 190/3 of the Criminal Code of the RSFSR.

It is for you to determine the degree of punishment. The character of the accused is of importance in determining the degree of punishment. At first sight, a variety of people are sitting here: a father with three children and a youth just starting in life; a candidate of science and a student who failed to complete his course. Their extreme political immaturity and ideological instability bring them together. Soviet power gave them everything and provided them with scope to develop their creative abilities. I think that the accused obstinately tried to overlook the wonderful things that are happening in our world. They did not obtain their news from Soviet newspapers or radio; they drew their corrupting information from murky foreign sources. As the file shows, accused Dremlyuga said in a burst of honesty that nothing good comes from such things.

Busy searching for information and disseminating it, three of the accused – Litvinov, Dremlyuga and Delone – were not employed in any way when the crime was committed. Litvinov had not worked since January, having been dismissed for absenteeism. The file shows that Litvinov was warned by the police, but failed to get a job. He neglected his child's upbringing and provided no support for it during several months in succession.

Bogoraz-Bruchman also neglected her duties at work. She was severely reprimanded on 8 August and dismissed from work on 23 August. Delone was born in 1947, but, despite his youth appears in the dock for the second time. He was convicted by the Moscow City Court less than a year ago. His full and open confession and his assertion that nothing like this would happen to him again were believed at that time. His youth earned him pity and his crocodile tears secured belief. The court had clearly made a mistake. Delone did not last out his term of suspension.

Nor was Dremlyuga working when the crime was committed. Born in 1940 in the admirable town of Saratov on the Volga, Dremlyuga led a far from admirable life. I do not propose to enter into the details of this Saratov Don Juan's existence: the list of forty-eight women of 17 and above tells all about Dremlyuga's moral character. He was convicted for speculating in tyres and for bribery, but bearing his youth in mind the court then trusted Dremlyuga and awarded him a suspended sentence. Yet he failed to justify that trust. I ask the court to take this into account.

The following measures of punishment are suggested:

Bogoraz, Litvinov and Babitsky, taking into account the absence of previous convictions, by application of article 43 of the RSFSR Criminal Code: Litvinov – 5 years, Bogoraz – 4 years, Babitsky – 3 years of exile. Delone and Dremlyuga, in view of previous convictions – deprivation of liberty. Delone – 2 years' deprivation of liberty, but taking into account the suspended sentence of one year and conjoining it – 3 years' deprivation of liberty; Dremlyuga – 3 years' deprivation of liberty, to be served in a standard regime corrective labour colony.

I believe that such a sentence will receive the unanimous approval of the public in the city of Moscow.

SPEECHES FOR THE DEFENCE

Advocate D. I. Kaminskaya's Speech (defending Pavel Litvinov)

I have, as I see it, an extremely complicated task before me. Complicated not merely because the intensity with which we have been working has left us all very tired. And not simply and solely because the time available for the preparation of this speech was clearly insufficient.

The task confronting any advocate invariably strikes me as

complicated, regardless of the circumstances of the hearing. Whenever I appear in court I am aware of a very deep professional and human responsibility towards the way in which I shall be able to discharge my duty.

I feel this responsibility particularly deeply in the present case, since all the evidence convinces me that the guilt of the man I am defending is not established and that, in terms of our legislation, he should therefore be acquitted by the court. To substantiate this assertion, I shall naturally point out to the court why the accusation against Litvinov is not substantiated, as I see it, and which items of evidence and statements by witnesses and accused have led me to conclude that he is innocent.

I have already referred to the inherent difficulty of a defender's task. It must be said that in this particular case the task is more than usually difficult. The absolute lack of precision in the indictment, combined with its insistence on individual liability and a complete failure to discriminate between one accused and another, has resulted in an indictment which sets out the objective circumstances six separate times, starting with the description and ending with the charge. The latter is repeated in absolutely identical terms for each of the accused. The Prosecutor's speech did not make up this deficiency and the charge remains as insubstantial as it was before he spoke. Moreover, actions classified in the indictment under article 190/1 of the RSFSR Criminal Code have been described by the Prosecutor as grossly violating public order and therefore covered by article 190/3 of the RSFSR Criminal Code. Conversely, actions which the investigation regarded as violations of public order are treated as dissemination of slanderous fabrications by the Prosecutor who asks that they should be dealt with under 190/1 of the RSFSR Criminal Code.

The indictment treats all the slogans as slanderous in content. It also considers that raising them in Red Square and thereby making them known to many people constitutes a form of dissemination of deliberately false fabrications. Yet the prosecution asked that these actions in particular should be dealt with under article 190/1 of the Criminal Code. When he came to substantiate the indictment under article 190/3 the Prosecutor confined himself to the general statement that the actions of the accused were collective and violated public order. Therefore, the prosecution considers that the mere fact of seven people appearing at the Execution Ground with the intention of publicly expressing their disagreement with a specific action of our government represents an action grossly violating public order.

On 25 August of this year Litvinov was indeed at the Execution Ground with his friends. He did indeed raise the slogan 'For your freedom and ours'. Nevertheless I consider that these actions of his did not violate public order and that the slogan which he raised was not slanderous in content.

Let me begin with the indictment under article 190/1. A decision about Litvinov's guilt or innocence under this particular charge depends on the legal assessment of the actions imputed to him. I must therefore refer to the actual text of the law. (The advocate then read out the text of article 190/1 of the Criminal Code.)

Thus, the law punishes, first, the *systematic dissemination by word of mouth of deliberately false fabrications*. This was not imputed to the accused either in the indictment or in the Prosecutor's speech.

Article 190/1 also covers liability for the *preparation of slanderous works*. The defence considers that the slogan raised by Litvinov is not a work, that there is no proof on the file of the slogan being produced by Litvinov and that the text of this slogan is not of a slanderous nature.

It is not by chance that article 190/1 specifically refers to liability for the production of a work. The very fact of producing a work slanderous by its nature, regardless of whether or not it is further disseminated, is a breach of our law. Legislation proceeds from the assumption that fabrications and gossip of any kind are less dangerous by their impact than works.

A work is the product of a writer's, scientist's or artist's labour (the definition of the word given in the *Great Soviet Encyclopaedia*, Ushakov's *Standard Dictionary* and the *Dictionary of the Russian Language* published by the Academy of Sciences of the USSR) and it makes its impact not only through the meaning or substance of its text, but also through the emotional charge necessarily present in a work of art or the strict argumentation of scientific writing. The expression 'work' has a meaning in law. The rights of the author of a work are specially protected.

We have been examining the material evidence at this hearing and surely nobody can claim that these banners constitute *works*.

The wording of the indictment speaks of the *preparation* of banners. The investigation endeavoured to establish that Litvinov had taken part in preparing the banners, but neither the experts nor witnesses' statements have supported this, even though Volume Four of the file is entirely devoted to the preparation of the banners. Thus it is not known by whom, where and when the slogans—and, in particular, that held by Litvinov—were prepared.

The prosecution maintains that Litvinov and the other accused appeared with these slogans in Red Square on 25 August. In my opinion, this part of the indictment is undoubtedly proved, all the more easily so because this was the only matter confirmed by Litvinov and the other accused from the very start of the investigation. Nor do I contest the statement that Litvinov sat down on the parapet of the Execution Ground and raised one of the slogans – 'For your freedom and ours'. It is proved that he was sitting, not standing; there is no disagreement with the prosecution. But these actions – sitting on the parapet and holding a slogan – do not in themselves constitute a crime under article 190/3.

Our law does not punish mere collective actions or the public expression of opinion or belief, whatever their nature. It punishes people only when such opinion or belief is expressed in criminal form. The content of a slogan taken in isolation may provide grounds for criminal proceedings as insulting behaviour, if it is insulting; or hooliganism, if it is indecent; or under article 190/1, if it is slanderous. But the content of a slogan can never be treated as a violation of public order. Yet this is precisely how the prosecution regards it.

If the sole fact of appearing in Red Square and raising banners does not constitute a crime, what actions can be treated as a violation of public order? First, resisting the representatives of authority and, secondly, obstructing traffic and disrupting the work of state and public institutions.

There is nothing on the file to show that Litvinov refused to obey the lawful demands of the representatives of authority. Not one among the witnesses who detained the accused could be described as a lawful representative of authority. Only witness Davidovich claims in his statement that one of those detaining the accused produced a document, but the Prosecutor rightly pointed out that the nature of this document was not known. In general, the investigation failed to identify those who detained Litvinov. Litvinov resisted nobody, however offensively or violently the detaining was done. Witness Yastreba stated that the accused quickly threw up their hands and unfolded the slogans, whereupon several people ran up almost immediately and took them away. The accused sat on without rising, even though they were being beaten up.

Was traffic disrupted? I suggest it was not. During the preliminary investigation there was no mention of any traffic. During the court hearing there were statements by witnesses on this score, but they differed. As it all lasted only a few minutes one cannot speak with any accuracy of the presence of cars. According to one witness's statement, cars could get past because the citizens stepped aside and made way. A traffic-control policeman confirmed this.

Judge: Please do not go beyond the terms of the indictment.

Kaminskaya: I need hardly mention that disruption of the work of public and state institutions was not even suggested.

One is left with the general statement about collective actions which grossly violated public order. We must define in practical terms what constitutes a violation of public order. It has been said that the text of the slogans caused indignation among bystanders and that this might – rightly or wrongly – have manifested itself in their actions. But we are dealing with Litvinov's actions, not those of others. There were statements about a quiet conversation (by witness Yastreba) and speeches being made (by Davidovich). There is nothing in the evidence to show that Litvinov shouted out slogans – this is not claimed by any of the witnesses.

Let us now pass on to the last point: was the slogan raised by Litvinov – 'For your freedom and ours' – slanderous? I confine myself to this slogan alone, but not because I consider the others to be criminal. Indeed, I am bearing in mind that my defendant does not disclaim responsibility for the other slogans as well and I am at one with him in this. The other slogans held by the defendants will, however, be dealt with by their own advocates.

Litvinov held the slogan 'For your freedom and ours'. The Prosecutor considers this slogan slanderous and therefore criminal. Instead of supporting this part of the indictment by an analysis in legal terms, the Prosecutor did no more than ask: 'What did Litvinov have in mind when he raised the slogan? Perhaps,' said the Prosecutor, 'he had in mind the freedom to organize a disorderly assembly or the freedom to indulge in slander?' The Prosecutor's speech contained no other arguments to support this charge.

And yet slander is a legal term. It deals with the communication of false information and, what is more, deliberately false to the knowledge of the perpetrator. Deliberateness is a subjective attitude of an individual to the information which he imparts. An individual may be wrong in believing that the information which he imparts is correct, but such is his inner conviction and he can therefore not be charged with the dissemination of information which is deliberately false insofar as he is concerned.

And now, specifically, as to the slogan raised by Litvinov:

Not so long ago the film *For Your Freedom and Ours* was shown at the Rossiya cinema. The title of this film is identical with the slogan raised by Litvinov in Red Square. Nobody considers this title slanderous. In other words, it is not the meaning of the slogan, but the implied context, the alleged purport which are now considered incorrect and criminal.

I personally think that the slogan 'For your freedom and ours' *can never* be considered slanderous. I always say 'for your freedom' and 'for our freedom', because I regard it as the greatest good fortune for a human being to live in a free state. I completely associate myself with that part of the Prosecutor's speech in which he spoke of the great merit of the Soviet people and the Soviet army in bringing freedom to Czechoslovakia. At that time, in the difficult years of the Great Patriotic War, our people and our soldiers had every right to raise the slogan 'For your freedom and ours'. In the text of this slogan I see nothing that is incorrect, let alone criminal. Moreover, it conveys no information, no message, true or false.

But this was not the only slogan raised. Moreover, it was raised in connection with definite and specific events, which agitated our entire people, events towards which no one could remain indifferent. In order to complete my argument in favour of Litvinov's innocence, I must therefore also deal with Litvinov's purpose in going to Red Square with this slogan.

At the preliminary investigation and in court Litvinov has said that he felt obliged openly to express his attitude towards the decision – with which he did not agree – to introduce troops into Czechoslovakia. And whether he was right in his assessment or wrong, the expression of his personal opinion cannot be treated as a crime.

In deciding this unusual case, the court cannot deny the undoubted sincerity and conviction of those whose fate it is deciding. This inner conviction that they were right, this wish to express their attitude and opinion openly, makes it impossible to convict them of communicating a conscious and deliberate lie, in other words, slander.

I end my exposition where I began it: all the evidence in the case convinces me of Litvinov's innocence. My request to the court is the only possible request under the circumstances, a request for acquittal.

Advocate Yu. B. Pozdeev's Speech (defending Konstantin Babitsky)

My client, Konstantin Iosifovich Babitsky, is a scholar, a learned member of the Russian Language Institute. Before his arrest, he

worked in a scientific field which has developed at the inter-
section of two disciplines – linguistics and mathematics. He
graduated from both the Communications Institute and the
philological faculty. During his short period of employment at
the Russian Language Institute Babitsky has proved a capable,
even talented scholar. Babitsky was not merely performing
socially useful work, but stood in the forefront of scientific
development. The authorities in charge of the preliminary
investigation were unduly hasty in ordering his arrest before
trial and separating him from his work and family. Can one
believe that this measure was necessary, particularly since
Babitsky did not acknowledge that his action provided grounds for
the indictment laid against him?

The defence has no wish to turn the courtroom into a debating
club. Its intention is not a discussion of Babitsky's political
opinions, but a demonstration in legal terms that his guilt cannot be established. The wording of the indictment is remarkably
similar for each of the accused. This is all the more surprising
because article 190/1 of the RSFSR Criminal Code does not
cover collective actions. Not one of the elements of article 190/1
is specifically imputed to Babitsky in the indictment, or fits his
actions.

No commentaries on article 190/1 have been published so
far. Let us therefore examine commentaries covering the article
on slander for purposes of comparison. This article also deals
with deliberately false fabrication, but against a single person
rather than society as a whole. In other words, a person charged
with slander must know that the fabrications he is disseminating
are false. First of all, this element of deliberateness was absent
in the present case.

Babitsky was in the Square with the slogan 'Long live free
and independent Czechoslovakia', written in Czech. This
slogan contains no information whatsoever. Such is his belief,
expressed in this form. Is a man to be tried for a text or a context? This question is very difficult and important. The Prosecutor has told us that troops were brought in to safeguard the
freedom and independence of Czechoslovakia, in other words,

precisely the subject of the slogan. No doubt Babitsky gave these words a different meaning. But criminal liability must proceed from the text itself, not from an interpretation of it.

Babitsky is an honest man and if he expresses an opinion believes in it. In that case, however, the element of deliberateness is absent. The wording of article 190/1 is specific. Fabrications, slander or the dissemination of deliberately false fabrications – not one of these elements is present in Babitsky's actions.

A board was found at Babitsky's home with the text of a slogan, which did not appear in Red Square. As he is not charged with preparing this slogan nothing need be said about its content. Babitsky could not have brought the slogan which he held to the Square because it would not have fitted into his pocket. His wife confirmed that he left the house without a slogan. Witness Davidovich stated that the slogan in Czech was taken from the pram. The Prosecutor mentioned Babitsky's remark: 'We are losing our best friends.' But if he is charged with uttering this sentence, is it under article 190/1 or 190/3? Article 190/1 requires persistent dissemination by word of mouth. Maybe 190/3 is intended? Yet the sentence was spoken quietly, in an ordinary voice in reply to some remark. And it does not discredit the Soviet state and social system.

Thus there is no proof of preparation, none of deliberateness, none that the slogan discredits the Soviet state and social system, none that Babitsky brought the slogan to Red Square. Babitsky should therefore be acquitted under article 190/1.

Article 190/3 sets a more complicated problem. It refers to collective actions which grossly violate public order. These were certainly collective actions. Was there necessarily collusion? Perhaps they all shared the same information. But it is less a matter of whether there was or was not collusion than of whether the actions of the accused resulted in a gross violation of public order.

First of all, we are dealing with a small group of seven people. They sat down on the parapet. Traffic does not use the side there. I take it that a violation of order must be an action by the accused. None of the witnesses mentioned Babitsky's actions. Neither he nor the group as a whole could have impeded traffic. It is claimed that the actions of the accused collected a crowd. I am not convinced that a crowd is a fixed concept. The witnesses mentioned 30–40 people. But 30–40 people in Red Square are nothing. It is claimed that when they had been taken away the crowd grew to 400. But the accused cannot be held responsible for what happened after they were taken away. All that is left is the single sentence about losing our friends, the Czechs and the Slovaks, which Babitsky himself mentioned to the court. I take it that Babitsky should be acquitted under article 190/1 in the absence of criminal liability and under article 190/3 in the absence of proof that a crime was committed.

I also ask the court to take into account in passing sentence that Babitsky works in a unique scientific field and that specialists in this field are rare.

Advocate S. V. Kallistratova's Speech (defending Vadim Delone)

Comrade Judges, may I ask you to overlook any imperfections my speech may contain, as I am embarking on it after twelve hours of constant work.

As lawyers we deeply respect the law and know that even the best motives do not justify its infringement. In the light of the law, and only the law, it is my professional duty to ask the court to acquit Vadim Delone, because neither the law nor the evidence give grounds to treat his actions as criminally liable. And if there is no crime, there is no call for the application of punishment.

I shall not devote much space to legal analysis of the evidence, because I must try to avoid repeating the arguments of my fellow advocates. But before entering upon a statement of the defence's basic position, I must point out that even from the point of view of the Prosecutor, who considers that Delone's guilt is proved, one cannot understand that he should demand such a severe penalty for Delone.

By his ruthless unfairness the Prosecutor even infringes the law. He asks for a total sentence of two years' deprivation of liberty under the two articles imputed to Delone, with the addition of a further year's deprivation of freedom in respect of an earlier sentence, whereas articles 41 and 44 of the Criminal Code lay down that only the unexpired part of a sentence may be added. As you know, Comrade Judges, Delone spent over seven months in prison until his release on the strength of the 1967 sentence. Following the letter and spirit of the law therefore the Prosecutor had no right to ask for a further year's deprivation of freedom on the strength of the previous sentence.

But this is far from being all.

When one looks at Vadim Delone, when one knows the evidence, when one sees him in court and compares him with the others – and such comparison is inevitable – one cannot avoid the painful feeling that the punishment which the Prosecutor demands for Delone has nothing to do with that which is formally laid to his charge.

The Prosecutor, a qualified lawyer, has said that Delone, like the other accused, had committed a serious crime. As lawyers we must use legal terms only in strict accordance with the law. I am forced to draw your attention, Comrade Judges, to the fact that the second footnote to article 24 of the RSFSR Criminal Code gives an exhaustive list of the crimes considered serious in law. This list contains neither article 190/1 nor 190/3 under which Delone is charged. The Prosecutor must know and understand this.

Comrade Judges, you are well aware of the sanctions available to the law and know that both articles under which Delone is charged provide for punishment not only in the form of deprivation of liberty, but also of corrective labour without deprivation of liberty, or a fine of up to 100 roubles. The law therefore states that a person found guilty of a crime described in these articles can be sentenced to a fine, or corrective labour without deprivation of liberty, or a term of deprivation of liberty from three months to three years depending on circumstances.

Yet the Prosecutor, without even referring to mitigating circumstances as provided by law, demands the maximum sentence possible for Vadim Delone. That is why I speak of the painful feeling that the punishment demanded by the Prosecutor for Delone has nothing to do with that which is formally laid to his charge.

The range of sanctions available to the law is broad. And if you were to consider how Delone should be punished you would decide not arbitrarily, but in terms of the law, since articles 35, 38 and 39 of the RSFSR Criminal Code state what is to guide a court in selecting one measure of punishment rather than another.

You must take into account the nature of the actions imputed to Delone and the seriousness of the threat they offer to society.

This is where I perceive a serious internal contradiction in the Prosecutor's speech.

At one point, the Prosecutor stated that the accused are an insignificant little group of wrong-minded people submerged in the unanimity of the entire nation. Does this mean that their actions were not all that dangerous? At another, however, he demanded the most severe sentence – three years' deprivation of liberty – clearly because he considers that these actions are unusually dangerous, a point of view which there is nothing in the evidence to justify.

In deciding the sentence the court must also take into account the personality of the accused.

Vadim Delone is twenty. He is not a hero. He has done nothing during his life that would enable us to lay before the court notes of commendation or evidence of his untiring productive work. The characters of people take shape in different ways. Some are already established, with a definite profession and an outlook of their own, by the time they are nineteen or twenty. Others develop and take shape only later.

But it is both callous and pedantic to describe a twenty-year-old youth as 'a person without fixed occupation', simply because he has not been at work for the past few weeks.

The fact of the matter is that Vadim is a young man who is still searching, because he has not yet found his way of life.

If those who search, wandering from job to job, from place to place, had always been so harshly and unjustly described as 'people without fixed occupation', not only Alexander Green would be missing from our bookshelves, but also Konstantin Paustovsky and many others. It is precisely people with a bent for creative literary work who are most frequently subject to this restlessness, this wandering instinct, this inability to find their place in life straightaway.

That is why I feel one cannot hold it against Vadim Delone that he was not working when he was arrested. He simply was unable to find his bearings quickly and get a job. Nor can one hold it against him that he abandoned his studies at Novosibirsk University. You have heard, Comrade Judges, how Vadim Delone, a young, inexperienced poet was terrorized by a devastating newspaper article which suddenly hit him like a bolt from the blue. I have in mind the article by a correspondent of *Vecherny Novosibirsk* which is on file. All that is dear to Delone, all his creative work, was not merely blackened in this article – it was besmirched. Indeed, Vadim himself was written off as a man, a personality and a poet. One must be hardened and strong-willed to stand up to such a blow.

Look, Comrade Judges, at the difference between a newspaper correspondent who puts the words 'creation' and 'poems' in inverted commas with hardly a thought and the considerate, sensitive reaction to the young poet's verse of that great poet and wonderful man, Kornei Ivanovich Chukovsky. We have put Chukovsky's letter on file. He spared neither time nor trouble to scan this young man's lines and wrote that Vadim Delone would become a great and strong poet if he persevered.

The spirit failed this twenty-year-old boy to such an extent that even the diploma he received from the regional committee of the Komsomol and the board of the 'Pod Integral' Club failed to make up for the devastating newspaper article. This diploma, now on file, awarded a second prize in a poetry contest dedicated to the fiftieth anniversary of the October Revolution. It and Chukovsky's letter entitle me to claim that Delone is indeed a poet.

Timorously, Vadim ran away from Novosibirsk – and where

did he go? Back to his mother. To the same mother for whom, as he was being led away from home after the search, he left the simple and touching note: 'Forgive me for causing you grief again.'

If the Prosecutor has a right to his opinion, so have I. Ours is a competition. We debate. The Prosecutor attempts to prove Delone guilty. I attempt to prove him innocent. And you, Comrade Judges, will mete out the sentence and establish the truth. But should a human being really be put out of mind while this debate proceeds and should three years' deprivation of liberty be requested for Delone in the light of a variety of abstract considerations?

The Prosecutor, I know, has an answer ready for me. The Prosecutor can say to you, Comrade Judges: 'I demand a sentence of this severity for Delone because he was previously convicted and, by law, previous conviction aggravates the crime.'

Yes, he was previously convicted and, what is more, under one of the articles now imputed to him. That 1967 sentence has force of law and I may not criticize it. I would not even think of questioning its legality.

But I would remind you, Comrade Judges, that article 39 of the RSFSR Criminal Code enables a court to disregard a previous conviction as an aggravating circumstance.

You cannot fail to take into account that Delone was barely nineteen when he was first arrested. All we are allowed to say about that case at present is that Delone received a conditional sentence. We did not hear that case and could not have heard it. The Prosecutor therefore overstepped his rights in talking about 'crocodile tears'. Delone may have had quite different reasons for his attitude in that court than the wish to soften somebody's heart with his tears.

The Prosecutor cannot point to any further aggravating circumstances under the law. There simply are none.

On the contrary, the uncontested absence of any selfish aims whatsoever, of any hope of securing personal advantage or gain from his action and, lastly, the lack of any serious aftermath should be regarded as mitigating circumstances.

All this entitles me to assert that a previous conviction for a crime committed at nineteen would not justify the application to Delone of the maximum sentence, even on the assumption that he is guilty.

But, Comrade Judges, I cannot in defending Delone merely restrict myself to arguing about the degree of punishment.

I expressed my firm conviction at the start that Delone had not committed a criminal offence and should be acquitted by the court.

I am no less entitled than my fellow advocates to point out that Delone neither prepared slogans, nor brought them to Red Square and that the slogan which Delone held – 'For your freedom and ours' – contains no slander. But I shall not dwell on this. Let me say quite simply that this particular slogan came into Delone's hands by chance and that he did not choose it. I must therefore discuss all the slogans figuring in the indictment.

But, in discussing them, I cannot refrain from pointing out that, as I honestly believe, some of them only got into the indictment through a misunderstanding.

How can the words: 'Long live free and independent Czechoslovakia' or 'For your freedom and ours' be called slanderous?

'For your freedom and ours' is spelt out in big red letters on the wall of the Rossiya cinema foyer as the title of a film.

Newspapers advertising this title have been distributed throughout the country in their millions. And I take exception to a criminal indictment relying only on context.

How can a slogan be treated as intrinsically slanderous if it merely contains a call to freedom and no opinions, not even objectively false opinions, about any developments, let alone providing information of any kind about facts?

I do not forget that there are other slogans and that I undertook to discuss them all. But at this point I shall endeavour to maintain a strictly juridical point of view and not step outside the law even for a moment. Equally, I will avoid repeating the arguments adduced in the other speeches for the defence.

The verbal dissemination of deliberately false, slanderous

information is only punishable under the law as a criminal offence if it assumes a systematic character.

These slogans do not represent works, the production or dissemination of which on a single occasion is punishable, a point well argued by Advocate Kaminskaya.

Thus, even from a strictly juridical point of view and regardless of the content of the slogans there is no criminal liability in the actions of the accused.

What, in strictly legal terms, are deliberately false fabrications? They are the communication of alleged facts or events by a person who knows that they did not really occur. In other words, responsibility exists under law for the dissemination of deliberately false, slanderous items of news or fabrications – in short, of information – about non-existent facts.

Not a single slogan imputed to the accused contains such information.

Slander may indeed be a different matter. It may be a deliberately false interpretation, an intentional false assessment of actual facts or events by the person concerned. This would also cover peculiar and slanted information which may be deliberately false in subjective terms.

But if any assessment is stated in accordance with inner, subjective conviction it may be objectively correct or incorrect, harmful or harmless, but cannot be deliberately false in subjective terms.

How can it be claimed that an assessment which he who makes it believes – let me repeat, even though it is objectively incorrect – how can it be said that such an inner conviction, even though objectively harmful, is *deliberately* false in so far as that person is concerned?

In legal terms, I am entitled to claim that our law does not recognize criminal liability in respect of convictions, thoughts or ideas, but legislates solely for actions containing specific elements of a recognized crime. This is the position of the defence and it entitles me to claim that Delone had no intention of discrediting the Soviet state system and that he was guided by completely different motives. If the Prosecutor defines these motives, these peculiar opinions and convictions, as political immaturity and unreliability, these do not incur criminal liability.

We possess a whole arsenal of means for struggling with and correcting those afflicted with political immaturity and political irresponsibility. Criminal liability is not among them.

I therefore suggest that there is no substance of the crime provided for in article 190/1 of the Criminal Code in Delone's actions and that he should be acquitted under this article.

The defence point of view with respect to article 190/3 may be stated even more briefly.

In maintaining that Delone is guilty, the Prosecutor only refers to Delone's own admission that he was in the Square on 25 August and unfolded a banner there, together with Yastreba's statement incriminating him.

Although the law concerns collective actions, each member of such a collective body is individually responsible for his actions and not for those of the group as a whole, according to the principle: individual responsibility for individual guilt.

And so, Delone admits, Yastreba incriminates. That is *all* the proof produced by the Prosecutor in his final speech.

And how does Yastreba incriminate Delone? Of what violation of order? After all, she does not say that he struck anybody. She states that Delone himself was struck twice. She does not say that he shouted, made a noise, violated order. She 'incriminates' him of that which he himself has admitted when he said here quite plainly and openly that he went to Red Square to express his disagreement with the government's decision to send troops into Czechoslovakia, sat down at the Execution Ground and unfolded a banner with the slogan: 'For your freedom and ours'.

If, as the Comrade Prosecutor maintains, the very fact of expressing disagreement with individual government measures attracts criminal liability, Delone cannot be defended. But let the Prosecutor point out the law stipulating that this is an indictable offence.

But I can hear it being said that Delone is not indicted for disagreeing with individual measures, even less for disagreeing for some dirty reasons not in any way mentioned in the indictment, but solely for the manner in which he expressed his disagreement. If so, such a criminal manner is not to be found in Delone's actions. Because it will not do to assert five times in succession that a violation of public order *was* committed, it must be shown and proved *how* in practice Delone's actions constituted such a violation.

The Prosecutor talks about article 13 of the Criminal Code, about the need to defend . . .

Judge (interrupting): You pay much attention in your speech to what the Prosecutor said. Please take up the case for the defence as such.

Kallistratova: Comrade Chairman, I am highly disciplined and unquestioningly submit to instructions from those who are entitled – as you are – to instruct me in court.

But I ask you to bear in mind that, as an advocate, I need not offer proof of Delone's innocence. By law, I am here to refute and criticize the proofs presented by the Prosecutor. The tenor of my speech therefore seems to me to be in order.

I shall not, however, engage your attention much longer. I am nearing the end of my speech.

Article 13 of the Criminal Code cannot justify illegal actions. Did article 13 make it necessary to beat up Delone who was not offering resistance? I think not. Moreover I would have welcomed a reproof in the Prosecutor's speech to those unknown, un-identified people who did this. We make very great demands on young Delone. Let us make the same demands on those who by their unrestrained behaviour brought about a violation of public order.

The responsibility for their actions cannot be placed on Delone: he did not make a noise, did not shout, insulted no one, disturbed no one and committed no violation of public order.

I shall not touch on other points to avoid repeating Kaminskaya's and Pozdeev's excellent arguments. I look, not for indulgence, but for a just and lawful verdict from you.

I ask you to acquit Delone for lack of criminal substance in his actions.

Advocate N. A. Monakhov's Speech (defending Vladimir Dremlyuga)

Comrade Judges! A group of Soviet citizens going to Red Square to express their disagreement with official policy in one of its most sensitive and important aspects constitutes an event unusual in our way of life and naturally gives one food for thought. It is easy enough to understand that the people and official departments concerned should disapprove of such actions. I have reason not to doubt that the court itself does not share the views summed up in the slogans of the defendants.

I would nevertheless point out that one's own attitude to political views should not have any bearing on the assessment of evidence collected for a court case or on the legal evaluation of 'those actions by the accused which a court regards as proved. In such matters we are entitled to expect absolute impartiality from a court.

By the text of the law under which Vladimir Dremlyuga is brought before the court the dissemination of deliberately false fabrications which discredit the Soviet state and social system is imputed to him. Objectively, this indictment is confined to the content of the five banners which he and his colleagues unfolded on 25 August near the Execution Ground on Red Square. I personally understood the State Prosecutor to say that all remarks singly or collectively uttered in Red Square by the accused are imputed to them under article 190/1 of the RSFSR Criminal Code. These remarks are described in the indictment as analogous to the texts of the banners. I therefore feel entitled to discuss the content of the banners only.

It must be recognized that, even without analysing personal intentions, the content of the banners (with one exception, which I shall take separately) is hard to reconcile with the specific legal formula about the dissemination of fabrications. The slogans convey no communication of any facts, false or true. They express a subjective and personal attitude to an event which took place on 21 August, an event, moreover, so well known that there is no point in asking whether it is true or not.

Yet a personal attitude, be it of approval or disapproval,

cannot be described as a fabrication. These personal reactions rate as emotions and opinions, not as substantial transmission of information. Disagreement, whether oral or in writing, with the opinion of even the most authoritative institution of the Soviet state is not, in itself, subject to criminal law.

Only premeditated distortion of information aimed at deluding somebody falls under article 190/1. In the present case, whom could the banners displayed near the Execution Ground have deluded and about what specific facts?

Now as to the remaining banner. The prosecution maintains that the very demand for the release of the First Secretary of the Czechoslovak Communist Party implies in context a false communication that he had been deprived of his liberty. This is not quite so. First, neither the text nor the context indicate in any way to what state or individuals this demand is addressed. This slogan would obviously have remained merely incomprehensible to people who had not heard foreign broadcasts. The context cannot be understood without recourse to the comments of foreign radio stations. But can an indictment really be constructed on a context supplemented by other information for which none of the accused is responsible and which the prosecution itself does not believe? I regard an indictment constructed in this way as legally incorrect and unfounded.

From the subjective point of view and with regard to the slogan in question, there is no substance in the imputation of disseminating deliberately false fabrications in so far as Dremlyuga's actions are concerned.

Let us refer to Vladimir Dremlyuga's statements. He maintains that he believed the information from Israel radio about Dubcek's internment. This subjective conviction was further strengthened, according to his statements, by the fact that the press did not mention the name of the First Secretary of the Central Committee, Czechoslovak Communist Party again until 27 August, while the events described in the indictment took place on 25 August. Objectively, therefore, one can understand and explain the honest belief acquired by the accused, so that the display of the slogan in question certainly does not provide evidence of a conscious attempt to disseminate deliberately false information.

Vladimir Dremlyuga is also indicted under a second article – for active participation in collective actions which grossly violated public order and led to the disruption of traffic. I would first point out under this heading that the wording of the indictment does not entirely tally with the law, that is to say article 190/3 of the RSFSR Criminal Code.

An essential feature demanded by the law in defining this crime is the presence of definite and specific results, such as actual disruption of traffic. Instead, the indictment employs a vague formulation incapable of more accurate definition about the abnormal movement of traffic. The prosecution does not elucidate what is 'normal' or 'abnormal' and would be unable to do so. Moreover, there is not enough evidence in this case to show that even one vehicle was brought to a halt as a result of the actions of the accused in Red Square.

A closer analysis of the indictment is required at this point, because the statements of the accused and a number of the witnesses differ on this subject. In accounting for their actions the accused made not the slightest attempt to deny the facts on which the indictment under article 190/1 is based. Yet they categorically denied taking part in any actions which could be construed as a violation of public order resulting in the abnormal movement of traffic.

In assessing the statements of the accused, the Prosecutor apparently found it necessary to speak of the immaturity of their political judgement. Immature judgement and the Prosecutor's resulting distrust towards the accused does not entitle the Prosecutor to accuse them of perjury or release him from his duty to analyse their statements thoroughly and objectively. The statements of two groups of witnesses are available to us, apart from those of the accused. The first group, produced by the prosecution at the preliminary investigation, comprises members of the military unit known to you, and of the police. If the Prosecutor casts doubt on the statements of the accused, I have grounds for asking you to look equally critically at the statements of the prosecution's witnesses. One feature of these witnesses' behaviour stands out from the evidence. When the events described in the indictment were in progress these witnesses did not simply express their dislike of the slogans they saw, but considered it their duty to detain the accused and hand them over to the police, in other words, acted as representatives of authority. This is a very serious matter, because if any harm had been caused to even one of those detained as a result of their actions, these witnesses would become directly or indirectly involved in the outcome of the case.

One should turn, in order to dispose of conflicting evidence, to the disinterested and objective statements of those witnesses who are neither related nor known to either side.

Witness Yastreba, for instance, gave evidence identical with that of the accused. She confirmed that the accused behaved with studied correctness at the Execution Ground. Their restraint was deliberate and, as they themselves claim, planned in advance. Yastreba also confirmed that the accused did not in fact shout out any slogans. Their conversation with the assembled citizens was quiet, so quiet that the witness was unable to hear a single word of it in the immediate vicinity of the accused.

Witness Leman was also examined and said that, having by chance been detained by citizens in plain clothes, they subjected him to physical violence. Leman is among those who do not share the views of the accused.

Judge: You are aware that the accused are indicted on account of their actions, not their views.

Monakhov: Leman does not display the slightest identity of views with the accused. Since he was at the Execution Ground he could not allow anything to happen which might darken his reputation. Yet he underwent detention and a beating up, thereby objectively confirming the statements of the accused about being beaten up and subjected to violence.

Thus the unbiased statements of the witness concerned, as well as those of witnesses Fedoseev, Korkhova, Velikanova, Medvedovskaya and Strebkov, coincide in almost every detail with the accounts given by the accused and confirm the basic facts related by the accused themselves, namely: no violation of public order was committed by the accused in Red Square; the individuals who assumed the functions of representatives of authority or acted in this capacity allowed themselves a number of unjustifiable actions, in the form of physical violence; this, for one thing, cannot be imputed to the accused as part of the violation of public order and, for another, certainly did not help to fulfil that educational function towards the accused which according to their statements these citizens wished to carry out.

The defence can also not accept the prosecution's conclusion that the indignation of citizens should in itself be regarded as evidence of violation of public order by the accused.

If the reaction went beyond orderly limits, those who overstepped these limits are guilty. The intentions of the accused did not include the actions of these citizens and they cannot be held responsible for them.

Even from the Prosecutor's point of view, one must disagree with his conclusion that Dremlyuga's past appearance before a criminal court should lead to a more severe sentence under the present indictment. The actions Dremlyuga was charged with six years ago represented a self-interested act; he is now accused of actions which did not, and could not, have any self-interested aims. In view of the difference in the underlying intent there are no grounds for linking these actions.

Thus the substance of the crime covered by article 190/1 of the RSFSR Criminal Code is absent from the actions of Vladimir Dremlyuga, while the indictment under article 190/3 of the Criminal Code is not supported by reliable evidence. Criminal punishment should be applied in strict accordance with criminal law and only when adequate proof exists.

Dremlyuga may be good or bad, but he has not committed a criminal offence and should therefore be acquitted.

Defence speech by Larissa Bogoraz

I shall try not to repeat in the speech for my defence the arguments adduced by the advocates, the more so since lawyers are able to formulate the legal aspect of the case better than I can.

We are indicted individually. But the charges against me are, for the greater part, similar to those against the other accused. In defending my own interests I shall therefore be forced to touch on questions that concern us all.

First, I draw the court's attention to that part of the indictment against me which differs from the others. It states that 'disagreeing with the Party's and government's policy, she sent two statements to the trade union organization and the Director.' Towards the end of the investigation Advocate Kaminskaya petitioned that this reference be excluded from the indictment, because the submission of statements at one's place of work could not be treated as a criminal act. She was told that these statements were not imputed against me, but were included for character purposes and to confirm my disagreement with the Party and government policy. These statements are, nevertheless, imputed against me in the indictment. I ask that the wording of this part of the indictment be amended.

The Prosecutor touched in his speech on the reference from my place of employment which mentions my lack of conscientiousness towards my duties, in being habitually late, and a failure to appear at work on 21 August. I was certainly late at times, but no more so than other colleagues. I did not appear at work on 21 August because I was a witness at my friend Anatoli Marchenko's trial. I had in fact warned my superiors of this. The Prosecutor also stated that I had been dismissed on 23 August. In fact, I warned the management of the institute on 22 August that I was going on strike in protest against the despatch of troops to Czechoslovakia and I sent written statements about this on 23 August to the trade union committee and the management of the institute. No mention whatsoever was made of dismissal in this connection. I learnt about my dismissal from the investigation documents.

I now turn to the substance of the indictment. First, the actions imputed to me under article 190/3. The article deals with the organization of or active participation in 'collective actions which grossly violate public order, or are connected with blatant non-compliance with legal demands by the representatives of authority, or involve the disruption of the operation of traffic, state or social institutions or undertakings.'

I shall not launch into a repetition of the lawyers' arguments. When I petitioned during the hearing for the inclusion in the file of additional documents on this point and the calling of further witnesses, I intended to show that this particular part of the indictment was unfounded and thereby achieve the removal of the indictment under this article. I understood – perhaps I understood wrongly – that if the court rejected my petition, this would mean that it did not doubt my innocence on this particular point. Else the rejection of these petitions would represent a breach of my right to defence.

But it is clear even from existing statements, particularly those of the two members of the Traffic Department, that we could not have disrupted the movement of traffic by sitting on the parapet.

It can therefore only be imputed to us that our actions *could have* provoked crowding which *could have* caused a disruption in the normal movement of traffic. Yet we are only accused of disruptions which occurred and not of those that might have done so.

Even if one assumed that traffic disruption had taken place, it would still have to be proved in order to secure a conviction under article 190/3 that this was the result of *our* actions.

According to the statements of witnesses a crowd gathered at the Execution Ground. Witnesses give various estimates of the numbers in this crowd. It was clearly a large crowd. But let us consider how it came to assemble.

I deliberately put to each witness the question: 'Why did you run (or walk) to the Execution Ground?' Most of them said something like: 'I saw others running, so I ran too'. 'I saw others walking there and also walked across'. Ordinary curiosity is easy enough to understand – we often see it on the streets of Moscow. People are running and shouting – I will run too and have a look at what's going on.

Those who first rushed to the Execution Ground form a special group of witnesses. There were a few of them and five of them serve in Military Unit 1164. All five state that they happened to be in Red Square at the same time entirely by chance and without previous agreement. It was they who took away the banners, or at least three of the banners; the investigation did not establish who took away the other slogans and the flag. It was they who insulted us. The remaining witnesses, on the other hand, stated that, seeing these few running and shouting, they ran along as well. It was this group of people, therefore, running, shouting and removing our banners who whipped up the crowd and the indignation. And it was only among these few that our actions stimulated an active response. We did not hinder the normal movement of traffic and we did not provoke the formation of a large crowd which could have hindered this movement.

A substantial error has been introduced in drafting the indictment: the latter is stated in general terms and does not describe specific actions, as it should under article 190/3. No commentaries exist on this article. What is the meaning of 'a gross violation of public order'? Different people may interpret this differently.

I shall adopt analogy as my method, also used by the Prosecutor when he compared the Czechoslovak events with events in Hungary in 1956 during his speech. If a lawyer can use this method, I assume that I may model myself on him.

Let me quote as an example an event I witnessed. I watched a mass demonstration in Insurrection Square against the latest case of American aggression. A huge crowd carrying home-made slogans packed the Sadovoye roundabout. It covered the roadway and the sidewalks and the traffic was brought to a standstill. The demonstrators were shouting and throwing ink bombs at the American embassy building. All that the authorities did was to divert the traffic. Disruption of the normal movement of traffic was far greater here than we could possibly have caused by our small demonstration. Moreover, those taking part in the other demonstration behaved very violently. We, on the other hand, a few people in all, sat quietly on the pavement with our slogans up.

I would regard the demonstration at the American embassy as much the grosser violation of public order. None of the participants, however, was brought to court.

Let us turn to our own actions. Witnesses vary in their statements as to whether any of us said anything or not. I do not cast doubt on any of these statements: it is their adequacy, not their reliability which is in question. The court lacks adequate grounds for maintaining that we 'shouted out slogans similar to the banners'.

As to my own actions. Witnesses' statements show that I was in Red Square and raised a slogan – the statements confirm my own words. I do not deny it – yes, I was in Red Square; yes, I raised a banner. No witness stated that I had said anything. There is *my own* statement that I said something. In reply to someone who asked what was going on, I said: 'We are holding a peaceful demonstration, but our banners have been taken away.' The statements of witnesses add nothing to that.

The statements about the rest of my actions are not clear. Davidovich said that I was not holding a slogan, but I know I was. Witness Yastreba said: 'I don't exactly remember whether she was holding anything or not'. Apart from that, witness Davidovich said that we, including myself, made speeches. But I could not have made a speech in that short space of time.

There is no evidence whatsoever as to how I was detained, because no one saw it. One witness stated that when pushed into the car I shouted: 'Freedom for Dubcek' or 'Freedom for Czechoslovakia'. He merely said however that a woman shouted this when she was being put in the car and I was not the only woman involved. Besides, his description of my appearance and clothes tallies neither with what I was actually wearing nor with the statements of other witnesses in this respect. Perhaps, therefore, it was not I.

But maybe it was. I may really have shouted or spoken these words aloud or shouted something in my indignation at the violence. This refers, however, to the time when I was being pushed into the car and has no bearing on the demonstration. The demonstration covers only those few minutes when we sat at the Execution Ground until we were detained. What I said in the car, or at Police station No 50, or later in prison is irrelevant to the present trial.

In any case, whatever may have been said by me and my comrades was no ruder than the words used during the similar event which I witnessed in Insurrection Square.

I therefore assume that this disposes of the indictment against me under article 190/3. I consider that in view of the evidence available there are no grounds for indicting me under this article and I ask that the indictment be withdrawn.

I now pass on to the indictment under article 190/1. This covers liability for 'the systematic dissemination in verbal form of deliberately false fabrications discrediting the Soviet state and social system and also the preparation or dissemination in written, printed or any other form of works of similar content'.

I shall not repeat the advocates' arguments to show that our slogans cannot be described as 'works' and shall deal only with the substance of the texts. Were the texts of our slogans deliberately false fabrications?

I stress that I do not disclaim responsibility for any single slogan that appeared in the demonstration. Our actions were collective by nature and I took part in them. As to whether there was collusion or not, this is not proved and is irrelevant.

Can the texts of our slogans be considered *deliberately* false? The question of falsity only arises in connection with one text, 'Freedom for Dubcek', because all the others only expressed feelings concerning the despatch of troops to Czechoslovakia, a fact known to all and not subject to doubt.

The slogan 'Freedom for Dubcek' expressed emotion about the fact that Dubcek was not free. Between 21 and 25 August the name of the First Secretary of the Czechoslovak CP, Alexander Dubcek, was mentioned only in the following context. I quote comments from *Pravda* of 23 August.

Judge: The court does not permit you to quote this. One must not talk about one's convictions. You may only speak here about the actions imputed to you.

Bogoraz: Very well, I shall paraphrase these comments. Dubcek's name is mentioned only in connection with his passivity, which led to an intensification of counter-revolution; he is also described as the leader of the rightist minority in the Central Committee of the Czechoslovak CP.

Judge: The court does not permit you to paraphrase the content of these comments.

Bogoraz: Why?

Judge: The court does not render explanations for its injunctions.

Bogoraz: But I must refute the assertion about the deliberate falsity of this slogan.

Judge: You can say that you were convinced of it – that will do.

Bogoraz: But the Prosecutor devoted half his speech to this question. May one talk about what the Prosecutor said?

Judge: Yes, you may.

Bogoraz: I considered . . .

Judge: We are not interested in what you considered. Speak only about the actions imputed to you.

Bogoraz: In that case I shall say simply that, on 25 August, I was certain that Dubcek was not free. I am not certain even now that he was free at that time. I was convinced of this and *deliberate* falsity was therefore absent. I consider that in so far as the slogan 'Freedom for Dubcek' is concerned the accusation of deliberate falsity is without justification.

As to the banner I was holding – 'Hands off the CSSR'.

The Prosecutor asked a series of questions in his speech and I presume that they were not rhetorical. In particular, 'What does this slogan "Hands off the CSSR" mean? Whose hands? Perhaps the hands of the German revanchists?' I will make it plain – it meant that I was protesting against the introduction of troops into the CSSR and demanded their withdrawal. I considered then, as I do now, that the despatch of troops to Czechoslovakia was a mistake on the part of our government and, to protest, I chose the traditional form for this kind of demonstration.

As to the slogan 'For your freedom and ours', the Prosecutor asks: 'What freedom are you talking about?' I do not know whether the Prosecutor and others present realize that this is a well-known slogan. I know its history and understand it in its historical and traditional sense. It is the slogan of the combined Polish and Russian democratic movements in the nineteenth century. I value the idea of the continuity of common democratic traditions.

As to the slogan: 'Down with the occupiers'. The Prosecutor said in his speech that occupation meant Babi Yar, Auschwitz and Maydenek. Yes, we all know the meaning of fascist occupation. But the word 'occupation' also has a direct meaning, the occupation by the troops of one country of the territory of another. And this is what occurred.

Judge: Troops were sent in but there was no occupation. Do not talk about your convictions, but only about the actions imputed to you.

Bogoraz: I am talking about my understanding of the word 'occupation'.

Judge (irritated): You are not on trial for your convictions, they are clear enough to us anyway.

Bogoraz: Well, if everything is clear to you anyway, we might as well have an acquittal on the spot. But I am accused of raising slogans and it is about the texts of those slogans that I am talking.

I think that the other accused read the slogans in the same sense. I repeat: that there is nothing false or deliberately false, or insulting in the slogan 'Down with the occupiers'. If the fact of despatching troops is not insulting, then the slogan is even less so.

Article 190/1 covers liability for fabrications discrediting the Soviet social and state system. The texts of the slogans, however, referred to a *specific action* of the government and Communist Party of the Soviet Union and had nothing whatever to do with our system. I do not think that a critical attitude towards any particular action by the government or CPSU would imply a slur on the Soviet social and state system. These texts criticize one specific action . . .

Prosecutor: Bogoraz is abusing her right of defence to propagandize her convictions. I demand she be reprimanded and deprived of her speech for the defence on the next occasion.

Bogoraz: I do not understand. Make it plain what I may and may not say.

Judge: One must not carry on propaganda for one's views here.

Bogoraz: I would not even try to propagandize my views here. I remind you of the text of article 190/1. (She read it out in full.) I am ·countering the indictment against me under this article. Do I not have that right?

Judge: You do, but within the limits allowed by legal procedure. Do not elaborate your convictions.

Bogoraz: My convictions go far beyond what I have been elaborating here. At present I am only saying what is relevant to the indictment under this particular article.

Thus our slogans did not contain deliberately false fabrication discrediting the Soviet social and state system. There was nothing of this in our slogans. They merely carried criticism of an individual error by the government – and no system is insured against mistakes.

(From the courtroom, with surprise: 'Revisionist . . .')

The Prosecutor cast doubt on our motives in choosing a venue for the demonstration. There is no room for doubt. All the accused are at one over this. I repeat that there was a combination of motives: first, appeals to the government are by tradition made in Red Square – and our protest was an appeal to the government; second, to the best of my knowledge there is no public traffic in Red Square.

Dremlyuga also spoke of publicity as a motive. Yes, I too undoubtedly wished to publicise our protest – I had no other purpose in mind. The Prosecutor suggested Alexandrov Square, for example, as a venue. I doubt whether the consequences would have been any different in that case. Wherever it had happened, the result would have been the same.

Did we agree in advance about meeting in Red Square? I now turn to this question even though such collusion cannot be imputed to us under this article.

The Prosecutor claims that the statements of witnesses confirm 'criminal collusion'. Yet *there are no* witnesses' statements on this subject, while no one among us either confirms or denies collusion – we simply refuse to give evidence. We have made no attempt to lie, but any one of us who talked about this would have to talk about other people and none of us wishes to do this.

When Litvinov was asked whether it was a matter of collusion or coincidence, he suggested another probable alternative. Let me repeat it, although I do not claim that this was exactly how it happened. It would imply information from some third person that a protest would be made at a certain time and place. Apart from this, as I have said, I made no secret of my intention to go to Red Square. But neither do I claim that I mentioned it to those particular people who are sitting in the dock.

I say it again – I would have made my protest even had I been alone.

I consider that I have answered all the points raised by the indictment under articles 190/1 and 190/3.

As to the reference to article 125 of the USSR Constitution, I too know the Constitution. While quoting individual articles of the Constitution, the Prosecutor blamed us for failing to comply with article 112. I know not only the articles dealing with our rights, but also those concerned with our obligations. I tried to carry out my working duties conscientiously.

The Prosecutor reminded Litvinov of the second part of article 125 of the Constitution and maintained that freedom to demonstrate was guaranteed only when the demonstration was directed to strengthening the socialist system. As I understand this article, freedoms are *guaranteed in order to strengthen* the socialist system and in the interests of the workers of the USSR.

Finally, as to the terms of punishment proposed by the Prosecutor. Exile is certainly a milder form of punishment than a camp sentence. I draw the court's attention, however, to the fact that articles 190/1 and 190/3 provide for a maximum of three years' deprivation of liberty. It is true that exile represents a restriction rather than a complete deprivation of liberty, but the lengths of sentence proposed *begin* with three years. Four years is more than three and five still more than that. This measure turns out to be harsher, bearing in mind that the article itself provides for milder types of punishment.

All the more so since this punishment does not end there and later entails very limited freedom of movement, the inability freely to choose a place of residence, to pursue certain occupations, etc.

I ask nothing on my own behalf. I ask the court to give thought to Delone's sentence.

Judge: Each of the accused has his own advocate. Speak about yourself.

Bogoraz: Very well. My last contribution to a discussion of the sentences is that I still consider that my guilt has not been established and that criminal proceedings under articles 190/1 and 190/3 are therefore not justified. I therefore ask the court for a decision to acquit.

End of second day. 22.45.

FINAL PLEAS OF THE ACCUSED

11 *October* 1968, 10.00
The court grants the accused their final plea.

Final plea by Larissa Bogoraz

To begin with, I must raise an issue unconnected with my final plea; my friends and relatives have not been admitted to the courtroom – neither mine, nor those of the other accused. This infringes article 18 of the Code of Criminal Procedure which guarantees the open nature of court hearings.

I cannot and do not intend to substantiate here and now in my final plea my point of view on the Czechoslovak question. I shall deal only with the motives for my actions. Why did I, disagreeing with the decision of the CPSU and the Soviet Government concerning the introduction of troops into Czechoslovakia, not only send a statement about this to my institute, but also demonstrate in Red Square?

Judge: Do not talk about your convictions. Do not overstep the limits of the hearing.

Bogoraz: I am not overstepping the limits of the hearing – the Prosecutor had a question about this. The question of motive was raised during the hearing and I am entitled to touch on it. Mine was not an impulsive act. I acted with forethought and fully understood what the consequences of my action would be.

I love life and value freedom. I understood that I was risking my freedom and I did not want to lose it.

I do not look upon myself as a public figure. Public activity is far from being the most important and interesting aspect of life to me and political life even less so. In order to bring myself to demonstrate I had to overcome my own inertia and my dislike of publicity.

I would have preferred to act differently. I would have preferred to support those of a like mind who were well known – well known in their profession or by their position in society. I would have preferred to merge my anonymous voice with the protest of such people. There proved to be no such people in our country, but their absence was hardly sufficient reason to alter my convictions.

I was faced by the choice of protesting or staying silent. Staying silent would have meant for me sharing in the general approval of actions which I did not approve. Staying silent would have meant lying. I do not consider mine the only right action, but to me it was the only action *possible*.

Knowing that I had not said 'Yes' was not enough. It was important to me that my 'No' had not been heard.

It was the meetings, the radio, the press reports about universal support which moved me to say: *I am against this, I do not agree*. Had I not done this, I would have considered myself responsible for these actions of the government, just as all adult citizens of our country bear the responsibility for all the actions of our government, just as our whole people bears the responsibility for the Stalin-Beria camps, the death sentences, for . . .

Prosecutor: The accused is going beyond the limits of the indictment. She is not entitled to talk about the actions of the Soviet government and the Soviet people. If this should recur, I ask that accused Bogoraz be deprived of her final plea. This power is vested in the court by law.

Advocate Kaminskaya: There is some failure to understand what Bogoraz is saying. She is speaking about the motives for her actions. The court should take these motives into account when arriving at its decision in the conference room and you must hear them to the end.

Advocate Kallistratova: I agree with Kaminskaya. I would wish to add on my own behalf that the Prosecutor is wrong in referring to the possibility of depriving the accused of her final plea. This is not in the Code. The law merely says that the chairman is entitled to delete from the speech of the accused parts that are not relevant to the case.

Judge: I consider the Prosecutor's statement well founded. (To Bogoraz) You keep on trying to speak about your convictions. You are on trial not for your convictions, but your actions. Tell us about specific actions. The court reprimands you.

Bogoraz: Very well, I will take account of this reprimand. I can do so all the more easily because I have not yet touched on my convictions or said a word about my attitude to the Czechoslovak question. I was speaking solely about what impelled me to undertake the actions imputed to me.

I considered a further reason against attending a demonstration – I insist that the events in Red Square should be described by this particular word whatever the Prosecutor may call them. It was the ineffectiveness of a demonstration which would not alter the course of events. Ultimately, however, I decided that it was not a matter of effectiveness in so far as I was concerned, but of my responsibility.

When asked whether I admitted my guilt, I answered: 'No, I do not admit it.' Do I regret what happened wholly or in part?

Yes, I have one regret. I very much regret that Vadim Delone should have appeared in the dock beside me. His character and his life have yet to take shape and may be wrecked in a camp. The remaining defendants are mature personalities capable of choosing for themselves. But I am sorry that a talented and upright scholar, Konstantin Babitsky, is to be removed for a long time from his family and his work.

(From the courtroom: 'Talk about yourself, can't you!')

Judge: These exclamations are to cease forthwith. If necessary, I shall order ejections from the courtroom. (To Bogoraz) The court gives you a third reprimand. Talk only about what concerns you personally . . .

Bogoraz (sharply): Should I perhaps submit an outline of my final plea to you? I do not understand why I may not talk about the other accused.

The Prosecutor concluded his speech by assuming that the sentences he proposed would be approved by public opinion.

The court does not depend on public opinion and should be guided by the law. But I agree with the Prosecutor. I have no doubt that public opinion will approve these sentences, as it has approved similar sentences in the past, as it would approve any other sentence. Public opinion will approve three years of camps for a young poet, three years in exile for a talented scientist. Public opinion will approve the prosecution's sentences because we shall be presented to it as parasites, renegades and purveyors of hostile ideology. Moreover, if there proved to be people whose opinion differs from that which is 'public' and who found the courage to express it, they would soon find themselves here (pointing to the dock). Public opinion will approve of summary treatment for a peaceful demonstration comprising a few people.

Yesterday, when I was defending my interests in the speech for the defence, I asked the court for a decision to acquit and I am just as convinced at present that the only correct and only legal decision would be acquittal. I know the law. But I also know legal practice and today, in my final plea, I do not ask the court for anything.

Pavel Litvinov's final plea

I will not take up your time by analysing the evidence at the hearing. I do not admit that I am guilty. Our innocence of the actions imputed to us is obvious.

The sentence that awaits me is, however, equally obvious. I was aware of it in advance, even as I made my way to Red Square.

I am perfectly certain that members of the State Security agencies mounted a provocation against us. I have watched the surveillance over me. I have read my sentence in the eyes of the man behind me in the metro. I saw this man in the crowd in the Square. I had on previous occasions seen the man who detained me and struck me. For almost a year now I have been systematically followed.

What happened since has proved me right.

I went to the Square nevertheless. I never asked myself whether I should or should not go. As a Soviet citizen I considered myself obliged to express my disagreement with a mistake of the grossest kind committed by our government which had upset and angered me, my disagreement with an infringement of the standards of international law and the sovereignty of another country.

I knew my sentence in Police station No 50 when I signed the protocol which stated that I *had committed* a crime under article 190/3. 'You fool,' the policeman said to me then, 'if you'd stay quiet, you'd live in peace.' Maybe he was right. He did not doubt that I was a man who had forfeited his freedom.

What is imputed to us is not a serious crime. There were no grounds at all for keeping us in custody during the preliminary investigation. Nobody present imagines, I hope, that we would have tried to evade the trial or the investigation.

The investigation also prejudged the court's decision. The investigator collected only such evidence as might serve the prosecution. The question of whether or not I believed in what I had expressed interested no one and was not even mentioned to me. Yet, if I *believed* it, article 190/1 – covering *deliberately* false fabrications – was automatically inapplicable. In fact, I did not merely believe it, I was convinced of it.

The abstract nature of the indictment also did not surprise me. Its wording does not make it clear what exactly in our actions discredited our social and state system. Even the initial indictment put to us in prison during the preliminary investigation was more specific. The Prosecutor also stated in his speech that we had stood out against the Party and government policy, not against the social and state system. Some people may think that all our policy, including our government's mistakes, is determined by our social and state system. This is not how I see it. Even the Prosecutor would probably not say this, or he would have to admit that all the crimes of Stalin's days were determined by our social and state system.

And what is happening *here*? Infringements of the law continue.

The most fundamental of these is the infringement of trial in open court. Our friends are simply not admitted to the courtroom, my wife is only let in with difficulty. Strangers sit in the courtroom who obviously have less right to be here than our relatives and friends.

Both we and our advocates submitted a number of petitions to the court. All were refused.

A number of witnesses on whose examination we insisted were not summoned. Yet their statements would have helped to clarify the circumstances of the case.

I shall say nothing of other infringements. These will do.

I believe it to be of the utmost importance that the citizens of our country should be truly free. This is important apart from anything else because ours is the largest socialist state and, for better or worse, all that happens here is mirrored in other socialist countries. The more freedom we have, the more there will be there, and therefore in the world at large.

Yesterday, when he quoted article 125 of the Constitution, the Prosecutor introduced some transposition into the text – indeed, this may have been intentional. The Constitution states that in the interests of the workers and with the object of strengthening the socialist system citizens of the USSR are guaranteed freedom of speech, freedom of the press, freedom of assembly, meetings and demonstrations. But in the Prosecutor's version these freedoms are guaranteed *only in as much as* they serve to strengthen the socialist system.

Judge: Accused Litvinov, do not conduct a discussion. Talk only about the case.

Litvinov: It is the case I am talking about. Larissa Bogoraz answered this in part and I agree with her interpretation of this article. True, it is usually interpreted in the Prosecutor's sense. But if one were to accept such an interpretation, who then is to decide what is and what is not in the interests of the socialist system? The citizen Prosecutor, perhaps?

The Prosecutor calls what we did a disorderly assembly, we call it a peaceful demonstration. The Prosecutor speaks with approval, almost with tenderness, of the actions of those who detained, insulted and struck us. The Prosecutor calmly says that, if we had not been detained, we might have been torn to pieces. And that is a lawyer! This is the terrifying thing.

It is obviously these very people who decide what is socialism and what is counter-revolution.

That is what frightens me. This is what I have fought and will continue to fight with all the lawful means known to me.

Vadim Delone's final plea

I shall not set out to repeat everything that my advocate has said. I have said from the very start that I consider the indictment against me unfounded, nor have I changed my opinion after listening to the statements of the witnesses and the Prosecutor's speech.

It is quite plain to me that the text of our slogans contained no false fabrication discrediting our state and social system. The slogans very sharply criticised the actions of our government. I am convinced that criticism of individual actions by the government is not merely permissible and legal, but necessary. We all know what came of lack of criticism of the government during the Stalinist period.

I did not criticise the state and social system in any way, let alone disseminate slanderous information and my actions were not systematic. I shall not start on a long explanation of why the texts of the slogans are neither deliberately false nor discrediting. The slogan – 'For your freedom and ours' – expresses my deep personal conviction.

I shall not attempt to interest the court in my personal beliefs and how I arrived at my point of view, particularly since this was denied to the other accused. The Prosecutor in his speech referred to the sources of our beliefs. I should like to say that I did not listen – and seldom do – to foreign radio stations. I formed my opinion by studying the articles and speeches of a number of Czechoslovak leaders and through conversations with Czechoslovak citizens who came here during the post-January period.

The Prosecutor asked me and Litvinov in this courtroom: 'What freedom do you demand? Freedom to slander? Freedom to arrange disorderly assemblies?' No, I do not need 'freedom to slander'. This is how I understand this slogan: not only democracy in our country depends on freedom, but the free development of another state and of the citizens of another country.

In describing me, the Prosecutor referred to my 'shedding crocodile tears' at an earlier trial. He said that I had been convicted before under article 190/3 and knew that what I did was actionable. I do not see why the Prosecutor should refer to my previous trial since it is not in question. But he has done so, and I must also talk about it. Over a year ago, in the Moscow City Court, I did indeed condemn my actions connected with a demonstration in Pushkin Square in support of my friends who had been arrested. Yet I did not condemn them in legal terms. I did not admit that I was guilty in law. The sentence states that I admitted my guilt. I did not object against this at the time. That is understandable – I was free. On top of this, I was not sure that what I had demanded at the demonstration was legal: to release my arrested friends who had not then been sentenced. It was a difficult position to defend. I was also depressed because a friend, Alexei Dobrovolsky,[22] for whose freedom I had spoken up, slandered me during the investigation.

The fact that I was convicted and that the sentences in the case of Khaustov, Bukovsky and others were put into effect, certainly does not imply that actions such as mine are invariably criminal. I had earlier taken part in two demonstrations, including the silent demonstration on 5 December 1966 against the partial rehabilitation of Stalin, and no repression followed.

I understood that I was in a special situation and that the prosecution would undoubtedly make use of this if an action were to be brought against me. Unlike the other accused I know what prison is – I had spent more than seven months there. I went to the demonstration nevertheless. In making up my mind on the way to Red Square, I knew that I would do nothing illegal but I realized – I was almost certain – that a criminal action would be brought against me. But my previous conviction could not induce me to abandon the protest.

The court, I think, will understand that such a decision was not easy to take. An indictment would mean severe punishment. This does no more than show how deep was my conviction that I was doing right. As I entered the Square I inwardly resolved to do everything necessary to avoid violating public order. I did not react even when I was beaten up. I repeat – I was deeply committed to my point of view and I am sure that I did not break the law. I assumed that I would be deprived of liberty for a long time because I had voiced my protest. I realized that the price I might pay for five minutes of freedom in Red Square could be years of deprivation of liberty.

Judge: Do not talk about your convictions. You are not indicted on account of your convictions.

Delone: It would be wrong for me to distrust the members of the court. When I was asked at the start of the trial whether I trusted the members of the court, I answered that I did. On the strength of the advocates' speeches and mine I ask the court for a decision to acquit. I am a man deeply repelled by any kind of totalitarianism . . . .

The Prosecutor protested against 'impermissible expressions'.

The Judge issued a reprimand.

Delone: I am thinking of alien points of view being forced on people. I accept that differing points of view exist. I do not consider myself guilty, but neither can I claim that mine is the only valid point of view. If nevertheless you find us guilty, I should like to say to the court that I ask not for indulgence, but restraint. We are not, as you yourself said, being tried for our convictions. We are being tried for expressing them in public and for the form which our protest took. I would ask the court to bear in mind that, whether or not we infringed the law by the manner of our expression, we expressed our convictions openly, honestly, unselfishly and with a deep faith that we were right. I have finished.

Vladimir Dremlyuga's final plea

I do not know whether it is done to select an epigraph for a final plea but, if it is, I would take for my epigraph the words of Anatole France from *The Opinions of Jerome Coignard*: 'Do you think you can seduce me by the vision of a government of honest men that so hedges in all liberties that no one can enjoy them?'

I have taken an active part since the age of seventeen in protests against the Party's and government's policy (including that of a certain Nikita Sergeevich Khrushchev) if I did not agree with it. I know I shall be interrupted and must therefore choose my words.

Judge: Not interrupted, reprimanded.

Dremlyuga: All my conscious life I have wanted to be a citizen – that is, a person who proudly and calmly speaks his mind. For ten minutes, I was a citizen. My voice will, I know, sound a false note in the universal silence which goes by the name of 'unanimous support for the policy of the Party and Government'. I am glad that there proved to be others to express their protest together with me. Had there not been, I would have entered Red Square alone. If there had been other ways, I would have used them. I am convinced that, in Czechoslovakia, since the Central Committee's January plenum . . .

Prosecutor: Accused Dremlyuga is not indicted in connection with events in Czechoslovakia.

Judge: The court asks you not to dwell on your convictions. Take note of this reprimand.

Dremlyuga: Yesterday the Prosecutor devoted two-thirds of his speech to reading our *Pravda* leaders. He touched in his preamble on Kosice, and Lidice and the events in Hungary . . .

Judge: You may not criticise the Prosecutor's speech, least of all its preamble.

Dremlyuga: That was just what I wished to dwell on. It is in this preamble that he set out to prove we deserved to be punished. The Prosecutor said that some people fail to understand that the occupation of Czechoslovakia was an act of 'fraternal assistance'.

Prosecutor attempted to interrupt.

Dremlyuga: Don't interrupt me! (Animation in the courtroom.) I would like to know how the citizen Prosecutor would have regarded . . .

Prosecutor: I protest. The accused has no right to ask questions. Make this clear to him.

Judge: Take note of this reprimand: I say again, do not dwell on your convictions.

Dremlyuga: Unfortunately it is precisely my convictions that have brought me here. I can therefore not avoid touching on them. I consider that this trial, like other trials and Stalinism . . .

Prosecutor: Specific indictments have been made against the accused Dremlyuga. This is what he should touch on. The trial is not concerned with other, earlier events.

The Judge again issued a reprimand.

Dremlyuga: I did not finish my sentence, I wish to finish it.

Judge: The court reprimands you once more.

Dremlyuga: According to me, all the happenings I have enumerated came about because there is no right to criticise the government. I went to Red Square, and would go anywhere, so that this might one day become legal. I shall in future continue to voice my protest by all available means. After the anti-cult Congress . . .

Prosecutor: I ask the court to warn accused Dremlyuga, that on the strength of article 297 of the RSFSR Code of Criminal

Procedure, the accused can be deprived of his final plea if he persists in using impermissible expressions.

Judge: If you do not comply with this last demand we shall be obliged to take definite measures.

Dremlyuga: I . . .

Prosecutor: I ask for a five minute recess, so that the advocate can explain to the accused his rights and obligations in delivering his final plea.

Judge announced a ten minute recess.

(After the recess)

Dremlyuga: As a sign of protest against this and many other trials I renounce the right granted to me by law of making a final plea.

Konstantin Babitsky's final plea

Citizen Judges! You are about to take a difficult and responsible decision. The legal grounds for this decision have been examined here with sufficient thoroughness. The court hearing has not shaken my belief that I have not broken the law. I wish to draw your attention to that aspect of the case which means most to me personally. I have in mind the motives of our act and the significance of your verdict.

I can see that the unusual circumstances surrounding our appearance in Red Square could arouse hostility towards us in some people's hearts. This is exemplified by the behaviour of individual citizens, who saw in us enemies of all that is so dear to them and, without further thought, fell upon us. I suggest that they were in error.

Who, in fact, stands before you, Comrade Judges?

I will have to speak about myself. An ardent love and respect for the law, love for progress, our motherland, our people and the peoples of the whole world were instilled in me by my mother, a Soviet school, the great literature of Russia and the best Soviet and foreign writings. Each one of us can, I think, say the same about himself to a greater or lesser extent. I suggest that this is reason enough why people who respect the same values should show respect for divergences of views.

I ask you, Comrade Judges, to see in me and my comrades not enemies of Soviet authority and socialism, but people with views which differ in some way from those generally accepted, yet who love their country and people no less than others do and therefore have a right to respect and toleration.

I must reckon with the possibility that I shall suffer punishment. I will not conceal that this prospect gives me no pleasure, but – please believe me – what worried me far more are other, deeper consequences of whatever decision you reach.

I respect the law and believe in the educational role of court decisions. I therefore call upon you to consider the educational roles performed by a decision to punish and a decision to acquit. What moral habits do you wish to instil in the masses: respect and tolerance towards differing views legitimately expressed, or hatred and the desire to suppress and destroy anyone with a different way of thought?

I call upon you to take into account that, as my friend Litvinov rightly said here, everything emanating from the socialist camp, everything good or bad that happens in our country, is decisively significant for the course of events throughout the world. You are, I suggest, not merely about to decide the fate of a few people for the next few years, but one way or another – however remotely – you will be influencing the fate of mankind as a whole. Please carry out your duty with wisdom and in accordance with the law. I am convinced that you take your stand on the law alone and calmly await my fate.

(11.40. A recess was announced. The court retired to the conference room. The sentence was read out at about two o'clock.)

SENTENCE

In the name of the Russian Soviet Federal Socialist Republic
11 October 1968   Moscow

The judicial college for criminal cases of the Moscow City Court, consisting of the Chairman Lubentsova, V.G., the People's

Assessors Popov, P.I. and Bulgakov, I. Ya., and the Clerk of the Court Osina, V. I., with the participation of the State Procurator, Assistant to the Moscow City Prosecutor Drel, V. E. and the advocates Kaminskaya, D. I., Kallistratova, S. V., Pozdeev, Yu. B., Monakhov, N. A., – having examined in open court the case against:

Bogoraz-Bruchman, Larissa Iosifovna; Delone, Vadim Nikolaevich; Litvinov, Pavel Mikhailovich; Babitsky, Konstantin Iosifovich; Dremlyuga, Vladimir Alexandrovich. [The personal details included in the indictment follow each of these names; Dremlyuga is described as having no previous convictions.]

– in respect of crimes provided for by articles 190/1 and 190/3 of the RSFSR Criminal Code –

established that:

The accused Bogoraz-Bruchman, Litvinov, Babitsky, Delone and Dremlyuga, disagreeing with the Soviet Government's policy decided to organize a disorderly assembly in Red Square for the propagation of their slanderous fabrications.

To secure publicity for their designs, they prepared in advance banners with the texts 'Down with the occupiers', 'Hands off the CSSR', 'Freedom for Dubcek', 'For your freedom and ours' and others which represent deliberately false fabrications discrediting the Soviet state and social system.

On 25 August 1968, at about 12 noon, they all came to the Execution Ground in Red Square, having brought concealed about them the banners concerned and took an active part in collective actions: each of them unfolded a banner and, addressing the citizens who had gathered round, shouted out slogans similar to the texts of the banners concerned, grossly violated public order and disrupted the normal movement of traffic.

Bogoraz-Bruchman, Litvinov, Babitsky, Delone and Dremlyuga did not admit their guilt, but none of them denied that on 25 August 1968, at about 12 noon, they arrived at the Execution Ground in Red Square, where they sat down on the pavement and unfolded banners with the above-mentioned texts.

The fact that the accused Bogoraz-Bruchman, Litvinov, Babitsky, Delone, and Dremlyuga appeared in Red Square at the Execution Ground and raised banners with texts containing deliberately false fabrications discrediting the Soviet state and social system, shouted out slogans similar to the texts of the banners and grossly violated public order and disrupted the normal movement of traffic is confirmed by:

the statements of witnesses Yastreba, Davidovich, Dolgov, Strebkov, Savelev, Ivanov, Fedoseev, Udartsev, Savilov, Besedin and Rozanov;

the accused's own statements in which they do not deny the fact of coming to Red Square with the above-mentioned banners;

the fact of the detention of the accused in Red Square and the confiscation of the banners from them;

the material evidence – the banners with the above-mentioned texts confiscated from the accused;

the fact of the removal from Babitsky's flat of a plastic cover and Babitsky's statement that this plastic cover was used by him for the preparation of a similar banner;

the conclusion of the expert forensic examination that the plastic cover confiscated from Babitsky was used for the preparation of a banner;

the certificate from No 4 Section, Traffic Control Department which indicates that the part of Red Square between Kuibyshev Street and the Kremlin Spassky Tower (near the Execution Ground) is a thoroughfare and that an accumulation of people on this thoroughfare sets up an increased hazard for traffic.

The assertions of the accused Bogoraz-Bruchman, Litvinov, Delone, Babitsky and Dremlyuga that they did not violate public order and disrupt the normal movement of traffic by their actions is refuted by the above-mentioned proofs and their actions are correctly described under article 190/3 RSFSR Criminal Code.

The court considers that the inscriptions on the above-mentioned banners unfolded by the accused in Red Square are slanderous works containing deliberately false fabrications discrediting the Soviet state and social system. By unfolding these banners in a place as populated as Red Square they pursued the object of acquainting a wide circle of people with their content, which represents dissemination of these deliberately false fabrications, such actions being directly provided for by article 190/1 RSFSR Criminal Code and the actions of Bogoraz-Bruchman, Litvinov, Babitsky, Delone and Dremlyuga are therefore correctly described under that article.

In determining the measure of punishment for each of the accused the court takes into account that Dremlyuga had previously appeared before a court and that Delone committed the crime during the period of his conditional sentence and therefore considers it appropriate to select a measure of punishment involving deprivation of liberty for them; Bogoraz-Bruchman, Litvinov and Babitsky are first offenders and have dependent children under age. The court therefore considers it possible to apply article 43 RSFSR Criminal Code to them and select a measure of punishment not involving deprivation of liberty.

On the strength of the above and guided by articles 303, 315 and 317 RSFSR CCP the judicial college for criminal cases of the Moscow City Court

SENTENCED

Dremlyuga, Vladimir Alexandrovich,
Delone, Vadim Nikolaevich,
Bogoraz-Bruchman, Larissa Iosifovna,
Litvinov, Pavel Mikhailovich,
Babitsky, Konstantin Iosifovich – to be found guilty under articles 190/1 and 190/3 RSFSR Criminal Code and subjected to the following punishments:

Dremlyuga, Vladimir Alexandrovich, under article 190/1 RSFSR Criminal Code, to three years' deprivation of liberty; under article 190/3 RSFSR Criminal Code, to three years' deprivation of liberty.

On the strength of article 40 RSFSR Criminal Code concerning the accumulation of crimes committed, to set a term of *three years'* deprivation of liberty, the punishment to be served in a standard regime corrective labour colony with deduction from the term of the time spent in preliminary detention from 25 August 1968.

Delone, Vadim Nikolaevich, under article 190/1 RSFSR Criminal Code, to deprivation of liberty for a period of two years and six months; under article 190/3 of the RSFSR Criminal Code, to deprivation of liberty for a period of two years and six months.

On the strength of article 40 RSFSR Criminal Code concerning the accumulation of crimes committed, to set a term of *two years and six months'* deprivation of liberty.

On the strength of article 41 RSFSR Criminal Code to add the four months of deprivation of liberty from the punishment not served under the sentence of 1 September 1967 of the Moscow City Court for criminal cases and set a complete term of *two years and ten months'* deprivation of liberty, the punishment to be served in a standard regime corrective labour colony with deduction from the term of the time spent under preliminary detention in custody from 25 August 1968.

Bogoraz-Bruchman, Larissa Iosifovna, under article 190/1 RSFSR Criminal Code, with application of article 43 RSFSR Criminal Code, to be subjected to exile for a term of four years; under article 190/3 RSFSR Criminal Code, with application of article 43 RSFSR Criminal Code, to be subjected to exile for a term of four years.

On the strength of article 40 RSFSR Criminal Code concerning the accumulation of crimes committed, to subject her to exile for a term of *four years.*

Litvinov, Pavel Mikhailovich, under article 190/1 RSFSR Criminal Code, with application of article 43 RSFSR Criminal Code, to be subjected to exile for a term of five years; under article 190/3 RSFSR Criminal Code, with the application of article 43 RSFSR Criminal Code, to be subjected to exile for a term of five years.

On the strength of article 40 RSFSR Criminal Code concerning the accumulation of crimes committed, to be subjected to exile for a term of *five years.*

Babitsky, Konstantin Iosifovich, under article 190/1 RSFSR Criminal Code, with application of article 43 RSFSR Criminal Code, to be subjected to exile for a term of three years; under article 190/3 RSFSR Criminal Code, with application of article 43 RSFSR Criminal Code, to be subjected to exile for a term of three years.

On the strength of article 40 RSFSR Criminal Code concerning the accumulation of crimes committed, to be subjected to exile for a term of *three years.*

To allow Bogoraz-Bruchman, Litvinov and Babitsky time spent under preliminary detention in custody in calculating the term of punishment at the rate of one day of detention in custody for three days in exile.

The method of detention of Delone and Dremlyuga not to be altered – to be kept in custody.

The method of detention of Bogoraz-Bruchman, Litvinov and Babitsky, at present under detention in custody, to be cancelled on their delivery to the place where the punishment is to be served.

The material evidence – banners and the plastic cover – to be destroyed.

The sentence may be appealed or protested to the Supreme Court of the RSFSR within seven days of promulgation and by the accused Bogoraz-Bruchman, Litvinov, Babitsky, Delone and Dremlyuga, at present in custody, from the moment they are handed a copy of the sentence.

Chairman V. G. Lubentsova
People's Assessors P. I. Popov
I. Ya. Bulgakov

EXTRACTS ABOUT THE TRIAL

Trial of the case concerning the demonstration in Red Square on 25 August 1968, Human Rights Year in the Soviet Union, Chronicle of Current Events No 4. *30 October 1968.*

[The article reports on the proceedings and the background of the case. It ends with the following comment]

All the circumstances of this nominally open trial differed little from those already experienced in earlier open trials. Friends and sympathizers not admitted to the courtroom and freezing on the street in the rain and early autumn snow; State Security agents in plain clothes, Komsomol special squad members and young vigilantes from the Likhachev factory, none wearing armbands. Eavesdropping on what was being said, photographing of bystanders – a sense of provocation was in the air. As it happened, not one act of provocation came off despite the enlistment of the local inhabitants in an attempt to provoke incidents. People living in houses nearby had been tipped off that currency speculators would be on trial, a sure way of whipping up hatred among simple folk against the friends of the accused. On 10 October, fighting drunks began to arrive in large numbers outside the court building, among them, oddly enough, many drunken women. It turned out that a multitude of vodka bottles had been set out on a table in one of the neighbouring courtyards, free 'hospitality' being provided.

About a dozen and a half relatives were let into the court building through the normal entrance and the remainder of those present were then informed that the courtroom was over-crowded. The rest of the public in court – journalists from several Soviet newspapers, representatives of the Central Committee, the Moscow Party Committee, the KGB, the Prosecutor's office, the special squads, some sixty people in all, went into the courtroom through the back door because they were reluctant to run the gauntlet of the assembled crowd. Relatives of the accused were prevented from leaving the building during recesses by threats that their seats would be taken.

The flimsiness of the charges became even clearer during the hearing. Five of those who took part in detaining the accused stood out among the main prosecution witnesses. These five, all members of the selfsame military unit 1164, happened to be in Red Square at the same time on 25 August without prior arrangement and helped to detain the accused. They testified at the preliminary investigation that the demonstrators had violated public order by their actions. Under cross-examination on the first day, however, these people got completely mixed up in their statements as to whether they knew each other. This was obviously why three of them who had not yet appeared in court turned out to have been suddenly 'sent on duty travel' on the second day. The court decided not to examine them, despite protests from the accused and their advocates. The evidence of a further prosecution witness, Lieutenant *Oleg Davidovich*, on the staff of the severe regime camps at Vetyu station, Komi ASSR, served as one of the main props of the court's decision to punish, even though his statements gave a picture of the demonstration entirely different from all others. He also quoted the time of the demonstration as 12.30 or 12.40 and said that he had entered Red Square from GUM which is well known to be shut on Sundays.

A traffic policeman called as a witness is also noteworthy. His statements were important in connection with the issue of interference with the movement of traffic. This policeman handed in a report about the events in Red Square to his superior on 25 August in which there was nothing about traffic dislocation. On 3 September he handed in a fresh report referring to dislocation. It was shown in court that he had been summoned for interrogation to the Prosecutor's office between these two dates.

The accused did not admit their guilt. Their examination, their final pleas and the speeches of their advocates conclusively proved the absence of criminal liability in the actions of the demonstrators.

Prosecutor Drel devoted a large part of his speech to events in Czechoslovakia, while the accused were invariably interrupted as soon as they touched on these events as part of the description of the motives for their actions or an explanation of the content of the slogans.

The Prosecutor demanded three years' deprivation of liberty for Vladimir Dremlyuga and two years for Vadim Delone with the addition of one year, the term of his previous, conditional sentence, less the period of over seven months spent in custody during the investigation (in other words, a total term of two years, four and a half months). The Prosecutor proposed that the other accused, in view of the absence of previous convictions and the fact that all three had dependent children, should be given the benefit of article 43 RSFSR Criminal Code and sentenced to exile rather than deprivation of liberty: Pavel Litvinov for a term of five years, Larissa Bogoraz – four and Konstantin Babitsky – three years.

The court found the accused guilty under both articles. It more than satisfied the Prosecutor's demands in terms of punishment. Vadim Delone, had said in his final plea 'I call upon the court not for indulgence but for restraint'. He was awarded half a year more in camp than the Prosecutor had suggested – two and a half years and another four months of unexpired sentence, making two years ten months in all. The other accused received terms in camp and exile in accordance with the Prosecutor's demands.

The accused and their advocates have appealed for cassation.

Forensic psychiatric experts under Professor Daniel Lunts pronounced Victor Feinberg insane at the end of October. He will be tried in his absence in accordance with existing legislation to decide whether compulsory medical treatment is to be applied. As we know, Victor Feinberg's teeth were knocked out in Red Square.

THE SOVIET PRESS AND THE DEMONSTRATORS' TRIAL

An official announcement was published in *Moskovskaya Pravda* and *Vechernyaya Moskva* (quoted at the beginning of the present section).

On 12 October two articles (quoted below) appeared about the trial, 'Reckoning on a sensation' by N. Bardin in *Moskovskaya Pravda* and 'Their just deserts' by A. Smirnov in *Vechernyaya Moskva*.

In the first place, these articles, exactly like the official announcement, mention only one charge, that of violating public order under article 190/3. Secondly, the nature of the 'violation' is not revealed and there is no hint at all that a demonstration of protest against the introduction of troops into Czechoslovakia was involved. To make up for this, the authors have provided 'character sketches' of the accused which do not stop short of direct slander and are calculated to smear them in the estimation of the readers. It was precisely this kind of 'information' that Larissa Bogoraz had in mind when she said in her final plea on 11 October: 'The Prosecutor concluded his speech by assuming that the sentences he proposed would be approved by public opinion.

'The court does not depend on public opinion and should be guided by the law. But I agree with the Prosecutor. I have no doubt that public opinion will approve these sentences, as it has approved similar sentences in the past, as it would approve any other sentence. Public opinion will approve three years of camp for a young poet, three years in exile for a talented scientist. Public opinion will approve the prosecution's sentences because we shall be presented to it as parasites, renegades and purveyors of hostile ideology. Moreover, if there proved to be people whose opinion differs from that which is "public" and who found the courage to express it, they would soon find themselves here (pointing to the dock). Public opinion will approve of summary treatment for a peaceful demonstration comprising a few people.'

According to unconfirmed reports the correspondents of two Soviet newspapers present in court refused to write the articles commissioned from them.

Note: I reproduce the articles from *Vechernyaya Moskva* and *Moskovskaya Pravda* but am not entering into polemics with them. They are not worth the trouble of picking out what has been touched up from what is simply lies. To be honest, I find them so repellent that I almost decided to do without them, but find myself forced to include even these dirty articles for the sake of completeness and objectivity.

Moskovskaya Pravda, 12 *October* 1968
Reckoning on a Sensation

Five accused have appeared before the Moscow City Court. They are charged with anti-social acts, an amoral way of life and collective actions grossly violating public order.

In the dock are Larissa Bogoraz-Bruchman, Pavel Litvinov, Vadim Delone, Vladimir Dremlyuga, Konstantin Babitsky.

Apart from Babitsky, none of the accused has been at work anywhere. They have in effect been living as parasites.

The facts of the matter are that on 25 August at 12 noon the accused enumerated above appeared by previous agreement in Red Square, sat down near the Execution Ground and unfolded banners which they had prepared and which carried slanderous inscriptions offensive to Soviet citizens. They started to shout at the top of their voices, quoting the inscriptions and trying to attract the attention of passers-by.

But this disorderly assembly lasted only a few minutes. No longer than was needed for people near the Execution Ground to understand the truth of it. Indignant workers, collective farmers and students surrounded them. These snatched the banners from the hands of the screechers, tore them up and told the hooligans in thoroughly plain terms what they thought of them.

Policemen had some difficulty in conducting this bunch through the infuriated crowd. They were all taken to the police section with the help of eyewitnesses. .

What are they like, these accused?

The bond between them is not just a matter of their anti-social views, but of their anti-social deeds, their relentless passion for alcohol, for debauchery and for idleness.

Litvinov, having found time in the spells between his drunken bouts to marry and abandon a wife and four-year old son without means of support, led a life of debauch.

Delone was also 'celebrated' for his drunkenness and immoral behaviour. Delone had been arrested in 1967 for a gross violation of public order and conditionally sentenced to a year's deprivation of liberty.

Dremlyuga had also been sentenced in Leningrad in 1963 for speculating in car tyres. It transpired in court that during a search at Dremlyuga's home a long list of women with whom he had lived was discovered.

This is not the first time that Bogoraz-Bruchman and Litvinov, now in the dock, have come to the notice of the Soviet public. They had, over a number of years, become the joint authors of dirty, slanderous lampoons which regularly appear in the pages of the Western gutter press, including even émigré publications.

It also transpired in court that the Soviet administrative authorities had displayed humanity and lenience towards Bogoraz-Bruchman, Litvinov and Delone. The anti-social nature of their behaviour was repeatedly made clear to them and they were warned that they would inevitably be brought to book unless they stopped their illegal activity. They were also repeatedly advised to give up their parasitic way of life and engage in socially useful work. Yet they did not mend their ways.

Workers and employees of various Moscow enterprises and institutions who attended the trial came to feel that something else united the accused – all of them were looking for every opportunity to attract the West's attention to themselves, 'Famous' is what they wished to become at all costs. Well, no need to doubt that Western anti-Soviet propaganda specialists will endeavour to exploit this trial for yet another splash, one more cheap sensation. They will endeavour to lament in the loudest possible tones those five, so near to them in thought and action, who have come before a Soviet court.

N. Bardin

The court sentenced Dremlyuga, V. A. to three years and Delone, V. N. to two years and ten months of deprivation of liberty; Litvinov, P. M. to five years, Bogoraz-Bruchman, L. I. to four years and Babitsky, K. I. to three years of exile.

Vechernyaya Moskva, 12 October 1968
Their Just Deserts

The hearing of the criminal case against Babitsky, K. I.,

Bogoraz-Bruchman, L. I., Delone, V. N., Dremlyuga, V. A. and Litvinov, P. M. in the Moscow City court lasted three days. They were accused of violating public order and committing other illegal acts.

The indictment shows that the above-mentioned accused came by previous agreement to Red Square on 25 August of this year, unfolded, near the Execution Ground, banners they had prepared with slanderous inscriptions which insulted the Soviet people and set about shouting dirty slogans.

Workers, employers and students in Red Square, indignant at the actions of these people, surrounded the screechers, snatched the banners from them and tore them up. The hooligans were taken to the police station.

The unattractive complexion of the accused became increasingly clear in the course of the trial. They were relaxed in court, as indeed they are in daily life.

Here is Litvinov, rising to give evidence. He does so, now with affected bravado, now with studied carelessness. Litvinov has received a higher education, he is a physics graduate of Moscow University. Maxim Gorky said that man was born to better himself. People were endowed with life in order to do good. Litvinov, indeed, had every opportunity to become a man of honest toil. The prospect of serving the people and the motherland, however, clearly did not appeal to him. He 'had a go', first in one educational institution, then another. He did not last long anywhere, however, and either chucked the job or was dismissed.

Litvinov was offered a place as assistant professor in the department of physics of the Moscow Lomonosov Institute of fine chemical technology, but he did not stay there long either. On the other hand, he managed to 'get into the limelight'. He fell foul of the community, abused discipline and systematically absented himself from work. The inevitable end came – he was dismissed under article 47/E of the Code of Labour Laws. Since January this year he has done no work.

The misdeeds committed by Litvinov are fundamentally at odds with the standards applied in life by Soviet people. Having got a new flat he arranged one drinking bout after another. Next to Litvinov sit his 'comrades in arms'. There's Delone. He too is not employed anywhere. He was expelled from his institute. Delone was arrested in 1967 for a gross violation of public order and conditionally sentenced to a year's deprivation of liberty.

And there's another friend of Litvinov – Dremlyuga. One can judge his moral character from acts such as getting himself tried for speculating in car tyres and engaging in drunkenness and debauchery.

It's distasteful to list the doings of this bunch. The Muscovites in court looked at them with indignation.

It should be added that the Soviet administrative authorities displayed humanity and lenience towards Bogoraz-Bruchman, Litvinov and Delone. They were repeatedly advised to give up their parasitic way of life and engage in socially useful work. But they preferred to go on behaving in the same way.

Red Square – our people's shrine. To behave there as a hooligan, to commit blasphemy is a crime in a class of its own.

The court sentenced Dremlyuga, V. A. to three years and Delone, V. N. to two years and ten months of deprivation of liberty; Litvinov, P. M. to five years, Bogoraz-Bruchman, L. I. to four years and Babitsky, K. I. to three years of exile.

The accused got what they asked for. They got their just deserts. Representatives of Moscow public life present in court greeted the court's sentence with approval. Let the punishment meted out to Babitsky, Bogoraz-Bruchman, Delone, Dremlyuga and Litvinov serve as a serious lesson for those who perhaps still imagine that one can get away with violations of public order. It won't work!

A. Smirnov

BEFORE THE CLOSED DOORS OF THE OPEN COURT
by Ilya Gabai

With freedom's seed the desert sowing,
I walked before the morning star,

From pure and guiltless fingers throwing,
Where Slavish ploughs had left a scar,
The living seed, the procreator.
Oh vain and sad disseminator,
I learned then what lost labours are.
Graze if you will, you peaceful nations
Who never rose at honour's horn.
Should flocks heed freedom's invocation?
Their part is to be slain or shorn:
Their dowry, the yoke their sires have worn
Through smug and sheepish generations.

A. Pushkin (translated by B. Deutsch & A. Yarmolinsky)

We came to the building of the Proletarsky District Court at 9 o'clock on the morning of 9 October 1968, an hour before the hearing was due to start. We were the friends and comrades of the accused. We shared their convictions unquestioningly and completely. The forthcoming trial was of more than academic interest for us.

We already knew what would happen.

We entertained no hopes at all of seeing our comrades. It was concern for their fate which, first and foremost, had brought us here and we were prepared to spend long hours standing in the street in hopes of the tiniest crumb of information. Everything that had earlier preoccupied us – for instance, whether our comrades should have undertaken this deliberate act of self-sacrifice well knowing that it would achieve nothing in practice – everything that only yesterday might legitimately have provided fuel for a deeply felt argument, was now out of place: behind these doors firmly closed against us the fate of people we held dear was being decided.

We were already used to the cynicism and impudence of KGB and court administration employees. We were reconciled to being constantly shadowed and photographed. This time, however, fresh ordeals, a new and bitter range of experience awaited us and it is our duty to describe them.

Our duty in the first place is towards those whom a sentence of this court has sent to camp or exile. This will, perhaps, cut short idle arguments about the futility of actions such as a demonstration. Someone, perhaps, will also be better able to appreciate the spiritual greatness of those who, in the desert, sowed the concepts of honour, decency and dignity among the multitudes ever eager to give animal instincts free rein.

Now I am rid of surplus thoughts, surplus feelings, surplus conscience.

M. E. Saltykov-Shchedrin ' *Vialenaya Vobla* '
(*The Dried Roach*)

Everything did indeed happen as we had foreseen. There proved to be 'not enough seats' for us in the courtroom. They had been taken by people with special passes who got into the building by the back door.

At P. G. Grigorenko's suggestion a letter was prepared to demand that friends of the accused be admitted to the court room. That was when those who were to become stars in this story first made their appearance.

Individuals in overalls arrived on the scene and we were showered with a stream of colourful but not yet particularly full-blooded slang. It came rather indolently – maybe the 'working class' was saving its strength for the coming combats. At any rate, one merely heard some off-the-cuff threats behind one, gingered up with obscenities. Someone rushed forward to enlighten these 'ordinary workers'. He might as well have left them alone from the start: beside them stood a man in a light coloured raincoat, with a face we well knew, issuing instructions to them from time to time in a low voice. A few days earlier he had been in charge of a search at my flat. The hand that jerked the puppets was there for anyone to see. Yet, driven by an incurable faith in the power of the spoken word, we too occasionally became unwilling actors in this pantomime . . . Meanwhile some forty people found time to put their signatures to the letter written at Piotr Grigorenko's suggestion and more were waiting their turn.

A veranda opposite the entrance to the court building was to become the stage for many a colourful scene in this three day show. People were crowding round a table which stood there.

It was hard to differentiate between the motives which had brought them there and impelled them towards that table. Only as time went by did many of us come to believe that he who chooses sleuthing, denunciation and provocation as his way of life bears the unmistakable marks of his trade. One of them, however, was well known to us.

Most of us remembered him from the previous winter, during the trial of Ginzburg and Galanskov, but some had met him even earlier at Sinyavsky's and Daniel's trial. In those days, over two and a half years ago, he was still trying to play up to us. He launched into provocatively courageous tirades: 'Just think of it,' he would exclaim, 'trying writers! Where else could that have happened?' He fooled no one, however, either by his speeches or his appearance. The central feature of his make-up was obviously meant to be the little black beard – the mark of the 'intellectual'. At the demonstrators' trial that winter he was spotted on the very first day and did not even start to put on a show. He boldly took charge of the 'boys' who were knocking about. Were they vigilantes, or special squad members or paid informers? In the absence of armbands or other marks of identification it is simplest just to describe them by the common term 'finks'. Part of the bearded man's time was spent in court and then, in his role of 'just an ordinary member of the public', he would obligingly inform Western correspondents how the hearing was going. They, let it be said, clearly grasped what he was no less than we did and treated his information accordingly.

While the collecting of signatures was in full swing, this creature snatched away the letter and tore it up. He was immediately surrounded by an angry crowd. Something like this followed:

From the crowd: That's hooliganism and you shall answer for it. There are plenty of witnesses.

Man with beard: It wasn't hooliganism. Just like you, I wanted to sign the letter.

From the crowd: And so you tore it up?

A fink: He did not tear it up.

Man with beard: I did not tear it up. (To P.G. Grigorenko): You tore it up yourself.

P. G. Grigorenko: That is a lie.

From the crowd: That is a lie. We are witnesses to your hooliganism.

(It emerged from a confused and somewhat heated exchange that the man with a beard, alternately a Komsomol city committee representative or an engineer just passing by, was called 'Alexandrov, Oleg Ivanovich').

Alexandrov: I wanted to sign your letter and make some alterations in it, because you have no class instinct.

And so, quite apart from his regrettable references to instinct instead of sense, this young fink was trying to teach the rudiments of political science to a general with wartime service, a noted and qualified theoretician and a man of firm communist views (unlike some of us).

'Alexandrov', it seems, virtually stranded among a few dozen indignant people, felt somewhat at bay. It is just possible that what happened on the following day was caused by the difficulty of instigating provocations successfully, given such inequality of forces.

'Alexandrov' refused to give documentary proof of his identity. The policeman on duty outside the court building declined to check his documents when asked to do so. Finally, on his advice, a fair crowd led 'Alexandrov' off to the nearest police station. The finks tagged on behind.

Outside the station entrance, policemen were already waiting for the crowd. They threatened it with punishment and told it to disperse. 'Alexandrov' was admitted without further ado. A little later, Piotr Grigorevich was summoned and then two more witnesses.

While waiting for the outcome (not that it was in doubt, but one really could not leave Piotr Grigorevich alone with that lot), those who were outside discussed their ideas and impressions. It was already becoming clearer who was who. Then the conversation was taken over by a youthful looking individual who introduced himself as Stepanov, a student at

the Moscow University Economics Faculty, and was even prepared to show his student card. He spoke smoothly – but he
lied. His line was something like this: 'Personally, I am not
involved in any way . . . I heard about it by chance at the university and came along . . . I just happened to be present during the
incident . . . No one snatched away the paper, it was one of you
who tore it up . . . All I am interested in is the truth . . .'and so
on. The individual may really have been a student and been called
Stepanov. It is all the more sad that snoopers should be recruited
from the student body. We also quickly came to the conclusion
that studying at Moscow University was certainly not his main
occupation.

Nothing unexpected happened at the police station. 'Alexandrov' was found to carry no documents and everybody was asked
to disperse, while he was kept back to establish his identity.
Very soon, fifteen to twenty minutes later, he walked back to
the court building and set about his sleuthing with no attempt
at concealment. The unsuccessful performance as a simple
engineer was over.

The number of people supposedly 'from the factory floor'
near the court was growing. The volume of simple, heartfelt
bad language went on increasing in that old Moscow alley. One
of the most zealous agitators was a man wearing glasses, with the
look of a button-holing drunkard. These people seemed to
harbour some special loathing for beards (but not for that of
'Alexandrov' – 'instinct' was clearly at work in this case). The
man with the glasses threatened one of the beards: 'We'll shave
you'. This exquisite joke was hugely successful and never left
the lips of the 'representatives of the people' throughout the
next three days.

The end was not yet in sight. Groups formed, conversations
developed, here and there arguments arose. Things were fairly
peaceful, although 'workers' as they arrived contributed a
certain element of freshness to the highly theoretical discussions.
There was a touch of wit, for instance, about their standard
accusation: 'Why are you here and not at work?' Asking them the
same question proved fruitless.

That day, attempts to set off a row were doomed to failure. One might have thought that when the 'working class' insulted somebody part of the purpose was to draw an angry retort or stimulate a slanging match. But nobody reacted to provocation. One bystander happened to tread on a shovel left lying around in fallen leaves. People in overalls were round him in a flash and tried to stage a noisy scene. The bystander walked away, shrugging his shoulders, and the 'workers' were left to keep each other company.

When setting out to generate a row or an argument these people usually clustered round the current victim, someone who had been unable to restrain himself and had answered back – words with words, threats with arguments, insults with reasoned replies which were, however, entirely wasted under these circumstances. Regardless of whether he spoke up or fell silent, those who hemmed him in would mount a lively argument, often merely among themselves. Then, as soon as the victim left the circle – sometimes comprising more than twenty people – it would instantly dissolve.

It is a bitter thought that we ourselves, so far removed from these people in spirit and so hostile to their soulless mechanical outlook, should also be so deeply affected by the present moral climate. This is best exemplified by the lack of trust revealed here in the relations between people. Embarrassing situations kept on cropping up. One might be talking to someone, take him for an informer and let him know it, only to find out later that this was a perfectly decent person. There was a group of young students whom nobody knew outside the court building on the first day. One of them boasted rather childishly of someone he was acquainted with. This later proved not to be so and the whole group then met with solid distrust. That evening, as these boys were going away, very depressed, they said that they would not come back.

The agencies which have made shadowing, the reading of mail and the tapping of telephones into standard practices are to blame for this falsification of values. Yet we ourselves stick too closely to the rules of their game. After all, we commit no crimes that require concealment, while we are punished, as a rule, only for our convictions. And what is a conviction worth if it has to be hidden?

At the same time, some of us found a sort of perverse enjoyment in talking to individuals whose assignments were crystal clear. I have heard this justified by claims to an author's professional curiosity. A few have even nursed hopes of shaking the clear-cut views of red pass holders,[23] but the latter were on the look-out for this kind of thing. A young mathematician who taught at a factory technical college met some of his students, all keen to practise provocation, and began to tell them how badly they were behaving, bringing their worker's honour into disrepute and so on. A week later he was dismissed from his job.

The torn-up letter was rewritten and collected fifty-eight signatures. Again a young, shortish man with a boxer's face nipped in, snatched the letter and, covered by several colleagues, ran away with it towards the court building. Policemen cleared a way for him and he vanished through the doors of the court where lesser mortals could not follow him. No more signatures were collected but, fortunately, two copies had been made and the second was duly despatched.

Romanov, a Foreign Ministry press office representative, came out to talk to foreign journalists. He explained that he had found himself in court by pure chance, knew nothing ('Do you know of a cafeteria hereabouts?' he asked one of the pressmen), but, as he was there, would keep his colleagues informed of the course of the trial. He kept his promise and the correspondents were handed information of the most innocuous kind ('The examination of the accused has ended', 'The Prosecutor has started his speech' and so on), but even that was something as far as we were concerned, particularly since relatives in the courtroom were not allowed out during a single recess.

One journalist asked whether they might take pictures. This, Romanov replied, was not 'in the Soviet tradition'. Meanwhile Stepanov, that detached student of economics who had earlier thirsted for the truth and only the truth, was busily breaking these very traditions and flashing his camera around. To begin with, when angrily questioned by one of those whom he had snapped, he said with a smile that it was all for the Faculty's wall-newspaper. Later, he stopped answering questions and just got on with the job. There was no point at all in dreaming up a profession for several people who were constantly on duty at his elbow.

The first day of the trial was drawing to a close. The hearing ended at eight in the evening and we went home. Everything still lay ahead of us – the outcome of the trial and the experience of a street in elemental uproar. It was 'Alexandrov', 'Stepanov' and their like who marked that first day most clearly in our memories. At least these young people might conceivably have belonged to various professions. Now the time had come for raw reality before which everything that makes life worth living – books, exhibitions, scientific enquiry or just decent behaviour – must give way. Why talk of *surplus* thoughts, *surplus* feelings, *surplus* conscience when these were simply absent? The others kept on that day calling their animal substitute for conscience and feeling, *instinct*. Instinct. A sense of smell. Not just instinct – they call it class instinct. Caste instinct. They have gutted their fish for dozens of years on end, dried it, cured it. Now it has neither thoughts, nor feelings, nor conscience left – only instinct . . .

> *Farewell, you uniforms of blue*
> *Farewell, you people that obey*
> *them . . .*
>
> M. Lermontov

It is revealed to us by classical literature that reason cannot encompass Russia nor a yardstick measure her and a great deal more of this sort of thing besides. We are commanded to believe that her standards are unique, that, broad shouldered, she will clear a path for herself and that the gang of hired thugs who staged pandemonium on 10 October are the only true begetters of genuine values, the very soil from which Pushkin, Chaadayev, Dostoevsky, Scriabin and Vrubel sprang. Nor, surprisingly, did faith in all this suffer a setback that day. They whipped up a hundred drunks but might as easily have whipped up a thousand. They stuck to abuse, but might have killed had they been ordered to do so. Moreover, there may well have been among this mob some real grade 6 lathe operator with his picture really pinned to the board of honour at the factory. It is possible to pity these people – for being so ignorant, for having such crippled souls, for being cruel and blind beyond all hope. We, however, knew people better worth pitying. We owed sympathy to them because they are so intelligent, honest and courageous, because they have been torn away for many a long year from the work they loved, because their lives may have been hopelessly ruined ...

On 10 October at 9 o'clock in the morning the Black Maria drove into the courthouse yard. Many of us shouted greetings to the accused although we could not see them. A KGB official – the one mentioned earlier in connection with the search at my flat – came up to those who had gathered and said: 'Sticking your necks out, are you? We'll soon be round for you as well.' (A few hours later, he was pretending to be a worker.

'A worker, are you?' one of us, who had spent several years in camp and was later rehabilitated, said to him, 'Do workers carry out searches nowadays?'

'Anti-Soviet gaol-bird', the other snarled through his teeth and walked away. Later that day he disappeared for good.)

Several of those who had been let into the courtroom on the previous day were not allowed in this time, the wife of one of the accused among them. Around midday a middle-aged woman suddenly appeared near the doors of the court and began to shout obscenities. She attached herself to the wife of the accused, let fly a stream of abuse at her, (she seemed to have a special hatred for glasses) and threatened to have her lynched. A police officer was standing in the middle of this particular ring of people. He was requested to detain the hooligan. Someone threatened to lodge a complaint about police inactivity, at which the officer remarked: 'You are grown up and yet you say such silly things'. Presently, the woman vanished for the time being.

Just then a dishevelled drunk turned up near 'Alexandrov'

and began to yell at those present. All he now needed, he insisted, was a sub-machine gun to fire at the crowd. By some miracle all the people's tribunes were now thinking and talking alike. In the course of this day many of them complained that they were not given a chance to shoot or drown the lot of us in the Yauza or, if the worst came to the worst, have a go at us with a bull-dozer.

The drunk was threatened with the sobering-up station and reluctantly took himself off. Someone asked 'Alexandrov' why he had not intervened in this disgraceful piece of behaviour instead of condoning it with all his might. 'Alexandrov' very properly reminded all concerned that in our country freedom of speech was guaranteed to every citizen and that he could not prevent a working man from speaking out what was on his mind.

'But incitements to hatred are, I believe, forbidden and hooliganism also is quite severely punished.'

'You feel that there has been incitement to hatred, do you?'

'And do you feel that a call for lynching by a drunken hireling represents a supreme manifestation of humanitarianism?'

Somebody lost his temper.

'You should do your recruiting in the sobering-up station or, better still, let the thieves and brigands out of gaol for such days. You have nothing else to fall back on – the ground is burning under your feet.'

Groups kept forming all over the place. Accusations of idle-ness, parasitism and contact with capitalists would suddenly be showered on one or other of us – it is astonishing how well they knew whom to attack. Very many of us, unfortunately, suc-cumbed to the temptation to enlighten the masses. This became increasingly difficult. As soon as a group began to form, 'specials' rushed across, threats and curses spurted. Conversation is impossible with militant louts while extricating someone from the middle of a ring of people, or persuading him not to get involved in an argument. The ubiquitous 'Alexandrov' stood in one of the groups where the argument had taken a particularly bellicose turn. We succeeded in dragging away the man who had tangled in argument with the hirelings – and 'Alexandrov' was told: 'Don't nurse any hopes. Nobody will get into a fight, nobody will fall for provocation'. 'Alexandrov' just smiled sardonically.

Elsewhere, a 'worker' in glasses was holding forth. He had found time to slip away and change out of overalls into a suit in the fashion of the forties. His message was perfectly predictable and most accessible to the 'open-hearted' people around him. He threatened to shave someone's beard and hang him from a branch by certain parts of his anatomy and so on. Here everything happened exactly as in badly dubbed Chinese films: the 'worker' would utter some witticism and a laboured, threefold 'ha-ha-ha' greeted it. This kept on happening and these 'ha-ha-ha's' sounded just as rehearsed as the slogans shouted out at ceremonial line-ups by Young Pioneers.

Among this ever-growing throng there were probably some who had simply been misinformed. A worker who named the factory where he was employed said they had been told that currency speculators were on trial. Even this lacks logic: why leave one's work to go to a court where such crimes are being tried? The majority, however, were hand picked and briefed. The man who beat up Feinberg at the 25 August demonstration was in this crowd for a while on the first day. He was recognized, noticed it and vanished.

A slight lull followed. Some of the crowd reeled away for a rest in a neighbouring courtyard. It was large and spacious, with long ping-pong tables set up in it. One of these carried a whole battery of vodka bottles, open tins of fish and mounds of cut bread. The 'working class' opponents whom we had come to know in the course of those stormy arguments were elbowing each other about around the fare provided.

It began to rain and everyone huddled on the veranda. Conversation continued in small groups, but disputes did not flare up. A drunken voice suddenly rang out – the 'worker' in glasses was addressing a foreign correspondent:

'Why are you interfering in other people's business? Go away from here'.

His drunken, illiterate, unconnected speech was not taken up even by his boon companions. The bystanders smiled in embarrassment. Some turned to Stepanov whose camera was working overtime that day and who wore an unbelievable white suit – 'A uniform?', as one of us had asked him that morning.

'Stop him', Stepanov was told, 'it's a disgrace'.

'I'm not a policeman,' he replied, 'and things would have come to a pretty pass if I were to stop a working man's mouth!'

The most painful part came in the evening, at about seven or eight o'clock. Patently drink-sodden people, mouthing oaths and threats, were promenading close to the policemen while these preserved a sphinx-like calm.

The woman who had started a row at midday reappeared. She was nearing the last stages of drunkenness, although she may have been playing up a little, because there was definitely system in what she was doing. Drunken workers crowded round her. The choicest and most vile abuse came gushing forth. The drunks seemed to be competing in abominations and low threats, with the woman as their ring-leader. Anything would do – the same wretched beards and glasses, the cut of the men's suits or the girls' hairstyles. A pregnant woman was insulted. Men accosted girls with vile obscenities. The police listened and kept silent. One drunk spent five minutes or more next to a policeman threatening, not people at large, but a particular person. He kept on threatening to tear out this man's duodenum (that, for some reason was as far as his knowledge of anatomy went) while the policeman took it all in and stayed silent.

The KGB man who had snatched away the letter with signatures on the second occasion stood in the centre of it all, almost beside the drunken woman. He seemed to be an inevitable participant in and organizer of these mass manifestations.

'I am a working woman,' screeched the inebriated female, 'and if I've had a drink or two, it's my own money I'm spending.'

An elderly man said to her:

'You're lying. You're no worker. You lack honour. You are just a hired hooligan.'

The crowd closed in on him while the woman cursed him in a most elaborate way.

'What gives you the right to talk like that to an old man?' a bystander asked her.

The crowd now turned on him.

'What are you here for anyway?'

'My friends are being tried here. And what about you?'

'Your friends are fascists and murderers. And you're no different.'

The familiar lamentations about the absence of a sub-machine gun followed.

'Who is a fascist?' the bystander asked. 'What about you, asking for people to be mown down?'

Then, for a while, this riff-raff kept to itself. A bunch of them, including the man who had snatched away the letter, still surrounded the drunken woman. Presently she pointed out the opposite side of the street to a young drunk with a dirty white bandage over his eye. The youth crossed over, peered into people's faces and went back to her. Whereupon she suddenly rushed across to Grigorenko followed by her entire escort, several dozen strong.

'I have no wish at all to talk to you,' said Grigorenko.

The crowd determinedly hustled him. One of his friends fetched a policeman. The latter expressed surprise at being summoned – he saw nothing out of the ordinary in a few dozen drunken louts importuning an old man. The policeman's lack of interest encouraged the crowd. Several of them turned on the man who had fetched the policeman. When he turned aside and quietly walked away, shouts of: 'Bloody yid – doesn't want a chat', followed him.

If any single factor prevented an outbreak of physical violence that day it was the presence of foreign journalists. The hooligans had been well briefed. This was obvious, not only from the obligatory presence of KGB men at all clashes or the arrangements clearly made in advance with the police, but also from scenes such as this, which all of us witnessed. One of the liveliest troublemakers went up to a foreign correspondent, but politely withdrew when he discovered that he was dealing with a foreigner. Some time later the troublemaker heard the correspondent speaking good Russian, went back to him and, fetching out as though to hit him, said: 'You're as much of a (string of unprintable epithets) American as I am an Eskimo.'

The uproar, it seems, was going beyond what had been planned. In due course the idol of the crowd – the drunken woman – was packed off home. By 11 o'clock, when the hearing ended, everything had more or less got back on the rails. A telephone call to the Ministry for the Preservation of Public Order also may possibly have had some effect.

There were just as many people present on the last day as before. Arguments between friends and enemies of the accused continued, but in a calmer and more academic vein than on the previous day. The majority of the earlier troublemakers were absent.

Money was collected to buy bunches of flowers for the advocates and these were stored in the car of a relative present at the hearing. The car was parked round the corner from the court building, but in full view of one of the policemen on point duty. It was, of course, locked. When we went to fetch the flowers the car turned out to be open and empty. Needless to say, we collected money and fetched other flowers, because there was no way of finding the thieves. When told of this, the police captain remarked: 'One of your lot stole them – Yakir, for sure' – and chuckled at his own joke.

At about 2 o'clock the Foreign Ministry representative came to invite foreign journalists to hear the promulgation of the sentence in court.

The whole crowd moved towards the doors of the building and waited for news of the sentence in tense silence. At long last the doors opened and those who had got in every day by the back entrance with special passes filed out one by one. This was the first time that we had seen them. The crowd opened a narrow passage through which they walked in silence, with solemn, stony faces. 'What was the sentence?' someone asked. They did not answer, as though afraid of contact with 'undesirable elements'. One of them merely snapped out: 'What sentence? A mild one. . .' A voice from the crowd said: 'Why ask them?'

Then the relatives of the accused emerged and we heard the sentence.

A rumour went round that an attempt would be made to take the advocates out through the back door. Part of the crowd rushed round the building and came up against a police cordon. Finally, the advocates came out of the main doors. The crowd surged forward. The bouquets were handed over with hasty explanations why they were so small.

'Little flowers, don't forget the little flowers!' the man who had snatched the letter away shouted after us. Those around him dutifully giggled.

As we were leaving, the same old threats, the same old abuse followed us, but now rather lazily. The police in their uniforms dispersed. The grey rabble made up of self-styled workers also faded away.

'I have always thought that the commonly held opinion is by no means identical with clear reason; that the interests of the masses are infinitely more affected by passion, infinitely narrower and more selfish than those of individuals; that so-called popular wisdom is not real wisdom; and that truth does not spring from the crowd.'

P.Chaadayev
A Madman's Apologia

Just so.

That is how these scattered notes, composed from memory, ought to end. It seems too much to hope that after reading them people will come to see things as we did. Perhaps they may at least cure some reader of his illusions.

The agencies of repression rely on a riff-raff of thugs, of evil and irrational beings. These beings are capable of doing much harm, lacking as they do the habit of reasoning and a desire for liberty and civil dignity. The cages were only opened a little during these three days and the animals inside did no more than show their claws. Some day, the entire zoo may be turned out into the street. Early Christians were thrown to the lions. This made sense: one can only do away with ideas and concepts and personal ties by resorting to the law of the jungle, because such action defies human standards.

A distinction was drawn during the nineteenth century between the people and the mob. In our century, however, all that could be destroyed was annihilated in the name of the people. Everything dirty and cruel in our history was covered up in the name of the people and greeted with roars of popular approval.

These notes may perhaps help some reader to be more strict with himself; after all, the difference between the hooligan's hand raised against his neighbour and the intellectual's hand raised against his fellow in a vote is not so great as might appear.

These notes may also help somebody to understand the behaviour of our comrades who were sentenced for demonstrating. So-called 'popular wisdom' is not real wisdom and so there is nothing left but to uphold one's honour and freedom, one's living soul in this morass, surrounded by these militant boobies. Even if it is still too early – before the dawn . . .

A FEW MORE WORDS ABOUT THE TRIAL

Of course I failed to get into the courtroom. By the middle of the second day I could stand it no longer and wrote to Lubentsova asking to be admitted at least for the sentence. I based my request on the fact that I had undergone investigation in connection with the case. But who would pay attention to requests by the insane? I was aware of this, but faintly hoped to arouse the Judge's curiosity; in her position I would have wished to know who this Gorbanevskaya was from whose pram, as the Prosecutor asserted, all the slogans had been taken. It was an empty hope and I spent the third day, like the two previous ones, at the doors of the court.

As soon as I heard the sentence, or rather the Prosecutor's proposals, it came to my mind that, if I had been tried along with the rest of the friends, I would have been given corrective labour. The 'mitigating circumstances' (no previous convictions and children) applied equally to me, while banishment and exile are not applicable to women and children under eight. And do you know what I thought? I thought that the sentence had been more or less known at the time when I was found insane. I made up my mind to ask about it, but was told on good authority that everything had been fixed a week before the trial at a meeting in the Prosecutor General's office. I do not know how much more there was in this rumour than in dozens of others, equally claimed to be on good authority, about actions and intentions in the 'upper echelons'.

I had the same experiences as everybody else outside the court, except that I did not witness passions at their height, because I left early to collect my child from the kindergarten. That evening, however, various people phoned me with news of the trial and said that terrible things had been happening round the courthouse. Next day, they were all full of their past experiences. Ilya Gabai has given a very accurate account of the days we spent during the trial. What is more, his characteristically emotional approach heightens the veracity of his story. He conveys not only the facts, as we saw them, but the feelings which we all experienced.

I have only three additions to make to his story.

1. *About information, foreign correspondents and Citizen Romanov*

Ilya mentioned that such meagre information as we received about the progress of the trial came from foreign correspondents. Romanov, of the Foreign Ministry Press Office 'who happened to be at the trial' emerged to give them short items of information from time to time. He then began to take them occasionally, in twos and threes, into the court building where the Deputy President of the Moscow City Court, Almazov, was giving short press conferences. The value of Romanov's 'information' is clear from his statement that he had not heard that the texts of the slogans were part of the indictment against the demonstrators; he made this statement towards the end of the second day, when the entire court examination had been concluded. Almazov's press conferences were not worth much either. At the time, the entire Western press printed his statement that those exiled would be offered a chance of work in their own profession. A naïve press! The agencies carrying out the sentences, including that dealing with exiles, belong to the Ministry of Internal Affairs and not to the judicial authorities. Almazov's statement therefore did not bind them in any way, while he was not bound by any promise the fulfilment of which was beyond his control.

2. *About the witness Davidovich*

It might be thought that I am so insistent about this witness because I fell foul of him during the investigation. That is not so. Various people who attended the hearing spoke of Davidovich with disgust. Everybody remembered his blatant lying and his arrogant assumption that he would be believed no matter what absurdity he volunteered. On the third day, when only the final pleas and the sentence were yet to come, witnesses were kept out of the courtroom – 'there's no room', they were told. Yastreba arrived, a tall girl and ungainly, or perhaps merely feeling awkward among us. She was not admitted and quickly went away again. Sania Daniel told me about her: 'She is no sympathizer of yours, in fact she is definitely against you. But she is the kind of girl whom Mother taught that one must always tell the truth. And so she tells the truth and does not understand how it can be that barefaced lies are told in such a place.' The latter referred to Davidovich's statements. Yastreba left, but Misha Leman, who had also been excluded, stayed on. Whereupon Davidovich arrived and was admitted without further ado. 'Misha!' someone yelled, myself maybe. 'They've let Davidovich in.' Misha raced after him waving his witness summons. Davidovich had to be turned away. He walked off, but was at once intercepted by one of Alexandrov's henchmen who took him towards the next alley and the back entrance of the court building through which all the 'spectators' had got in and where the Black Maria pulled up. A crowd of indignant people set off after this pair. The two quietly talked it over as they went along and obviously decided not to bring matters to a head.

Davidovich took leave of his companion and made off. His address is known: Komi ASSR, St. Vetyu, V/ch [Military Unit] 6592. Severe regime camps are located at Vetyu Station.

3. *To Ilya Gabai – about some of the 'stars' of his tale*

And so, Ilyushenka, while you sit in Tashkent prison, in God knows what conditions, without news of your relatives or friends, we have met a few of Alexandrov's bunch as well as the man himself. He and the other character who stuck so close to him, the horse-faced one who wore a black peaked cap – which, for some reason, you insisted was a student's cap – these two, and perhaps others as well, are to be witnesses in, of all things, your own case and that of Piotr Grigorevich (Grigorenko). Nadia Emelkina saw Alexandrov when she went to Berezovsky for interrogation; I saw the other one the following day. They both came before Berezovsky for whom they were, of course, as valuable and trustworthy witnesses as the wretched Dobrovolsky, whom he also summoned. This was in July. In June, we all went to the Moscow University Club, to see the revue 'As You May Like It', and caught sight of Stepanov. He was still wearing that unforgettable white suit, but (how people do grow!) he had already become the leader of a gang of lads as unkempt and unwashed as himself, and just as vigilant. While the entire audience went mad with delight and wore out its hands clapping, while most respectable citizens in the circle shouted, 'Stepanov' stood mute and motionless at the end of the front row in that circle and just scanned the hall with a hunter's look, trying to memorize who had been clapping and with how much enthusiasm. Later, the members of the orchestra were called one by one to the Party Committee to be questioned about their social origin and their attitude to the work that they had performed. Their questioners also revealed an intimate knowledge of what had been said in the foyer and backstage. The director of the club, who was accused of permitting 'a meeting by an anti-Soviet organization in public premises', had a heart attack.

So, as you can see, life carries on.

AFTER THE CASSATION HEARING

[On 19 November 1968 the Supreme Court of the RSFSR heard and rejected the cassation appeal of the demonstrators. It confirmed the sentence of the Moscow City Court without any alterations.]

The day on which the cassation appeal was heard was marked for us by several house searches. The hearing had started and, as usual, we had been left outside (we were kept out of both the courtroom and the narrow passage leading to it, while the audience, except for relatives, appeared from the opposite side without going past us). Several of our friends who had firmly intended to come were missing. Piotr Grigorevich had not arrived, neither had Galia Gabai, or Nadia Emelkina who was spending the night with Galia. Ilya Gabai was not in Moscow at that time: after a vain search for work he had gone off to be a teacher in the backwoods, in a village near Kineshma. The telephone in the Grigorenkos' flat was not answering.

We immediately suspected that a search was in progress there, and so it proved to be. The searches were connected with the case of the Crimea Tatars and that in Grigorenko's flat was carried out by Berezovsky, who had arrived from Tashkent, 'in person'. Mustafa Dzhemilev,[24] who was staying with Grigorenko, feared that he might be arrested and jumped out of the window. He broke his leg. 'Pity it wasn't his head', said Berezovsky.

The gathering of signatures to a letter in defence of the unjustly sentenced demonstrators had started in November, even before the Supreme Court hearing. It was a difficult time. The enthusiasm with which hundreds of people had signed letters during the spring of 1968 in connection with the Ginzburg-Galanskov trial had slumped. It had been dampened in some by repressions, in others because repressions had passed them by, but they could see elsewhere how one was liable to be slung out of the Party or one's job and be unable to find work, etc. Others again were tired of appealing to the authorities. In these circumstances, even the ninety-five signatures collected looked impressive: frankly, I had not expected more than fifty. I did not sign the letter, because I no longer wished to approach any representatives of authority. I also felt that I had said all I wanted to say by taking part in the demonstration and by the letter which gave an account of it.

To: The Deputies of the Supreme Soviet USSR
The Deputies of the Supreme Soviet RSFSR
Copies to: The editorial offices of
Izvestia Sovetskaya Rossiya

On 11 October 1968 the Moscow City Court promulgated a sentence convicting Konstantin Babitsky, Larissa Bogoraz, Vadim Delone, Vladimir Dremlyuga and Pavel Litvinov.

These five people were participants in a demonstration in Red Square on 25 August 1968 against the introduction of troops into Czechoslovakia.

Their participation in a peaceful demonstration, an attempt to express their protest by these constitutional means, has been qualified as 'a gross violation of public order'.

Their slogans: 'Long live a free and independent Czechoslovakia', 'For your freedom and ours', 'Hands off the CSSR', 'Down with the occupiers' and 'Freedom for Dubcek' have been qualified as 'deliberately false fabrications slandering the Soviet state and social system'.

We consider that the participants in the demonstration have been awarded a deliberately inequitable sentence: this sentence represented a reprisal for the open and articulate expression of their views. We consider that there were no legal grounds whatsoever for instituting criminal proceedings against them.

Citizen Deputies of the Supreme Soviet! We do not refer to the blatant violations of professional standards perpetrated by the court and the investigators. We refer to something more important. Civil liberties guaranteed by the constitution – freedom of speech, freedom to demonstrate – have been violated. It is your duty to defend these liberties. We therefore appeal to you, asking you to intervene and to insist upon the quashing of the sentence and the suspension of the criminal case in view of the absence of indictable matter.

AVRUTSKY, G.	Engineer
AKIMOV, B.	Student
AMINEVA, E.	Office worker
ASANOVA, Z.	Physician
BAEVA, T.	Employee
BERNSHTEIN, S.	Writer, Party member
BLIUMENTAL, A.	Student
BLIUMENTAL, YU.	Musician
BUIMISTR-BULANOV, G.	Actor
VASILEV, L.	Lawyer
VELIKANOVA, T.	Mathematician
VOLPIN, A.	Post-graduate student in physical and mathematical science
VRUNOV, A.	Student
GALKIN, V.	Engineer
GABAI, G.	Teacher
GABAI, I.	Teacher
GINZBURG, L. I.	Pensioner
GLEZIN, E.	Construction Engineer
GORINA, A.	Pensioner
GRIGORENKO, A.	Senior technician
GRIGORENKO, P.	War pensioner
GRIKEVICH, V.	Junior research officer
DZHEMILEV, M.	Worker
DZHEMILEV, R.	Construction technician
DIKOV, YU.	Geo-chemist
EVGRAFOV, M.	Student
EMELKINA, N.	Office worker
ZIMAN, L.	Teacher
ZIMIN, N.	Editor
KANAEV, A.	Geologist
KAPLAN, A.	Master of Physical and Mathematical Science
KATS, L.	Office worker

KVASHA, I. V.	Distinguished artist of the RSFSR
KIM, YU.	Teacher
KISELEV, YU.	Artist
KOVALEV, S. A.	Master of Biology
KOZLOVSKY, D.	Student
KOMODROVA, N.	Chemist
KORSUNSKAYA, I.	Post graduate
KOSTERIN, A.	Author
KOSTERINA, I.	Member of the Union of Artists of the USSR
KRAVTSOVA, G.	Engineer
KRASIN, V.	Economist
LAVUT, A.	Mathematician
LAPIN, V.	Literary journalist
LEBEDEVSKY, V.	Editor
LEVITIN, A. E. (KRASNOV)	Orthodox writer
LITVINOVA, N.	Student
MAIOROVA, M.	Student
MALTSEV, YU.	Philologist
MELNIKOV, O.	Senior laboratory assistant
MILASHEVICH,V.	Hydrologist
MURTAZAEV, M.	Worker
MIKHAILOV, V.	Engineer
MURAVEV, D.	Philologist
MUSTAFAEV, M.	Engineer, Party member
NEIFAKH, A.	Doctor of Biology, Party member
NEKRASOV, V.	Writer, Party member
PANOVA, L.	Mathematician
PARAMONOV, L.	Student
PETROVA, G.	Pensioner
PETROV, I.	Student
PETROVSKY, L. P.	Historian, Party member
PINSKY, L.	Writer
PISAREV, S.	Pensioner, Party member since 1920
PLIUSHCH, L.	Mathematician

PRIMAK, L.	Doctor
ROKITIANSKY, V.	Translator
RUDAKOV, I.	Worker
RODNIANSKAYA, I.	Literary writer
RUSAKOVSKAYA, M.	Engineer
SAENKO, YU.	Office worker
SATRAEV, YU.	Teacher
SELIVANOV, E.	Mathematician
SEMIDLIAEV, V.	Teacher
SMORGUNOVA, E.	Philologist
SOKIRKO, V.	Engineer
SOLOVEVA, E.	Teacher
SOROMETOV, KH.	Engineer
STRELNIKOVA, E.	Pensioner
SUSHKO, B.	Historian
SYROECHKOVSKY, E.	Biologist
TELESIN, YU.	Mathematician
TERNOVSKY, A.	Doctor
TIMACHEV, V.	Engineer-Geologist
TIMOFEEVA, O.	Officer worker
TUMANOVA, L.	Philosopher
TURIYANSKY, V.	Fitter
KHALILOV, A.	Worker
SHTEIN, YU.	Producer
SHTELMAKH, A.	Engineer
YUDINA, M. V.	Professor at the Conservatoire
YAKIR, I.	Student
YAKIR, P.	Historian
YAKOBSON, A.	Translator

The present document would have been signed by a fair number of other like-minded people who have approved it. They did not do so because others have been subjected to discrimination at work for signing similar documents. Some also refused to sign because they considered that no useful purpose was served by appeals to the public authorities.

Despatched 1.12.69

We ask you to reply to 1) Moscow G-21, Komsomolsky Prospekt 14/1, kv. 96, Grigorenko, P.G., 2) Moscow E-397, ul. Shkolnaya 44, Krasin, V.A., 3) Moscow Zh-280, ul. Avtozavodskaya 5, kv. 75, Yakir, P.I.

For signing this letter S. Bernshtein, A. Neifakh and S. Pisarev were expelled from the Party;

V. Rokitiansky was dismissed from work;

V. Sokirko was excluded from his post-graduate course;

Yu. Dikov was removed from his teaching post and not allowed to present his thesis.

In connection with the letter demanding admittance to the courtroom during the trial, rather than the present document, O. Melnikov was expelled from the University biological faculty before taking his diploma and dismissed from his post there. Among the signatories of the above letter, Yu. Telesin was recently dismissed for 'having been unsuccessful in a competition'.

Yu. Shtein was forced to leave his job 'at his own request';

Irina Yakir was expelled from evening classes at the Historical Archive Institute.

In the meantime, all three had signed several other documents objectionable to the authorities, such as the appeal to the United Nations Organization by the Action Group for the Defence of Human Rights in the Soviet Union.

Ilya Gabai and Piotr Grigorevich Grigorenko were arrested in May 1969. In the course of interrogation Investigator Berezovsky asked witnesses for statements concerning the above letter, among other documents.

The convicted demonstrators were moved from Moscow early in December, either to exile or the camps. Not long before she was taken away Larissa managed to do time in the Lefortovo Prison punishment cell for communicating by tapping. She was released from isolation after two days as a result of protests by her father. Vadim Delone was put in handcuffs during transit in Krasnopresnenskaya prison – for reciting Mandelshtam's poems aloud.

Kostia Babitsky was sent to Krasnozatonsky, 12 kilometres from Syktyvkar. He works as a joiner in a ship-building yard and was given a room in a hostel. His family stayed in Moscow, but his wife and children spend their holidays with him. After the winter holidays his eldest daughter Natasha remained with her father and finished the ninth class of school there.

Pavel Litvinov was sent away farthest of all, to the village of Verkhnye Usugli, Chita Region, an air and bus journey from Chita even today. There is also no long-distance telephone communication with it and mail remains the only form of communication with his friends and relatives in Moscow. Pavel is employed as a fitter although the local school is desperately in need of a physics and mathematics teacher. Yet Pavel likes his work. His wife, Maya Rusakovskaya, was, however, refused a job at the school and has to work as a plasterer.

Of all the exiles, Larissa Bogoraz was the worst off; prison and especially the journey to her place of exile ruined her health. At Chuna, Irkutsk Region, where she was sent she was, of course, told that there was no question of employing her in her profession. Until recently Larissa worked in a timber processing plant, first as unskilled labour, then as a hoist operator alternately moving and stacking heavyish planks. She was medically certified sick for a long time, hardly earned anything as a result and was half starved. When she wanted to switch to working in the post office, where there was a vacancy, the police would not allow it. It is only recently that she obtained a medical certificate recommending lighter work and she is now in the drying-shop, where the job is more fully automated.

Volodia Dremlyuga was sent to Murmansk, where he sews mittens, just like our friends in Ozernoye or Yuli Daniel until he was recently taken for a 'rest' to Vladimir prison. Volodia was first given permission to meet his wife for three whole days at the beginning, but this was later cut down as a punishment for some violation of the camp regime.

Vadim is having a very hard time. He is in a timber felling camp in Tyumen and the camp administration makes quite sure that he does not get transferred to lighter work. Vadim is delicate and has a heart condition resulting from rheumatic fever. He finds the physical privations and hunger hard to endure and isolation among criminals even harder. His 'Ballad of disbelief' was recently confiscated during a search and this earned him a six month suspension of parcels and visits.

PART FOUR

THE FATE OF VICTOR FEINBERG

Victor Feinberg, born in 1931, worked as a fitter in a factory until he completed his university course in 1968. He graduated from the English department of the Leningrad University Philological Faculty, won top marks with a thesis on Salinger and worked as a guide in the Pavlovsk palace museum right up to the time of the demonstration.

Victor had at one time been classified as disabled because of a head injury, but had not been registered for psychiatric purposes or hospitalized in this connection. He was under investigation in 1957 for fighting a policeman who had called him a yid. He was found to be sane and given a conditional sentence of one year.

Victor is the typically wretched Jew in appearance, the kind jew-bashers jump on with a shout of 'Beat up the yids' almost by reflex action. I hardly noticed him being beaten up because I was so absorbed in my own fight for the flag. It was only in the 'Half-rouble' that I saw him with his bleeding, swollen lips, holding his blood-smeared teeth in his hand. Tatka later told us how he had been hit: he was punched in the face and about the head and kicked at least half a dozen times.

Four of his teeth were knocked out – all the upper incisors. It stands to reason that he was not fit to be produced in court in that state when it was a question of showing that the demonstrators had violated public order, while those who beat us up, took away the slogans and tried to provoke the crowd were indeed acting in accordance with, and in the interests of, the law. The accused and some of the witnesses did tell how Feinberg was beaten up and had his teeth knocked out, but words are as nothing compared with the evidence of one's eyes and the sight of a man disfigured.

The simplest way of keeping somebody out of court is to pronounce him insane. I still wonder why they did not make up their minds to pronounce all seven of us insane and describe the demonstrators as a 'bunch of lunatics'. After all, who other than lunatics would openly say 'No' amid the universal shouts of popular approval? The intention, so it seems, must have been to observe a certain appearance of both legality and publicity. They therefore confined themselves to pronouncing Victor and me insane. As far as I know, Victor's diagnosis refers to 'residual symptoms of schizophrenia', 'residual symptoms of concussion of the brain' and 'exophthalmic goitre'. Victor does in fact suffer from the latter, but it is by no means a mental ailment and it grew more acute under prison conditions in Lefortovo. 'Delusions about reforms' are mentioned in the experts' report among the grounds for a diagnosis of schizophrenia. Thus any private dissent from the existing system, any statement about the need to alter or improve it will be interpreted as 'delusions' if they should wish to pronounce you insane. It is also said that the doctors treating Feinberg in Leningrad informed him that his diagnosis was 'schizo-dissension'. Who can tell whether a bored doctor was showing off his wit to his patient or whether such a diagnosis really exists in Soviet psychiatry? Personally, I am prepared to believe the latter.

The trial to impose compulsory medical treatment on Victor Feinberg was held on 2 December under Judge Monakhov, whom we later saw presiding over Ira Belogorodskaya's trial. The proceedings took place in Feinberg's absence. According to the Criminal Code, the court would have had the 'right' to call him, but made no use of this right. In so far as I know, the 'insane', or rather those whom a court is to pronounce insane, never do appear at the trial. It may be that the judges are afraid of being confronted, not with a piece of paper, but with a real – and possibly sane – person.

Victor's counsel, Advocate S. L. Ariya, contested not only that Feinberg's actions fell under the corresponding articles of the Criminal Code, but also that Feinberg's condition and the threat to society from his actions required his removal to a special psychiatric hospital. After all, articles 190/1 and 190/3 under which Feinberg's actions were impugned do not cover offences classified as especially dangerous or serious.

Indeed, I know of a trial in Leningrad under article 190/1 which resulted in the individual concerned being pronounced insane and placed in the custody of his relatives with observation by a psychiatric centre in accordance with the experts' recommendation. The difference was that this individual agreed that, in writing a 'criminal' letter to the Central Committee, he had acted in a state of agitation while temporarily deranged. I am sure that Victor, on the contrary, would have claimed that he was completely in his right mind when he appeared in Red Square.

Predictably, the court simply repeated the conclusions of the expert examination in full, pronounced Feinberg insane and prescribed compulsory treatment in a special psychiatric hospital.

Early in February 1969 Victor was lodged in the Leningrad Special Psychiatric Hospital in Arsenalnaya Street. Little is known about his stay there. He was transferred from the 11th medical department where he was receiving treatment for his thyroid condition to the stricter 4th department. The orderlies – and orderlies in this hospital are no more than criminal inmates – beat up a patient until he bled. Victor heard his cries and met him next day covered in blood. His face had been smashed and his pyjamas were blood-stained. Victor set about composing a complaint against the orderlies. He was immediately transferred to another department without being allowed to finish his complaint. The latter 'got lost'. Victor's worried parents were told that he had done nothing wrong and were promised that he would be returned to the medical department.

Victor's father has been appointed his custodian since 1 June. This may help to speed his return home. One board convened in June did not, however, authorize his release from hospital. The next board was due to meet in December 1969.

His wife wrote to Victor that he should leave hospital as soon as possible in order to secure the peace and quiet which was lacking there and which he must have if his health was to improve. This letter never reached him.

As a minor, his fifteen-year-old son is not allowed to visit relatives in prisons and camps. Part of the money sent to him is held back because he spends it on subscriptions to newspapers and magazines.

I quote two documents about compulsory treatment in special hospitals to enable the reader to form an idea of Victor's present circumstances. The first is an extract from *The Chronicle of Current Events*. The second was written by Piotr Grigorevich Grigorenko shortly before his arrest.

It should be pointed out that if Victor had been declared sane, and given the court's attitude to dependent minors, he would have been awarded exile rather than camp and would have encountered far more humane conditions.

Victor Feinberg's fate is the most tragic among that of the demonstrators. It is also, I think, the only one in which the intervention of world public opinion and international organizations – the International Red Cross first and foremost – could be of assistance. If this book should reach any readers in the West, I ask them to do all they can to alleviate Victor Feinberg's treatment within the walls of a prison mental hospital and hasten his release.

THE FATE OF DISSENTERS PRONOUNCED MENTALLY ILL

Extracts from 'The Year of Human Rights in the Soviet Union Continues'. The Chronicle of Current Events No. 30 (8) 30 June 1969

Individuals who have committed serious criminal offences (brutal murders, rape and gang violence) while insane and psychologically disturbed and therefore not fit to plead are sent to special psychiatric hospitals for compulsory treatment. It also happens that people are pronounced insane in order to isolate them from society when the investigation cannot establish that they are guilty of serious crimes, but is satisfied that they have committed such offences. The term of detention in hospital is not laid down by the court and may be extended indefinitely. People who are not ill in any way get sent to these hospitals on account of their convictions together with others who are genuinely sick. They are thereby deprived of their right to defend themselves by legal means and end up in conditions far worse than those in present-day camps and prisons.

The first of such 'hospitals' was already operating in Kazan before the war. There is still a special department there for political prisoners. A special type colony was opened in Sychevka, Smolensk Province, after the war for incurable mental cases and political prisoners who were regarded as most dangerous by special hospital managements and the KGB. People sent to this colony are driven to total mental breakdown. Special hospitals were opened in Leningrad, Ul Arsenalnaya St 9, P/ya [Post Box] US-20, st-5 in 1952; in the building of the former German convict prison at Cherniakhovsk, Kaliningrad Region, P/ya 216, st-2 in 1965; in Minsk in 1966; and in Dnepropetrovsk in 1968.

All these institutions have the following features in common: political prisoners who are sane in every way share cells with the seriously deranged; those who do not wish to recant are subjected to torture under the guise of treatment and given injections of aminazine and sulphazine in large doses, which cause shock and severe physical disorders; the regime is that of a closed prison with one hour of daily exercise. The prisoners are sometimes given intravenous injections of sodium amytal, a potent sedative which suppresses the personality, and are then interrogated. The staff comprises warders from the Ministry of Internal Affairs (MVD) troops wearing white coats over their uniforms; orderlies recruited among convicted criminals (thieves and gangster second offenders), also in white coats; and, lastly, the medical staff proper, many of whom wear officers' epaulettes under their white coats. The brick walls which surround these 'hospitals' are even more awe-inspiring than those around other prisons.

. . . Prisoners in special and severe regime camps who find the conditions unbearable sometimes try to simulate insanity. Some succeed in this, but when they reach a psychiatric prison hospital immediately realise that they have come to something far worse than the most severe camp. Some of them even implore the doctors on their bended knees to 'let them go back'.

People released from such 'hospitals' are issued with passports in a special series, as though they had served a prison sentence. Whoever is stubborn enough not to admit his illness has practically no chance of gaining his freedom.

CONCERNING SPECIAL PSYCHIATRIC HOSPITALS (FOOLS' HOUSES) BY P. G. GRIGORENKO

My comrades have asked me for a brief account of these institutions based on my personal experience.

There is nothing inherently wrong with the idea of special psychiatric hospitals, but what we have in fact made of it is as criminal and as inhuman as anything can be.

Undesirable people have been disposed of by declaring them insane and putting them into psychiatric institutions for long periods, or the whole of their lives, ever since insanity was recognized for what it is. In view of this, progressive people have for many years now fought to ensure that the treatment of mental patients was under the effective control of society. Society has also insisted that those who commit crimes in a state of mental derangement should not be subjected to criminal sanctions, but sent for psychiatric treatment. Bekhterev and Serbsky, two outstanding Russian psychiatrists, were among those who fought for this and Soviet legislation set out to satisfy these demands.

It is unfortunate that the whole subject was, at the same time, completely removed from public control and entrusted to an agency with hand-picked staff, including the doctors, who are only appointed after a special process of selection in which medical qualifications play almost no part. Other factors are given priority, the most important being a capacity to take orders and not to assert oneself as a medical man.

A look at the arrangements for treating mentally sick criminals shows that the main fault is not in the special psychiatric hospitals as such. If, as I have been asked, I were only to describe the conditions in which the inmates are kept, nothing terrible or illegal would transpire.

The conditions in which most of the patients in the Leningrad Psychiatric Hospital are kept are less severe than those obtaining in prison. Cells are only used in five departments. Everywhere else the wards are open from first call until lights out. Most patients are employed in the workshops. One department is fitted out like a sanatorium, with radio and television provided. There is a very good library. True, many library assistants are reluctant to replenish the shelves of the department, but a little determination will secure you anything you need. Books, newspapers and magazines can be obtained from outside. There is a film show twice a week. Local residents are allowed two visits a week and people who have come a long way three days in a row. Food parcels are allowed at visiting times. The food provided is considerably better, more varied and more appetising than in prison. There is white bread. Those who need a special diet get it. Butter, milk and sometimes fruit is included in the menu. There is much more meat than in prison. It is no exaggeration to say that the medical care provided is exemplary. I imagine that ordinary mental hospitals are far from being so well served. The very high qualifications of the intermediate grade of medical personnel are striking (considerably higher rates of pay obviously have something to do with this). Hospitals such as the Leningrad Special Psychiatric Hospital could therefore be shown to any visitors, even to foreign tourists. The more trusting might even express admiration. But let us take things easy and have a look at the arrangements as a whole.

One must start at the beginning and establish whether it is really the mentally sick patients who are placed here and whether conditions which make for the grossest form of arbitrary behaviour are not built into the system. It is an investigator's order which sends one for psychiatric examination to the infamous 'Professor Serbsky Institute of Forensic Psychiatry'. The institute is nominally subordinate to the Ministry of Health USSR, but I have often seen Professor Lunts, the head of the department in which I underwent examination, come to work in a KGB colonel's uniform, though he was always wearing a white coat by the time he reached the department. I also saw other doctors belonging to this institute in KGB uniform, but never succeeded in discovering the connections between these KGB men and the Ministry of Health.

It is said that only one department is subordinate to the KGB, that which carries out expert examinations in political cases. Personally, I suspect that the KGB's influence – a decisive influence, moreover – extends over the entire work of the institute. Even if things are as they are rumoured to be, the question arises whether psychiatric examinations are *capable* of being objective in political cases if the investigators and the experts are subordinate to the same individual – and bound by military discipline.

To avoid lengthy speculation on this topic, I will relate what I saw. I arrived in the second (political) department of the Serbsky Institute on 12 March 1964. I had not until then even heard of a means of retribution whereby healthy individuals could be found insane, apart from what history had taught me about Piotr Chaadayev. It had not ever crossed my mind that systematic *Chaadayevisation* might exist in our country. I only realized this when the order sending me for psychiatric examination was imparted to me. The following conversation then took place between me and the investigator.

After reading the order, I looked at the investigator: 'Well, so you have found a way out of the dead end, have you?' I asked him. (I had previously often told him that if the investigation were to continue and yet observe all the standards of procedure, it would soon run into a dead end.) He was most upset and started to reply in a disjointed and muddled way:

'Piotr Grigorevich, what are you thinking of! Oh no, this is simply a formality. You are completely normal. I have no doubt about it, but there is a note about concussion in your medical record and a psychiatric examination is obligatory in such cases. The court would not accept the case without it.'

I remarked that before sending a case anywhere there first had to be a case. He went on assuring me that the investigation would continue after the examination and that a case would be drawn up. It became increasingly clear to me however that there would be no sort of investigation and that it was a padded cell for me for life, or so I thought at the time. Having arrived at this logical conclusion, I looked at all subsequent events from this standpoint.

There were nine people in the department when I got there. Two more arrived during the next five or six days. Working on my assumption about the purpose of ordering an examination I predicted the outcome of all eleven cases, basing myself solely on the extent to which each case could be proved or not, rather than on the mental condition of each individual concerned. In fact, it was quite clear even without medical training that only one of us, Tolia Edamenko, was mentally defective, yet he was the only one for whom I forecast camp. In my opinion, the 'fools' house' awaited only three of us: me, Pavel Borovik (an accountant from Kaliningrad) and Denis Grigorev (an electrical fitter from Volgograd). In all three cases there was nothing for the investigation to go on and no possibility whatsoever of building anything up.

All the rest, in my opinion, would be pronounced normal, although three of them had very skilfully 'put it on' to simulate insanity and another really was insane. I was only doubtful about one person, Yuri Grimm, a Moscow crane-driver who had distributed a leaflet caricaturing Khrushchev. 'If you don't repent', I told him, 'you'll go to the "fools' house"', if you do, to a camp.' I arrived at this because the investigator visited him several times a week and tried to convince him of the need to 'repent', while promising him all sorts of benefits. In the end, Yuri 'repented' and got three years in a severe regime camp. All my other forecasts proved completely correct. Grimm's case is noteworthy. When I demanded to see the prosecutor and the investigator in my case, I was told they did not have access to the individual under examination as long as the latter was in progress. This rule was not observed in Grimm's case, an excellent illustration of the fact that this so-called institute was merely a branch of the investigator's office. The medical expert and the investigator talked only of repentance to Yuri. While this was going on, the doctor behaved even more foully than the investigator and painted a lurid picture of Grimm tucked away for life among the 'psychos' if he did not repent.

Even in Leningrad I had already met people who had been interned in a psychiatric hospital without being mentally ill. Engineer Piotr Alexeevich Lysak made a particularly painful impression on me. He had been sent to the Special Psychiatric Hospital for opposing some expulsions on the grounds of political unreliability at a student meeting and had spent seven years there by the time I arrived. His fury at this terrible retribution and at the thought of his ruined life had overwhelmed his brain. Every day he indicted furious missives which were, natually enough, never forwarded and merely went to swell his medical file, to serve as justification for further 'treatment' (people who refuse to admit that they are ill are seldom released from a special psychiatric hospital). I tried to bring this truth home to him. His judgement was absolutely normal in all other matters, but he was, as one might say, armour-plated on this point. What was worse, he would agree with the force of my arguments, but when I finally put the crucial question: 'Well then, we stop writing as from tomorrow, don't we?', he would suddenly flare up again: 'No, I'll prove it to the swine yet!' Once, during such a conversation, when Piotr got particularly carried away by the thought of how he would prove it to them, I said somewhat irritably: 'You talk in such an irrational way that I am beginning to doubt your sanity!' He suddenly stopped and gave me a look which I shall not forget until my dying day and asked quietly, very, very quietly, with a kind of bitter scorn in his voice: 'You surely don't imagine one can spend seven years here and stay sane?'

His question sums up our inhuman system of compulsory treatment. It is obvious that even if normal people were only very occasionally detained among the insane, the strongest possible protest would still have to be raised. The real moment of horror for a healthy person placed in these conditions comes when he begins to realize that he may in time turn into one of those whom he sees around him. This is particularly frightening for the easily vulnerable, those who suffer from insomnia or cannot shut out extraneous noises – which reverberate with incredible violence in such places.

The Leningrad Special Psychiatric Hospital occupies what was formerly a women's gaol next to the famous Kresty Prison. As in ordinary prisons, only the cells have ceilings and the centre of the building is hollow. One can see the glass lantern on the roof above the fifth floor from the first-floor corridor. Sound travels well and is even amplified in this echo chamber. One of the mental tortures inflicted on the inmates in Stalin's time made use of this particular effect.

The hospital was established in 1951. At that time, no attempt was made to conceal that it had been instituted to house people who were undesirables in the eyes of the regime. There were as many doctors in this 'hospital' then as in a prison and their duties did not differ from those of prison doctors. The guard-changing drill in those days went like this: the warder who was handing over on the first floor would shout at the top of his voice: 'Guard duty over the most dangerous enemies of the people – handed over', and the guard taking over would reply: 'Guard duty over the most dangerous enemies of the people – taken over. . . .' All this could be heard in every cell on every floor. The procedure was repeated on all floors up to the fifth, day in, day out, with every change of guard. This no longer happens. Doctors are now in charge of this institute and have a decisive say in everything which concerns the living conditions of those who have become inmates in the hospital. Even they, however, cannot alter the acoustic properties of the building which are part of its design. I could therefore hear only too clearly all that happened on every floor.

Everything turned out well for me personally. The hazards of my profession, or the iron constitution inherited from my parents, soon enabled me to insulate myself from everything which did not directly concern me. Something that occupied the whole prison for more than two hours entirely passed me by – the recapture of a violent lunatic who had somehow succeeded in breaking free from the orderlies and was rushing round naked from floor to floor. I trained myself not to notice the unending tap-dance which went on above my head, round the clock, practically non-stop (breaks only came during short periods when the dancer collapsed, completely exhausted). There were many other things I did not notice and in this way I survived my time in this hospital without any great psychological damage. The only thing I cannot forget and which still sometimes wakes me up when I am asleep was, at night, a wild cry accompanied by the sound of breaking glass. I failed to insulate myself against this. It would seem that one's nerves are more vulnerable to such effects in sleep. I can, however, imagine the impact on somebody whose sensitive nervous system registers direct everything that surrounds him and whose defences in this respect are less well developed than mine.

I repeat that even if people were to be placed in such conditions only occasionally and by chance, every case should be very carefully scrutinized and certainly given the widest publicity. With us, however, it is not a matter of chance but the product of a system, and one in common use at that. As I have already said, during the mere three months which I spent under psychiatric investigation the Serbsky Institute promoted three normal people to insanity and sent one man who was undoubtedly mentally abnormal to a camp. The latter is also part of the system, although I only understood this after I had read Anatoli Marchenko's *My Testimony*. Such people, it turns out, are needed in camps to make life even more unbearable for the sane.

The extent to which bogus psychiatric examinations are used in the course of investigation can be seen from the following case. During exercise at the Leningrad Special Psychiatric Hospital I met a very interesting man to talk to, endowed with an exceptional memory and the knack of telling a story. Indeed, he had a story to tell; despite his relatively tender years, he had already managed to accumulate ten years in various places of detention, mostly in centres for juveniles. He had landed in a special psychiatric hospital as a result of being arrested for petty theft and would probably have been released without trial if the investigator had not had the bright idea of disposing of an un-solved – and rather stale – murder case with his help. Not much was expected of him: merely to testify that one of his closest friends had been in the vicinity when the crime was committed. My new-found companion knew that this was not so and refused to make a statement to this effect. Whereupon the investigator said: 'So you don't want to assist the investigation do you? Well then, I'll pack you off somewhere where you'll remember me for the rest of your life' – and sent him for psychiatric examination. He was pronounced insane as a matter of course and had spent his time ever since fighting this decision.

Volodia Pantin proved lucky. He chanced upon an intelligent and honest woman who handled the case so well that the experts' conclusion was set aside. A doctor who liked me told me that this was exceptional. As a rule, the experts' conclusion could not be annulled because this invariably required the concurrence of the doctor responsible for the initial diagnosis. Volodia got by all this, but six long years had passed.

When the diagnosis had been set aside, the case was heard in court as a crime committed by a mentally sound individual. The court was well aware of Volodia's period of confinement, awarded him four years, the maximum sentence provided for under the relevant article, and set him free. He had thus served two extra years for refusing to 'assist the investigation'.

A psychiatric hospital is terrifying for the sane because they are thrown among people who are psychologically disturbed. Yet the total absence of civil rights and the hopelessness of their position are no less terrifying.

A special psychiatric hospital patient lacks even the meagre rights enjoyed by other prisoners. He simply has no rights at all. The doctors can do anything they like with him and no one will interfere or defend him. None of his complaints or those of his fellow patients will ever get outside the hospital. His one and only hope is in the honesty of the doctors.

The doctor who was treating me told me this when I sketched out my state of complete legal helplessness and vulnerability at our first interview. He gave me an open, honest look and asked: 'Don't you set any value at all on the honesty of the doctors?' 'On the contrary', I told him, 'it is the only thing I count on. If I lost my faith even in this, I would just have to look for a way to commit suicide.'

I never had cause to regret my faith in the doctors' honesty, but I insist now – as I insisted then – that *a system is worthless* in which *the honesty of the doctors* is the only hope. Supposing you hit upon a dishonest one? This is by no means out of the question and is solidly substantiated in practice, if only by the fact that people who are mentally perfectly sound are at present being pronounced insane. It is also, when all is said and done, a perfectly logical development of the system: if the authorities wished to aggravate the circumstances of healthy 'psychos', they would begin to remove honest people from the system and replace them by those who would be prepared to do anything for money and position. Why believe that there are fewer 'wrong ones' of this kind among psychiatric doctors than in any other profession?

It is particularly harrowing to realize that one had been put into this position indefinitely. Some scale of minimum periods of detention is applied by the doctors, but I have not seen it. I know that murderers are held for not less than five years. It is said that in this respect political prisoners are equated with murderers, but that if they do not recant they may not be released even then.

It should be added that even reliance on the honesty of the doctors does not provide a complete answer, because the KGB maintains its own undercover agents in these institutions and their reports carry at least as much weight as the doctors' conclusions. Cases may occur in which a court does not sanction the medical board's decision to release an individual from hospital on the grounds that 'the period of treatment does not correspond to the seriousness of the crime'.

To sum up, the conditions in a lunatic asylum, the total absence of civil rights and the lack of any real hope of release, represent the most important and most horrifying circumstances encountered by anybody interned in a special psychiatric hospital. People who are psychologically vulnerable may as a result quickly develop real mental disturbances: in the first instance, suspicion of the doctors and a fear of being deliberately subjected to treatment aimed at breaking down a normal psychological make up. Worst of all, this is a perfectly rational possibility given that the patients are deprived of all rights and that society has no control whatsoever over the system.

Public opinion must therefore fight for a radical alteration of the system of expert examination and detention in special psychiatric hospitals and for real control over the conditions in which patients are detained and treated there. As long as these aims have not been achieved, if you are sent to such an institution you must put great faith in the doctor's better nature. You must believe and trust him. This can only do good, all the more so because you will achieve nothing at all by being distrustful. After all, if they make up their minds to use illegal methods of treatment on you, the outcome will be the same for the suspicious and the trusting. And even then, the trusting may be better off.

EPILOGUE

During the night of 21 to 22 August 1968, Boguslavsky, a twenty-year-old inhabitant of Leningrad, wrote 'Brezhnev get out of Czechoslovakia' on the three horses by Klodt. He was arrested there and then on the Anichkov Bridge and sentenced two weeks later to five years of severe regime under article 70. In the course of a cassation hearing in October the Supreme Court of the RSFSR reclassified his action under article 190/1 and accordingly altered the sentence to three years of ordinary regime, the maximum sentence under the article concerned.

Chronicle of Current Events
No 4, 31 October 1968

I have been reading through the issues of the *Chronicle of Current Events* in search of reports about cases of dissent from 'universal support'.

These reports show that we were not alone in our wish to protest. I am not talking about those who *think* as we do – they are far more numerous than those who spoke up.

Among the various forms of protest, ours was not even the most hopeless and most certain to attract retribution. My heart bleeds for the Leningrad boy writing his desperate inscription on the bronze horses of the Anichkov Bridge that first night after the tragic news. Yet even him I would not have dared to stop or say: 'This is senseless, you are beating your head against a wall' – and other things of the same sort which were said to me in connection with our demonstration.

The decision to demonstrate was personal to each one of us. None of us pressed – or would have thought of pressing – such a decision on anybody else. The step I took was the only one possible for me and I was right to take it, on my own behalf and in my own estimation. Similarly, those who did not publicly voice their attitude towards the events were equally right, on their own behalf and in their own estimation, whatever their reasons – the political futility of protest or the likelihood of disproportionate consequences from their actions.

But it is not for them to judge whether we were right to demonstrate.

Some experiences are more stark than this. When I heard that an enthusiast at a party meeting in the Planning and Technical Research Institute where I worked had declared: 'They dared to set their dirty feet on the sacred cobbles of Red Square', I merely laughed. But when the resolution 'To hold her up for shame' was passed unanimously, including the votes of some of my fellow workers who were readers of my verse, it hurt. Even then I find it hard to condemn them, although Ilya Gabai's words are only too appropriate: there is not much difference between a thug raising his hand against his neighbour in the street and an intellectual raising his hand against his neighbour at a meeting.

The 'pointlessness' and the 'inappropriateness' of the demonstration were the talk of half Moscow for a while, not of Moscow the city, but of that 'left wing, radical and liberal' Moscow which I find it impossible to describe more accurately, that Moscow which completely agreed with our attitude to the fact of invasion.

Opinion about the demonstration changed only gradually as the trial approached, while it was being held and after it was over. The significance of our action became increasingly obvious. One of our friends, who had been strongly opposed to it and had tried to dissuade some of the potential demonstrators, told me that winter: 'Now I've understood: it was cowardice. I should have gone with you. What you did was right.' Another, very close to me, Larissa and Pavel, told me when he reached Moscow from the south just after the demonstration: 'Had I been in Moscow, I would have called off the demonstration!' By late autumn, almost in winter, he reluctantly admitted: 'Well, of

course, if I had been here, I too would have gone with you.'
And these are our closest friends.

I have also come across other arguments: 'Was it worth
going to prison for the sake of the Czechs?', followed by evidence
of the Czechoslovak leadership's retreat, and also: 'You demanded freedom for Dubcek, but has Dubcek stood up for
you?'

This is not the place to examine the thorny path travelled
by Czechoslovakia since 21 August 1968. I would merely like
to recall once more the Czech student's words: 'Think of
Czechoslovakia even when it is no longer a newspaper sensation.' Nothing has changed in my attitude towards that country
and its heroic people, whoever may be at the head of the party
and state machine. Just as I cannot hate Poland and the Poles
for the presence of Polish troops among those which entered
Czechoslovakia. Just as I can only bitterly regret that my people,
the multitude of nations inhabiting my country's soil, should
have been made accomplices to this crime. The purpose of our
demonstration was, so it seems to me, not merely to give expression to our own remorse, but also to redeem at least a
fraction of our people's guilt before history. This purpose was
fulfilled.

In Czechoslovakia, the first news of the demonstration appeared in *Rude Pravo* on 26 August. My letter became known
later. I am told that it was handed out as a leaflet in Charles
University. When they reproduced the official TASS report
about the trial of 'violators of public order in Red Square on
25 August 1968' some Czechoslovak newspapers also printed a
reference to other agency reports according to which the
accused were a group of intellectuals protesting against the
introduction of troops into Czechoslovakia.

The students of Charles University sent to the Soviet Union
(I do not know to what government department it was addressed)
a petition requesting the release of the demonstrators under
sentence. I have often received greetings from Czechoslovakia,
from individual citizens and from the Czech Union of Writers.
Someone was told in Prague: 'If it had not been for the demon-

strators in Red Square, we would not have talked to any of you Russians.'

The best answer to all those who cast doubt on the need for our demonstration is Anatoli Yakobson's letter. Anatoli Yakobson is a man of extraordinary stature, not only professionally (he is a brilliant translator, a favourite teacher, a profound literary critic), but by his humanity and depth of feeling. I believe that he was shattered not to have known about the demonstration in advance and not to have taken part in it. I will therefore conclude this book with his letter. (Yakobson relied on my letter for his facts and therefore omits one slogan and slightly misquotes another.)

ANATOLI YAKOBSON'S LETTER

On 25 August 1968, seven people – Konstantin Babitsky, Larissa Bogoraz, Natalia Gorbanevskaya, Vadim Delone, Vladimir Dremlyuga, Pavel Litvinov and Victor Feinberg – went to the Execution Ground in Red Square and unfolded slogans 'Long live free and independent Czechoslovakia' (in Czech), 'Shame on the occupiers', 'Hands off the cssr', 'For your freedom and ours'.

Secret service men in plain clothes threw themselves on the demonstrators with filthy yells reminiscent of a pogrom. Some were beaten up and all were pushed into a car. Lefortovo Prison and an investigation followed. Little time passed before the demonstrators were brought to court charged with 'collective actions grossly violating public order', except for Gorbanevskaya and Feinberg whom the authorities found it convenient to treat as insane.

All those in our country who seek the truth have heard of the demonstration; so have the people of Czechoslovakia; so has humanity at large. By speaking from London a century ago in defence of Polish freedom and against its oppressors on behalf of a Great Power, Herzen redeemed the honour of Russian democracy single handed. These seven demonstrators have undoubtedly saved the honour of the Soviet people. The importance of the demonstration on 25 August cannot be exaggerated.

Many people with humane and progressive views, however, who admit that the demonstration was both courageous and high minded, also assume that it was an act of despair and that a demonstration resulting in the inevitable and immediate arrest of its participants and retribution against them was unwise and ineffective. Even 'self-immuration' has made its appearance as a new word to match 'self-immolation.'

I believe, on the contrary, that even if the demonstrators had been unable to unfold their slogans and their demonstration had remained unknown to all, it would still have been a sensible and justifiable act. Actions of this kind cannot be measured by the yardstick of ordinary politics where every action must produce an immediate and substantial result, a material advantage. The 25 August demonstration was not the manifestation of a political struggle (for which, be it said, the necessary conditions are absent) but the manifestation of a *moral* struggle. One cannot forecast even the relatively short-term consequences of such a movement. One must begin by postulating that truth is needed for its own sake and for no other reason; that human dignity will not permit one to condone evil, even if one cannot avert it.

Leo Tolstoy wrote: ' . . . Discussions about the consequences for the world at large of one or other of our actions cannot serve as guidance for our actions and behaviour. Man is endowed with another and incontrovertible guidance – the guidance of his conscience, by following which he is certain that what he does is what he should be doing.' Hence the moral principle and guide to action – 'I cannot keep silent'.

This does not mean that everyone who is in sympathy with the demonstrators should follow them into the Square, nor that every occasion is suitable for a demonstration. It does mean that all who are of a like mind with the heroes of 25 August must, guided by their common sense, choose their own time and form of protest. There are no general rules. One thing only is amply clear: 'sensible silence' may turn into ultimate senseless-ness – the restoration of Stalinism.

Since 1966, after the trial of Sinyavsky and Daniel, not a single arbitrary or unlawfully violent act by the authorities has passed without *public* protest and reproof. That has the makings of a precious tradition, a start to people releasing themselves by their own efforts from humiliating fear and participation in evil.

Let us recall what Herzen said: 'Nowhere do I see free men and I cry – halt! Let us start by making ourselves free.'

NOTES

1 *Chronicle of Current Events*: A typescript publication, circulating unofficially, though not so far illegally, in the Soviet Union and dedicated to the defence of Human Rights. It has appeared at fairly regular two-monthly intervals since April 1968 to record infringements of legality in the USSR and report at greater length on major developments in this connection. An English translation of the first issue has been published in *Uncensored Russia*, ed. Peter Reddaway, London, 1971.

2 *Lubyanka*: Moscow headquarters, prison and interrogation centre of the secret police since the early days of the October Revolution.

3 *Marchenko*: Anatoli Marchenko, born 1938, sentenced to six years in a labour camp in 1960 for 'hooliganism', then attempted escape, wrote *My Testimony* about his experiences in 1967. He supported various causes disapproved of by the Soviet authorities and, in particular, the liberalization movement in Czechoslovakia in 1968. As a result, he was sentenced to a further term of forced labour for alleged offences against probation and passport regulations.

4 *Irina (Bogoraz)*: Irina Belogorodskaya, Larissa Bogoraz's cousin, born 1940, was sentenced to one year in a labour camp in 1969 for distributing 'anti-Soviet literature'.

5 *Letter*: For the letter referred to, see pp. 54–56.

6 *Vigilante squads*: Squads formed of Young Communists and other volunteers to act as police auxiliaries.

7 *Galanskov*: Yuri Galanskov, a writer born in 1939. He was arrested in 1967 for distributing an illicit periodical called *Phoenix*. Tried with Alexander Ginzburg and sentenced to seven years of forced labour.

8 *Ginzburg*: Alexander Ginzburg, a writer born in 1936. Imprisoned on an

insignificant charge and sentenced in 1968 to five years of hard labour. In 1966 he compiled and sent to the Soviet authorities concerned a collection of documents about the trial of the writers Sinyavsky and Daniel which was later published in the West.

9 *Article 70*: This deals with agitation and propaganda aimed at subverting the Soviet system and the production, dissemination or possession of literature for this purpose.

10 *Article 190/3*: The organization of, or active participation in, collective actions involving a gross violation of public order, or clear disobedience to the lawful demands of representatives of authority, or disrupting the work of transport, state or public institutions or services, is punishable by three years' deprivation of freedom, or one year of corrective labour, or a fine up to 100 roubles.

11 *Gabai*: Ilya Gabai, a teacher born in 1936. Took part in 1967, together with Bukovsky, Delone and Kushev, in a demonstration demanding the repeal of Article 70 RSFSR Criminal Code and protesting against the arrest of Galanskov and his companions.

12 *Yakir*: Piotr Yakir, born 1923, son of a brilliant Red Army commander executed during Stalin's purge of the army leadership in 1937. Sentenced at fourteen to seventeen years' forced labour and rehabilitated in 1956. Active in the Soviet civil rights movement since the early 'sixties.

13 *Article 190/1*: The systematic dissemination by word of mouth of deliberately false fabrications slandering the Soviet state and social system, as also the preparation or dissemination of such slanderous works in written, printed or any other form, is punishable by three years' deprivation of freedom, or one year of corrective labour, or a fine of up to 100 roubles.

14 *... still at home*: Natalia Gorbanevskaya was arrested in December 1968 and committed by a Moscow court to a 'special category' psychiatric hospital in 1970 after she had compiled the present book.

15 *Zolotukhin*: Boris Zolotukhin, a member of the Presidium of the Moscow advocates' board, defended Ginzburg at his 1968 trial. He was subsequently dismissed from his post and expelled from the Party for an 'anti-Party and anti-Soviet line of defence'.

16 *Grigorenko*: Piotr Grigorenko, born 1906, former Major-General and lecturer in cybernetics at the Moscow military academy. Active in defending civil rights since the early 'sixties. Dismissed from his post, discharged

from the Army and interned in a 'special psychiatric hospital' in 1964. Arrested in 1969 in connection with the protest of the Crimean Tatars deported by Stalin during World War II against the Soviet government's failure to arrange for their return to the Crimea.

17 *Kosterin*: Alexei Kosterin, 1896–1968, writer and journalist, active in defending civil rights from the early 'sixties.

18 *Yakobson*: Anatoli Yakobson, poet and translator, active in defending civil rights since the early 'sixties. Arrested in 1969 during demonstration in Red Square on Stalin's birthday, but soon released.

19 *Khaustov*: Victor Khaustov, sentenced in 1967 to three years' forced labour for participation in a demonstration against Article 70.

20 *Bukovsky*: Vladimir Bukovsky, born 1941, a writer active in the civil rights movement since the early 'sixties. Expelled from university and twice interned in a special psychiatric hospital. Sentenced to three years' forced labour in 1967 for demonstrating in favour of Galanskov and his companions.

21 *Kushev*: Yevgeni Kushev, a young poet tried together with Bukovsky and Delone in 1967.

22 *Dobrovolsky*: Alexei Dobrovolsky, a typographer born in 1939, repeatedly arrested since 1958 and sentenced to various terms of forced labour. Also twice interned in special psychiatric hospitals. Turned state evidence at the trial of Galanskov and his companions in 1968.

23 *Red Pass*: KGB identification card.

24 *Dzhemilev*: Spokesman for the Crimean Tatars.